Digital Working Lives

OFF THE FENCE: MORALITY, POLITICS, AND SOCIETY

The series is published in partnership with the Centre for Applied Philosophy, Politics & Ethics (CAPPE), University of Brighton.

Series Editors:

Bob Brecher, Professor of Moral Philosophy, University of Brighton

Robin Dunford, Senior Lecturer in Globalisation and War, University of Brighton

Michael Neu, Senior Lecturer in Philosophy, Politics and Ethics, University of Brighton

Off the Fence presents short, sharply argued texts in applied moral and political philosophy, with an interdisciplinary focus. The series constitutes a source of arguments on the substantive problems that applied philosophers are concerned with: contemporary real-world issues relating to violence, human nature, justice, equality and democracy, self and society. The series demonstrates applied philosophy to be at once rigorous, relevant, and accessible—philosophy-in-use.

Titles in Series

The Right of Necessity: Moral Cosmopolitanism and Global Poverty, by Alejandra Mancilla
Complicity: Criticism between Collaboration and Commitment, by Thomas Docherty
The State and the Self: Identity and Identities, by Maren Behrensen
Just Liberal Violence: Sweatshops, Torture, War, by Michael Neu
The Troubles with Democracy, by Jeff Noonan
Against Borders: Why the World Needs Free Movement of People, by Alex Sager
Digital Working Lives: Worker Autonomy and the Gig Economy, by Tim Christiaens

Digital Working Lives

Worker Autonomy and the Gig Economy

Tim Christiaens

ROWMAN & LITTLEFIELD
Lanham • Boulder • New York • London

Published by Rowman & Littlefield
An imprint of The Rowman & Littlefield Publishing Group, Inc.
4501 Forbes Boulevard, Suite 200, Lanham, Maryland 20706
www.rowman.com

86-90 Paul Street, London EC2A 4NE

Copyright © 2023 by The Rowman & Littlefield Publishing Group, Inc.

All rights reserved. No part of this book may be reproduced in any form or by any electronic or mechanical means, including information storage and retrieval systems, without written permission from the publisher, except by a reviewer who may quote passages in a review.

British Library Cataloguing in Publication Information Available

Library of Congress Cataloging-in-Publication Data

Names: Christiaens, Tim, author.
Title: Digital working lives : worker autonomy and the gig economy / Tim Christiaens.
Description: Lanham : Rowman & Littlefield, [2023] | Series: Off the fence: morality, politics and society | Includes bibliographical references and index.
Identifiers: LCCN 2022032751 (print) | LCCN 2022032752 (ebook) | ISBN 9781538173732 (cloth) | ISBN 9781538173800 (paper) | ISBN 9781538173749 (epub)
Subjects: LCSH: Supervision of employees. | Electronic surveillance. | Autonomy. | Gig economy. | Social control.
Classification: LCC HF5549.12 .C447 2023 (print) | LCC HF5549.12 (ebook) | DDC 658.3/02–dc23/eng/20220829
LC record available at https://lccn.loc.gov/2022032751
LC ebook record available at https://lccn.loc.gov/2022032752

To Noah and Hebe

Contents

Acknowledgments	ix
Chapter 1: The Creeping Uberization of Work	1
Chapter 2: Governing the Workforce: From the Factory to the Digital Gig Economy	19
Chapter 3: Exploitation and the Digital Capture of Social Cooperation	39
Chapter 4: Alienation in the Platform Economy	59
Chapter 5: The Human Limits to Growth	75
Chapter 6: Worker Autonomy as Collective Self-Valorization?	95
Chapter 7: Worker Autonomy as Conviviality	115
Chapter 8: Toward Convivial Platform Labor	135
Index	153

Acknowledgments

This book is the product of many conversations and discussions. In particular, I would like to thank Robin Dunford, Michael Neu, and Bob Brecher for the confidence they have held in me for writing this book. When I emailed my initial proposal, I was still a PhD student in political philosophy focusing on the exegesis of Michel Foucault and Giorgio Agamben. It was not self-evident, from their perspective, that this would end in a hopefully interesting book about the gig economy. I would also like to thank Natalie Mandziuk, Chris Fischer, and the staff of Rowman & Littlefield for their editorial care in getting the book published.

In the meantime, I have had many opportunities to discuss the content of this work with, among others, Stijn De Cauwer, Patrizia Zanoni, Koen Van Laer, Massimiliano Simons, Lode Lauwaert, Mauritz Kelchtermans, John Hoggan Morris, Natasha Lushetich, James Muldoon, Jeroen Meijerink, Oliver Davis, Chris Watkin, Eugenia Stamboliev, Lisa Herzog, Vladimir Bogoeski, Denise Kasparian, and many more. Some of the thoughts formulated in this book date from so many years ago that it is hard to remember everyone who has generously contributed. I remember, for instance, an evening eight years ago at the university cafeteria of KU Leuven, where Massimiliano Simons and I first read together the chapters from Marx's *Capital* that form the basis for the chapter about exhaustion in this book.

I would also like to thank the philosophy department of Tilburg University for the confidence and support I have received this last year for finishing this book.

Chapter 1

The Creeping Uberization of Work

This book is about broken promises. After the Global Financial Crisis of 2007, the so-called "sharing economy" became a new buzzword in Silicon Valley. Its proponents promised emancipation and autonomy to a workforce crippled by economic recession and government austerity. The hope was to use our collective wealth more effectively by crowdpooling it.[1] Individuals own resources that often remain idle, whereas the latter could be used to benefit both the owners and the general public. Why should everyone own a private car if we can share our cars via the Uber platform? Why would we book expensive hotel rooms, if we can get to know new tourist destinations by couch surfing with one of the locals via Airbnb? Why would we waste time assembling Ikea furniture ourselves if we can contact a neighbor through TaskRabbit to do it for us?

The promises from Big Tech corporations were not only directed at consumers. Workers were expected to profit from the emergence of so-called "digital platforms." Gone were the days workers at the bottom of the labor market had to surrender their autonomy to the commandments of a boss. Even low-skill workers like taxi drivers, delivery couriers, or admin workers could start entrepreneurial careers. Platforms like Uber, Deliveroo, or Amazon Mechanical Turk promised workers flexibility and expanded autonomy. People could now work for themselves and make their own money simply by downloading an app.

The reality of work in the sharing economy is, however, far less auspicious. The sharing economy is rarely about sharing at all. Big Tech corporations rather extract data from social cooperation to generate more private capital. For workers, the sharing economy is better named a "digital gig economy," where people scramble for underpaid gigs by obeying not a human boss but an opaque algorithm. Not a week goes by without some scandal breaking out about undignified working conditions at companies like Uber, Deliveroo, Amazon, or TaskRabbit.

In this book, I will study the problems generated by the digital surveillance of work in the newly emerging digital gig economy. I will study how the algorithms that control the labor process at these companies undermine human autonomy. Though the individuals working for their smartphone apps might not have a real-life boss telling them how to do their job, they still obey commands coming from elsewhere. In this book, I will study what problems come from heteronomous assemblages of digital technology and human labor, and how these entanglements between humans and machines must be redesigned to expand human autonomy. How should we remodel digital platforms to aid, rather than impede digital workers in cultivating an autonomous form of life? Before we delve into these questions, however, I would like to explain what the digital gig economy exactly is and which theoretical frameworks are most suitable to study its problems and opportunities.

1. WHAT IS THE DIGITAL GIG ECONOMY?

Observing the dominance of Big Tech corporations, some commentators warn for the so-called "uberization" of work.[2] In their view, the traditional labor contract with its steady pay, formal rights, and access to social security services is under attack from digital labor platforms. The decline of traditional employment in the global North is, however, not a new phenomenon. In the global South, traditional employment relations have remained the exception rather than the norm. This decline has been an ongoing process since at least the 1970s, long before the rise of ubiquitous digital platforms. But the fallout from the 2007 Global Financial Crisis, and the popularity of digital media, have aggravated the problem during the 2010s. Digital platforms exemplify a new stage in the precarization of labor in general. These platforms operate through smartphone apps that offer precarious "gigs" to isolated workers. Companies like Uber, Deliveroo, or Airbnb do not offer employment contracts, but they present their online platforms as services to "independent contractors" searching for work.[3] They see workers as consumers of their digital services, not as their direct subordinates. This grants platform companies the privilege to bar workers from the opportunities that traditional labor contracts secure. Some commentators fear that looming on the horizon of digitalization is the definitive breakdown of traditional employment relations to the detriment of workers' well-being.

Uber is generally put forward as the paradigmatic case. It offers cheap taxi services through an easily navigated app. Contrary to traditional taxi companies, however, Uber does not own a single car, nor does it employ many drivers. It rather presents itself as a digital service provider to both ends of the transportation transaction. Not only consumers, but also drivers are private users of Uber's app. These drivers are independent, self-employed contractors who merely use Uber as a means to reach clients. Uber itself only claims ownership over the mediating platform that connects the supply of drivers to the demand for transportation. In Uber's own self-understanding, the company is not a taxi business at all but a piece of software independent taxi drivers use for their own little business. Uber owns the marketplace where service providers and consumers meet, but it does not actively coordinate the labor process, or so it claims. Other platform companies use the same argument: Airbnb connects tourists to potential hosts with spare bedrooms, Deliveroo connects hungry consumers to restaurants and couriers, and Amazon connects book publishers to readers. In all kinds of social activities, so-called "Uber-for-X"-companies have emerged. Such companies claim to be mere digital middlemen between suppliers and consumers.

Whether this self-presentation is believable, if platform companies control the entire digital infrastructure of these transactions, is doubtful, as we will see in the upcoming chapters, but let us for now accept platform companies' self-understanding at face value. How do they plan to make money from their services? Downloading the app is often free, yet these companies claim to generate tremendous revenues. We will take a better look at the business model of labor platforms in chapter 3, but in the meanwhile, it is good to know that profits are purportedly generated in four ways:[4]

1. In exchange for their services, platform companies take a cut from every transaction conducted on their platform. When someone, for example, orders food through Deliveroo, the payment is split among the restaurant, the courier, and Deliveroo itself. Because platform companies avoid traditional labor contracts, they can easily expand their slice of the revenue without opposition from workers. The latter enter into a unilaterally predetermined contract of adhesion. They either accept the platform's terms and conditions or do not gain access to the app. Platforms, furthermore, profit from all made transactions because they transfer the risk of losses to workers: if a transaction fails to materialize, the loss is borne by workers alone. In the case of Deliveroo, for instance, workers take the risk of investing in a new bike or driving in busy traffic. If anything goes wrong, or if there simply are no orders, the driver loses time and money.[5] If the transaction is completed, on the other hand, not only the driver but also Deliveroo profits.

2. Platform companies extract data from online transactions to optimize their services. Sometimes they profit from selling this information to data brokers, but more often platforms keep these data in-house. Amazon, for instance, tracks users' behavior to predict and shape future demand. It analyzes information about consumers to create lists of

suggested purchases that encourage users to buy more.[6] Since Amazon takes a cut from every transaction made on its website, maximizing the money circulating on its platform is a sure strategy to enlarge its income.

3. The profitability of online platforms frequently depends on achieving monopoly status. By being the only platform for a specific service, platform companies take a percentage of all transactions in a particular economic sector and can harvest all available data in that domain. Uber, for instance, strategically underprizes its services whenever it enters a new city to outcompete traditional taxi companies.[7] Once Uber achieves a monopoly, it can raise its prices since it has, by then, become an inescapable resource for drivers and consumers. Two circumstances help platform companies acquire monopoly status. They, firstly, evade regulations applicable to traditional offline companies by presenting themselves as tech businesses. Because Uber is supposedly a tech firm and not a taxi business, government-mandated taxi regulations do not apply to Uber's services. By invoking "technological exceptionalism,"[8] platform businesses operate in a regulatory vacuum presenting unfair competition to nondigital companies. Platform companies, secondly, benefit from so-called "network effects": "the more numerous the users who use a platform, the more valuable that platform becomes for everyone else."[9] If all consumers are on Uber, it makes no sense for drivers or consumers to use a different service, even if the alternatives provide better working conditions or prices. Subsequently, the difference between Uber's platform and a city's transportation market, as such, tends to evaporate. Uber owns the market itself.

4. As we will see, many platform companies do not actually generate profits at all.[10] They rely on wealthy investors whose "venture capital" finances the firm until the latter acquires monopoly status. Venture capitalists are financial investors willing to spend high amounts of money over several years in the hope that some investees become the new Amazon or Facebook. If only a few of these investments succeed, the tremendous revenues will still suffice to make up for the losses in other investments. Many platforms, hence, start as promising entrepreneurial ideas in search of investors. Usually, these start-ups build their reputation not by financial prowess but by establishing a convincing narrative with charismatic business leaders, slick elevator pitches, and utopian promises.[11] Sometimes this model of growth-before-profit works spectacularly, as in the case of Amazon, which only started making profits seven years after its founding in 1994. More frequently, however, digital start-ups quickly collapse once their business model becomes visibly unviable.[12] This trend makes some critics doubt the long-term financial

viability of the "growth before profit" model, but it is currently a thriving sector.

Returning to the labor point of view, digital gig work provides some definite advantages to workers. Many workers do not wish to work full time. They might see their activity as a hobby or a small side job.[13] For some, driving an Uber or hosting an Airbnb is genuinely a nice hobby that generates some extra cash. These people are less affected by the downsides of algorithmic management discussed in this book. My focus, however, will be on the workers dependent on digital platforms for their everyday sustenance. This is the most vulnerable group of workers, but even there the story is not entirely negative. The low entry barriers in the digital gig economy, for example, help marginalized workers finding a source of income.[14] Workers who would not be able to find a traditional job—for instance, migrants who do not speak the local language—can often secure income through digital gig work.[15] This partly explains the prevalence of migrants from the global South among the Northern digital workforce. Furthermore, the rise of the digital gig economy responds to a real, widespread call among workers in low-level jobs for more flexibility at work.[16] The monotonous nine-to-five desk job under the direction of a boss no longer inspires a lot of enthusiasm among young people. Workers like the independence and flexibility offered in the digital gig economy.[17] Especially among low-skilled workers, platform gigs might be the best realistic alternative to low-paid precarious jobs in factories or service work. The latter—sometimes coined "McJobs"[18]—are often just as precarious and underpaid but lack the freedom of being one's own boss.

But escaping the human boss is no guaranteed route to freedom. Platform companies replace human surveillance with the algorithmic coordination of the workforce. Deliveroo, Uber, Airbnb, and others meticulously track and analyze their workers' conduct. They distribute rewards and punishments according to how individuals perform on their opaque metrics without actually communicating to workers how and when they are being monitored. The algorithm-as-boss system, thereby, fosters new forms of subjugation. For workers, these algorithms are black boxes that control their work and income with minimal accountability. This strategy of algorithmic control constitutes the core problematic of this book: I will study how the algorithmic management of the workforce in the digital gig economy generates new obstacles to autonomy and how these obstacles can be overcome. What problems emerge from the digital surveillance of gig workers and how can we imagine a more autonomous relation to digital technology in platform work? Some critics call for constraining or outlawing some of these technologies.[19] However, I would like to differentiate between different modes of human/machine entanglement in order to retain some of the emancipatory promises of the early internet, while minimizing the dystopian fallout. Digital technology is not inherently bad, so there is no need to generalize techno-pessimist suspicion, but there are clear problems that need to be addressed in the name of future human autonomy. Distinguishing the dystopic and utopian dimensions of digital platforms will require a theoretical framework to (a) determine exactly how the digital gig economy threatens human autonomy and (b) delineate the values that must be respected in digital gig work in support of workers' autonomy. For the first part of this project, I turn to the post-workerist critique of contemporary digital capitalism. For the second part, I move from post-workerist critique to Ivan Illich's philosophy of technology.

Focusing on the obstacles to and possibilities for workers' autonomy in the digital gig economy, however, means disengaging from other debates in its vicinity. Many thinkers in the post-work debate, for instance, emphasize how people ought to liberate themselves from the compulsion to work entirely in order to achieve human autonomy.[20] In their view, humankind can only be autonomous if it frees itself from "bullshit" jobs. These authors, hence, attack the economic system that forces people to hold and keep a job to survive. In these debates, policy proposals are discussed like the general basic income and the shortening of the work week as means of liberating humankind from the compulsion to work. Another debate I will not entertain is the automation debate.[21] Some argue that digital technology can one day entirely replace the human workforce, so that humanity could afterwards live in blissful unemployment. There are good reasons to be skeptical of such promises, but they are beyond the scope of this book. Both debates deal with autonomy *from* work, whereas I will focus on autonomy *in* work. I will not ask how people can liberate themselves from work as such, but how—now that we have to work anyway—digital gig work can be rendered more compatible with the aspiration of human autonomy. Remembering the etymology of "autonomy" as "self-legislation," can digital platforms be redesigned in such a way that workers rather than capital set the law for themselves?

2. POST-WORKERISM AND THE STRUGGLE FOR WORKERS' AUTONOMY

I will explore the obstacles to human autonomy in the digital gig economy with the help of post-workerist philosophy. Originally, workerism arose in 1960s Italy as an update to Karl Marx' critique of political economy.[22] In the journals *Quaderni Rossi* and *Classe Operaia,* activist thinkers like Mario Tronti, Antonio Negri, Raniero Panzieri, and Romano Alquati elaborated a Marxist philosophy opposed to the official doctrines of the Italian communist party. According to Tronti's magnum opus, *Workers and Capital*, "after Marx, no one has known anything new about the working class. It still remains an unknown continent."²³ To explore this *terra incognita,* workerists conducted workers' inquiries to acquire first-hand knowledge of working-class aspirations and struggles beyond the pages of sclerotic Marxist dogma. In workerist philosophy, proletarian class consciousness cannot be gauged in philosophical analyses of the dialectics of capital, but among workers themselves. By engaging directly with factory workers, workerists uncovered a proletarian class far more defiant of capitalist rule than their more theoretically inclined comrades had suggested.

Traditional Marxist sociologists, like the Frankfurt School, had described the postwar working class as an integrated and pacified mass of atomized individuals. In their view, the social compromise between capital and labor after World War II had turned the working class complacent to total administration, one-dimensional, and in fear of freedom. According to Adorno and Horkheimer,

> Capitalist production so confines [consumers], body and soul, that they fall helpless victims to what is offered to them. As naturally as the ruled always took the morality imposed upon them more seriously than did the rulers themselves, the deceived masses are today captivated by the myth of success even more than the successful are. Immovably they insist on the very ideology which enslaves them. [. . .] The result is a constant reproduction of the same thing.²⁴

For the Frankfurt School, the pacification of working-class subjugation was an accomplished fact. Italian workers' inquiries, however, revealed a working class far less complacent.²⁵ Workerists encountered subtle and multifarious forms of resistance that enabled workers to take control of the labor process.²⁶ For the workerists, capital was not an all-powerful apparatus capable of preemptively canceling all opposition, but a fragile obstacle to working class autonomy. They noticed, for instance, that absenteeism was often a hidden tactic to escape capitalist compulsion. Lunch breaks and informal social gatherings, secondly, fostered "invisible organizations" upon which workers could rely during insurgencies.²⁷ Workerists also revealed that workers could use the assembly line to their advantage by engaging in spontaneous actions of so-called *"autoriduzione."*²⁸ Instead of collectively going on strike, individual workers would take turns to strike or feign an injury. Such a dissemination of disruptions would incessantly interrupt the streamlined workflow of large-scale factories until the whole production process broke down. The factory would come to a halt, not through large-scale unionized opposition but thanks to a flood of microscopic acts of disruption. According to workerists, such subtle forms of work refusal (*rifiuto del lavoro*) demonstrated that the working class was perfectly capable of autonomously organizing its political and economic operations without the need for guidance from a Leninist party cadre or capital.[29]

Based on these observations of working-class resistance, Tronti argues that capitalist society can only integrate the working class in an antagonistic fashion. In his view, the Frankfurt pacification thesis does not align with working-class experience. Workers are first and foremost "living labor" (i.e., embodied living beings that modify their surroundings through labor.)[30] But, in order to survive, living labor must commodify itself as "labor-power." Workers must sell their potential for labor during specific sets of time in exchange for a wage. During those hours, labor-power is a "figure of capital," an integral moment of capital's own self-propelling accumulation cycle.[31] Capital determines how this labor-power is mobilized in the production process and at what pace. Concrete human labor becomes the mere phenomenal form that capital assumes to expand itself. So, even though capital can only exist by extracting value from human labor, the latter appears as a mere extension of capital.

Workers, however, do not coincide with their assigned role as capital's instruments. They remain living labor capable of much more than the capitalist production process requires.[32] As embodied living beings, workers are capable of autonomously and collectively directing their labor to fulfill common projects, yet capital restricts this capacity to generate private profit. According to Tronti, this excess living labor remains a constant source of friction "within and against" (*dentro e contro*) capital.[33] Living labor is always already capable of self-organization, and recurrent resistance shows that the working class does not need capital to steer its labor. Workers only submit to capitalist discipline because their social conditions render them dependent on wages. As Tronti writes, "constrained—not by juridical laws but economic ones—to sell labour-power, which is to say, to sell themselves on the market as a commodity, [workers] find themselves already individually united against the capitalist even before they begin to produce capital. . . . Workers enter into capital, are reduced to a part of capital, *as* a working class. Capital now has its enemy within."[34]

This theory of ineradicable working-class antagonism leads Tronti to defend a unique theory of capitalist development. Usually, capitalist development is explained as the outcome of capitalists' quest for efficiency. Capitalist entrepreneurs supposedly invent new technologies and organizational forms to maximize profit. For Tronti, however, innovations are not the product of inventive entrepreneurs but instruments for containing class struggle. Capital only changes its internal composition reluctantly, when working-class resistance compels it to change. According to Tronti, "the pressure of labour-power is able to force capital to modify its own internal composition; it intervenes *within* capital as an essential component of capitalist development; it pushes capitalist production forward from within."[35] Since capital needs the integration of labor-power to secure its expansion, labor-power can disrupt capital's operations from within. To contain this force of disruption, capital must regularly update its internal composition. With every new escape attempt from the working class, capital has to redesign the apparatus that keeps workers in check. Tronti illustrates this dynamic with Marx' depiction of industrialization in *Capital: Volume I*.[36] According to Marx, large-scale industrial technologies were not introduced because capitalists spontaneously explored efficiency gains in the production process. Capitalist management was *forced* to look for technical advances once the working class successfully acquired a legal reduction of the working day. If capital could no longer keep workers in the factory for more than twelve hours a day, it had to find different methods to guarantee profitability. It had to introduce technologies that make workers more productive during their restricted working hours. According to Tronti, not capital but the working-class desire for autonomy drives the capitalist system forward until it will eventually break.

The apocalyptic breakdown Tronti envisioned did not take place during the workers' revolts of the 1960s and 1970s. Many years later, Tronti reminisces that 'workers' struggles determine the course of capitalist development; but capitalist development will use those struggles for its own ends if no organized revolutionary process opens up, capable of changing the balance of forces."[37] The revolts in Italy and beyond for better wages, more freedom of expression, and alternative lifestyles were ultimately reincorporated into capitalism. In response to workers' demand for more autonomy, capital reconfigured its internal composition to accommodate for this desire without letting it undermine capitalism as a whole.[38] As I will show in chapter 2, since the 1970s, capital has moved monotonous factory jobs abroad and has replaced them in the global North with so-called "immaterial labor," (i.e., service jobs that demand individual creativity and social interaction). The digital gig economy is, in this field, just a small part of the immaterial sector, which also comprises research and development, elderly care, marketing, and so forth. Workerism consequently had to adapt as well, morphing into what is today commonly called "post-workerism," a Marxist philosophy that combines the experiences of Italian workerist activism with the critical philosophies of French thinkers like Gilles Deleuze, Michel Foucault, and Félix Guattari.[39] This new form of thought reached its climax in 2000 with the publication of *Empire* by former workerist leader Antonio Negri and his American collaborator Michael Hardt.

Negatively formulated, the basic thesis of *Empire* is that the factory is no longer the primary terrain of struggle and the traditional working class is no longer the obvious revolutionary subject. Instead, according to Hardt and Negri, once capitalist production spreads from the factory to all forms of social interaction, society itself becomes the site of struggle.[40] In this novel terrain, not merely the working class but "the multitude" is the new enemy of capital. Once not just the factory, but the home, social life, and the internet become sites of contestation, not just workers but all of humankind is involved in the struggle against capital. Hardt and Negri take the concept of multitude from Spinoza to reveal the opportunities for resistance and collective autonomy in this new political conjuncture.[41] They oppose this Spinozist notion to the Hobbesian concept of "people."[42] According to Hobbes, the masses can only constitute an organized political unity by submitting to a common authority, the state. If they refuse to be subjugated, isolated individuals purportedly come to nothing but anarchy and violence. People, in other words, need a transcendent leader to withhold them from killing each other. Political organization has to be imposed upon the people from above. According to *Empire*'s Spinoza however, individuals in the state of nature are perfectly capable of rationally perceiving that collective self-organization is in their own best interest. The multitude does not need a state to form a politically unified collective subject. Through spontaneous cooperation, individuals form an autonomous collective without the need for a sovereign. In Spinoza's worldview, human beings possess the common capacity for collective self-organization. According to Hardt and Negri, the internet is even the ideal instrument for this multitudinal cooperation. It provides an infrastructure for individuals to spontaneously communicate and collaborate. People form online communities without a center of power that tells them what to do or how to organize. The Spinozist promise of a humankind united as multitude beyond the state can finally become a reality thanks to the technological affordances of the internet age.

One can easily spot the affinity between Tronti's self-organizing working class and *Empire*'s multitude. Workerists had already perceived factory workers' capacity to autonomously organize struggles and the production process in the 1960s. Now that capitalist production has moved beyond the factory, this capacity for autonomous self-government also becomes apparent across the whole social spectrum. According to Hardt and Negri, contemporary capitalism even depends on people's multitudinal capacities for spontaneous self-organization. In today's work environments, people are expected to use their creativity and social skills to organize with each other as a multitude, as we will see in more detail in the next chapter. The potential for collective autonomy is hence present in the current age; it is merely a matter of wresting its force from the capitalist system that tries to control it. By encouraging virtues like creativity, social cooperation, and self-reliance, contemporary capitalism has purportedly incorporated its own gravediggers. "The multitude, in its will to be-against and its desire for liberation, must push through Empire to come out the other side."[43]

3. TOWARD CONVIVIAL AUTONOMY IN THE DIGITAL GIG ECONOMY

The influence of post-workerism on critical literature about the digital gig economy is considerable.[44] It forms the backdrop for the writings of Trebor Scholz, Christian Fuchs, Callum Cant, Jamie Woodcock, and many more. I will, however, only use it to criticize the obstacles to human autonomy in chapters 2 to 5. Chapters 6, 7, and 8 will, on the contrary, be devoted to discussing more emancipatory modes of relating to digital technology with the help of Ivan Illich's philosophy of technology and convivial autonomy. The *pars destruens* of this book hence follows post-workerist intuitions very closely, but the *pars construens* takes theoretical resources from elsewhere to investigate the possibilities for workers' autonomy in the digital gig economy. Two reasons explain the need for this shift of perspective:

(1) Though post-workerism values workers' autonomy as a key concept, it lacks a conceptual analysis of "autonomous working conditions."[45] It remains unclear what criteria have to be respected in order for work to qualify as autonomous. One scans the pages of *Workers and Capital* or *Empire* in vain for a definition of autonomy. This omission is, however, not due to a lack of intellectual rigor, but a consequence of the method of workers' inquiries. Post-workerists focus on political struggles in the here-and-now, not on the future these struggles are supposed to establish. As Tronti argues, "no worker who is fighting a boss is going to ask, 'And then what?' The fight against the boss is everything. The organisation of this struggle is everything. This constitutes a whole world."[46] Post-workerism is a theory born from class struggle; what futures this struggle is supposed to reveal lies beyond its horizon. As a result, many post-workerist writers researching the digital gig economy today focus on workers' struggles and strikes, not so much on the ethical values that should inform alternative economies.[47] This makes post-workerism extremely helpful in diagnosing the problems against which workers in the digital gig economy struggle, but it does not imagine alternative, better digital platforms. The normative guidelines for future human/machine-relations are hard to derive from the immediacy of class struggle.

(2) The central concepts of post-workerism, put forward over twenty years ago in *Empire*, were not designed for an age dominated by Google, Uber, and Amazon.[48] The first iPhone was released in 2007, Uber was founded in 2009, and almost all publications about the digital gig economy date from after 2015. It is, hence, not self-evident that concepts like "multitude," "immaterial labor," or "general intellect" can apply to the 2020s as they did to the 2000s. Hardt and Negri have had to update their original paradigm every few years with the publication of *Multitude* (2004), *Commonwealth* (2009),

and *Assembly* (2017)—not counting their other collaborative projects. If one thus wants to respect the situational specificity of workers' struggles in the digital gig economy, one should remain cautious of blind applications. To mention one example, the post-workerist thinker Franco "Bifo" Berardi has become critical of Negri's and Hardt's optimistic portrayal of the multitude's self-organizing capacities in the digital age. He argues that

> If we want to understand something more about the present social subjectivity, the concept of multitude needs to be complemented with the concepts of the network and swarm. A network is a plurality of organic and artificial beings, of humans and machines, who perform common actions thanks to procedures that make possible their interconnection and interoperation. If you do not adapt to these procedures, if you don't follow the technical rules of the game, you are not playing the game. If you don't react to certain stimuli in a programmed way, you don't form part of the network.[49]

Negri and Hardt believe the multitude can organize itself spontaneously and autonomously. For them, the internet is primarily a new medium and instrument for social cooperation. The internet is a "democratic network is a completely horizontal and deterritorialized model."[50] According to Berardi however, digital networks can subsume human interactions so pervasively that human conduct becomes preprogrammed. As we will see in the following chapters, algorithmic governance surreptitiously modifies human choices. It thus becomes hard to say whether human organization online is the product of the multitude's spontaneous potential for social cooperation or of decentralized nebulous planning. The internet does not *necessarily* serve the expansion of human autonomy, as Hardt and Negri still naively believed in *Empire*. Something needs to change about digital technology to make it compatible with human autonomy, but this "something" remains unthought in the classics of post-workerist thought.

To imagine workers' autonomy in human/machine-relations, I propose to move from post-workerism to degrowth philosophy of technology, particularly Ivan Illich. The degrowth movement is an ecological movement that stresses the limits to economic growth and subsequently tries to imagine alternative forms of life and economic conduct that do not rely on economic growth or environmental pollution. Though this summary seems a project alien to the Marxist heritage of post-workerism, the shift is less dramatic than one would expect: some of the founders of degrowth thought have roots in 1960s workerism (Cornelius Castoriadis) and both movements share an interest in anticapitalist and antistatist projects like the promotion of the commons (Michel Bauwens), citizen science (Ivan Illich), and ending wage labor (André Gorz). Ivan Illich plays a vital role in the development of degrowth thought for his critique of modern industrial technology. He argues that modern technology is often promoted with the promise of expanding the reach of human autonomy, whereas, in reality, these tools often subjugate their human users. According to Illich, "the hypothesis was that machines can replace slaves. The evidence shows that, used for this purpose, machines enslave men."[51] This disappointing conclusion resonates well with the experiences of workers in the digital gig economy. They were promised digital tools that would make their lives more autonomous, yet, in actual fact, they have become slaves to an algorithm. The advantage of Illich's critical theory of technology, however, is that he couples his critique to a positively formulated ideal. The technologies Illich wishes to promote, expand human beings' so-called "convivial autonomy." By this, Illich means that some tools make people independent from commodified or marketized services, enable their potential for collective self-determination, and allow them to construct a lifeworld imbued with human meaning. One of his key examples is the library: instead of imposing a fixed educational curriculum on people, libraries grant them access to a mass of intellectual resources with no preestablished instructions about how to navigate these resources or how to use them. Individuals can build their own intellectual world from the books they assemble along their random walks through the library hallways. Illich's analysis thus leads to a tripartite definition of convivial autonomy, a project that entails the promotion of (1) human independence, (2) collective self-determination, and (3) the cultivation of meaningful relationships to each other and the world.

In this book, I will attempt to imagine how digital labor platforms must be reformed to become convivial tools. I will take the experience of platform cooperatives as my template to think about what convivial autonomy can mean in the digital gig economy. In contrast to the privately owned platforms from Silicon Valley, platform cooperatives allocate ownership and control of the digital infrastructure to users themselves. In the case of labor platforms, this means workers themselves determine the operative systems of the platforms they work with. This arrangement is ideal for the formation of a kind of guild socialism reminiscent of the thought of G. D. H. Cole. Platform workers hold control over the algorithms that judge their performance. Consequently, their shared work experiences and values about the quality of work provide a basis for a meaningful common identity among platform workers. This collective identity can be a valuable resource for the establishment of more wholesome human/machine-relations.

NOTES

1. Alex Rosenblat, *Uberland: How Algorithms Are Rewriting the Rules of Work* (Oakland, CA: University of California Press, 2018), 31–32; Alexandrea Ravenelle, *Hustle and Gig: Struggling and Surviving in the Sharing Economy* (Oakland: University of California Press, 2019), 26; Juliet Schor, *After the Gig: How the Sharing Economy Got Hijacked and How to Win It Back* (Oakland: University of California Press, 2020), 16.

2. Trebor Scholz, *Uberworked and Underpaid: How Workers Are Disrupting the Digital Economy* (Cambridge: Polity Press, 2017); Sarah Kessler, *Gigged: The Gig Economy, the End of the Job and the Future of Work* (London: Random House Business Books, 2018); Rosenblat, *Uberland*; Colin Crouch, *Will the Gig Economy Prevail?* (Cambridge: Polity Press, 2019); Jamie Woodcock and Mark Graham, *The Gig Economy: A Critical Introduction* (Cambridge: Polity Press, 2020).

3. The classification of platform workers as independent contractors rather than employees has been repeatedly contested in court with mixed results. The European Commission has, for instance, suggested making the employee status the official norm. In California, however, the 2020 referendum over Proposition 22 has infamously blocked courts from recognizing platform workers as employees. For an overview, see Valerio De Stefano et al., "Platform Work and the Employment Relationship" (International Labour Organization, March 2021), https://www.ilo.org/wcmsp5/groups/public/---ed_protect/---protrav/---travail/documents/publication/wcms_777866.pdf.

4. See Srnicek, *Platform Capitalism*, 36–92; Shoshana Zuboff, *The Age of Surveillance Capitalism: The Fight for the Future at the New Frontier of Power* (London: Profile Books, 2019), 63–97; Nick Couldry and Ulises Mejias, *The Costs of Connection: How Data Is Colonizing Human Life and Appropriating It for Capitalism* (Stanford, CA: Stanford University Press, 2019), 83–112.

5. Callum Cant, *Riding for Deliveroo: Resistance in the New Economy* (Cambridge: Polity Press, 2020), 57.

6. Jake Alimahomed-Wilson, Ellen Reese, and Juliann Allison, "Introduction: Amazon Capitalism," in *The Cost of Free Shipping: Amazon in the Global Economy* (London: Pluto Press, 2020), 4–5.

7. Rosenblat, *Uberland*, 168–69.

8. Rosenblat, 34.

9. Srnicek, *Platform Capitalism*, 45.

10. Srnicek, 21; K. Sabeel Rahman and Kathleen Thelen, "The Rise of the Platform Business Model and the Transformation of Twenty-First-Century Capitalism," *Politics & Society* 47, no. 2 (June 2019): 183–85.

11. Adam Arvidsson, *Changemakers: The Industrious Future of the Digital Economy* (Cambridge: Polity Press, 2019), 82–93.

12. Schor, *After the Gig*, 37. One particularly spectacular case is the collapse of WeWork. This platform, led by the charismatic Adam Neumann, claimed to digitally connect available flexible office spaces to companies and freelance workers looking for a place to work. The project was almost entirely bankrolled by Softbank,

a Japanese bank specializing in venture capital investments. In 2019, the start-up attempted an initial public offering on Wall Street but failed miserably once it actually had to provide transparency about its finances. Neumann had to step down and the company never recovered from this embarrassment. See Antonio Aloisi and Valerio De Stefano, *Il Tuo Capo è Un Algoritmo: Contro Il Lavoro Disumano* (Bari: Editori GLF Laterza, 2020), 51.

13. See Rosenblat, *Uberland*, 50–65; Schor, *After the Gig*, 42–43.

14. Moritz Altenried, "The Platform as Factory: Crowdwork and the Hidden Labour Behind Artificial Intelligence," *Capital & Class* 44, no. 2 (2020): 153–56; Phil Jones, *Work without the Worker: Labour in the Age of Platform Capitalism* (London: Verso Books, 2021), 11.

15. Cant, *Riding for Deliveroo*, 90.

16. Woodcock and Graham, *The Gig Economy*, 30.

17. Schor, *After the Gig*, 29.

18. Douglas Coupland, *Generation X: Tales for an Accelerated Culture* (New York: St. Martin's Press, 1991), 5.

19. Zuboff, *The Age of Surveillance Capitalism*, 53.

20. See, among others, Kathi Weeks, *The Problem with Work: Feminism, Marxism, Antiwork Politics, and Postwork Imaginaries* (Durham: Duke University Press, 2011); Nick Srnicek and Alex Williams, *Inventing the Future: Postcapitalism and a World without Work* (London: Verso, 2016); David Graeber, *Bullshit Jobs: A Theory* (London: Penguin Books, 2019); Helen Hester and Will Stronge, *After Work: The Fight for Free Time* (London: Verso Books, 2021).

21. Paul Mason, *Postcapitalism: A Guide to Our Future* (New York: Farrar, Strauss, and Giroux, 2017); Aaron Bastani, *Fully Automated Luxury Communism: A Manifesto* (London: Verso, 2020); Daniel Susskind, *A World without Work: Technology, Automation, and How We Should Respond* (New York, NY: Metropolitan Books/Henry Holt & Company, 2020); Aaron Benanav, *Automation and the Future of Work* (London: Verso Books, 2020); Jason Smith, *Smart Machines and Service Work: Automation in an Age of Stagnation* (London: Reaktion Books, 2020).

22. For a full history, see Robert Lumley, *States of Emergency: Cultures of Revolt in Italy from 1968 to 1978* (London: Verso, 1990); Steve Wright, *Storming Heaven: Class Composition and Struggle in Italian Autonomist Marxism* (London: Pluto Press, 2002); Patrick Cunninghame, "Autonomia in the 1970s: The Refusal of Work, the Party and Power,"*Cultural Studies Review* 11, no. 2 (2005): 77–94; Tim Christiaens, "Uit Verzet Geboren: De Filosofische Erfenis van Het Operaismo," *Ethische Perspectieven* 28, no. 2 (2018): 87–111.

23. Mario Tronti, *Workers and Capital*, trans. David Broder (London: Verso, 2019), xxiii.

24. Theodor W. Adorno and Max Horkheimer, *Dialectic of Enlightenment*, trans. John Cumming (London: Verso Books, 1997), 133–34.

25. Franco Berardi Bifo, *The Soul at Work: From Alienation to Autonomy*, Semiotext(e) Foreign Agents Series (Los Angeles, CA: Semiotext(e), 2009), 49.

26. Antonio Negri, *Reflections on Empire*, trans. Ed Emery (Cambridge: Polity Press, 2008), 36.

27. Romano Alquati, "Struggle at FIAT," trans. Evan Calder Williams, Viewpoint Magazine, 26 September 2013, https://viewpointmag.com/2013/09/26/struggle-at-fiat-1964/.
28. Lumley, *States of Emergency*, 185.
29. Tronti, *Workers and Capital*, 10.
30. Tronti, 157.
31. Tronti, 13.
32. Tronti, 206.
33. Tronti, xix.
34. Tronti, 138.
35. Tronti, 21–22.
36. See Tronti, 22–35.
37. Mario Tronti, "Our Operaismo," *New Left Review* 73, no. 1 (2012): 128.
38. For an empirical description, see Luc Boltanski and Ève Chiapello, *Le nouvel esprit du capitalisme* (Paris: Gallimard, 2011).
39. For an overview of this evolution, see Matteo Mandarini, "Antagonism, Contradiction, Time: Conflict and Organization in Antonio Negri," *The Sociological Review* 53, no. 1 (2005): 192–214; Joost de Bloois, Monica Jansen, and Frans Willem Korsten, "Introduction: From Autonomism to Post-Autonomia, from Class Composition to a New Political Anthropology?," *Rethinking Marxism* 26, no. 2 (2014): 163–77.
40. Michael Hardt and Antonio Negri, *Empire* (Cambridge, MA: Harvard University Press, 2000), 209.
41. For more on Negri's reception of Spinoza, see Antonio Negri, *Subversive Spinoza: (Un)Contemporary Variations*, trans. Timothy S. Murphy (Manchester: Manchester University Press, 2004); Antonio Negri, *The Savage Anomaly: The Power of Spinoza's Metaphysics and Politics*, trans. Michael Hardt (Minneapolis: University of Minnesota Press, 2008); Antonio Negri, *Spinoza for Our Time: Politics and Postmodernity*, trans. William McCuaig (New York: Columbia University Press, 2013); Antonio Negri, *Spinoza: Then and Now*, trans. Ed Emery (Cambridge: Polity Press, 2020).
42. See Negri, *Reflections on Empire*, 79–95.
43. Hardt and Negri, *Empire*, 218.
44. Roberto Ciccarelli, *Forza Lavoro: Il Lato Oscuro Della Rivoluzione Digitale* (Roma: DeriveApprodi, 2018); Christian Fuchs, *Rereading Marx in the Age of Digital Capitalism* (London: Pluto Press, 2019); Cant, *Riding for Deliveroo*; Woodcock and Graham, *The Gig Economy*; Tim Christiaens, "Digital Biopolitics and the Problem of Fatigue in Platform Capitalism," in *Big Data: A New Medium?*, ed. Natasha Lushetich (London: Routledge, 2020), 80–93; Alessandro Delfanti, *The Warehouse: Workers and Robots at Amazon* (London: Pluto Press, 2021).
45. Though (post-)workerism is sometimes called "autonomist Marxism,' this name is predominantly a product of Anglophone interpreters of the (post-)workerist tradition, not of (post-)workerists themselves (Ben Trott, "Operaismo and the Wicked Problem of Organization," *Journal of Labor and Society* 20, no. 3 (2017): 316.
46. Tronti, *Workers and Capital*, xxiv.
47. See, for instance, Cant, *Riding for Deliveroo*.

48. See also Antonio Negri and Michael Hardt, "Empire, Twenty Years On," *New Left Review* 120, no. 6 (2020): 67–92.

49. Franco Berardi Bifo, *The Uprising: On Poetry and Finance* (Los Angeles: Semiotext(e), 2012), 14–15.

50. Hardt and Negri, *Empire*, 299.

51. Ivan Illich, *Tools for Conviviality* (London: Marion Boyars, 1972), 23.

Chapter 2

Governing the Workforce

From the Factory to the Digital Gig Economy

> To work at a machine, the workman should be taught from childhood, in order that he may learn to adapt his own movements to the uniform and unceasing motion of an automaton.
>
> —Karl Marx

After delineating the scope of the digital gig economy and the method of post-workerist critique, we should ascertain how workers are governed in the digital gig economy. What role do digital technologies play in labor coordination? As Lazzarato correctly remarks, one cannot write the history of technologies independently from the "social machines" in which they are embedded.[1] The logic of technological development expresses, to a large extent, the social conditions in which these technologies are invented and implemented. That is why, according to Marx, "it would be possible to write quite a history of the inventions, made since 1830, for the sole purpose of supplying capital with weapons against the revolts of the working class."[2] If we wish to outline the role of digital technology in today's digital gig economy, we should hence describe the social circumstances in which they are implemented and the strategic role they play in the struggle between labor and capital. I proceed in three steps: first, I briefly outline the role of technology in the factory-society of the nineteenth century until the end of Fordism in the 1970s. Second, I describe the post-Fordist corporation as today's successor to the Fordist factory. Working-class struggles rendered the factory-society unsustainable, so capital responded with a reorganization of the mode of production that sought to immunize firms from working-class tactics. In the third section, I specify the role of digital technologies in breaking up working-class resistance and adapting workers to the rhythm of capital accumulation.

1. THE INDUSTRIAL FACTORY UNDER FORDISM

From the days when Marx wrote his major works to the 1970s, the factory was the central social machine of capitalist production. Many conditions changed in those decades, but large-scale industry producing standardized commodities remained the norm. Cities and towns were organized around the factories that employed the majority of the urban population. The specificity of twentieth-century Fordism concerned how it combatted the capitalist problem of overproduction. Factories spewed out masses of cheap commodities, but since workers were too poor to buy them, capitalists were left with loads of unrealized value. Entrepreneurs like Henry Ford and economists like John Maynard Keynes addressed this problem by reinterpreting the problem of overproduction as an issue of underconsumption: by paying workers more, granting them political representation in unions and political parties, securing social benefits, and boosting overall employment, workers accessed higher levels of subsistence that allowed them to buy the products factories created. Mass producers were transformed into mass consumers.

Although workers were given many benefits lacking in Marx' days, labor conditions in the Fordist factory were not necessarily worker friendly. Mass production necessitated the fast pace of assembly-line production and a detailed division of labor that squeezed any craftsmanship out of the labor process. Workers were reduced to automated cogs in a self-sustaining production system. In Marx' eloquent prose,

> In handicrafts and manufacture, the workman makes use of a tool; in the factory the machine makes use of him. There the movements of the instrument of labour proceed from him; here it is the movements of the machine that he must follow. In manufacture the workmen are part of a living mechanism. In the factory we have a lifeless mechanism independent of the workman, who becomes its mere living appendage.... By means of its conversion into an automaton, the instrument of labour confronts the labourer, during the labour process, in the shape of capital, of dead labour, that dominates, and pumps dry, living labour power.[3]

To guarantee workers' compliance with assembly-line production, capital had to establish an intricate system of foremen, planning offices, production targets, and so forth. The production process had to discipline the unruly bodies of workers into docile "living appendages" of a self-propelling machine. A "continuous struggle against the element of 'animality' in man" had to transform living labor into moments of an autonomous production cycle.[4] Management scientists like Frederick Taylor, thus, spent their careers exploring how to displace control over the labor process from the workplace to centralized planning offices servicing the factory owners.[5] Taylorism effectuated a "psycho-physical adaptation [among workers] to the new industrial structure";[6] it employed all kinds of techniques to expropriate workers from control over the labor process. For capitalist production to remain operative, the factory owners had to determine the quality and pace of industrial production. This alteration of the labor process to fit capital's needs, Marx called "the real subsumption of labour under capital."[7] Instead of merely profiting from the labor process but leaving its precapitalist self-organization intact, Taylorist techniques altered the labor process itself directly to serve capital accumulation.

Technology played a crucial role in this real subsumption of labor. In section 3 of chapter 15 of *Capital: Volume I* on "The approximate effects of machinery on the workmen," Marx already outlined three possible ways in which factory technology affected workers: (1) deskilling, (2) prolonging the workday, and (3) intensifying labor productivity.[8] In the nineteenth century, all three were relevant, but by the time of twentieth-century Fordism, the third mechanism gained special prominence. Allow me to outline all three ways capital dispossessed workers of their control over the labor process:

(1) The machinery of large-scale industry rendered much of workers' expertise from previous eras redundant. An old-school car mechanic had to know the intricate details of his craft to assemble or fix cars, but working at a General Motors assembly line in Detroit required minimal skills or experience. A few days of instruction and the willingness to blindly follow orders sufficed in the industrial factory. Skilled workers subsequently lost much of their bargaining power. Employers could easily replace refractory workers with more docile subjects. Automation created a few skilled jobs in maintenance and office labor, but it mostly displaced expensive craftsmen with cheaper, deskilled workers. Not only were skilled resistant workers no longer in demand, but the deskilling of factory labor opened up the labor market for an "industrial reserve army" of unemployed workers. In the nineteenth century, women and children entered the factories, but even in the twentieth century, employers avidly attracted unskilled migrant workers to outcompete their more expensive Western counterparts. Deskilling, in other words, meant fewer jobs for more people so that competition among workers undermined working-class solidarity against capital.

(2) To constitute a profitable investment in the nineteenth century, many factory machines had to operate nonstop to recuperate their costs. Capitalists, thus, had an incentive to keep their labor force at work as much as possible, leading to twelve-hour workdays, six days a week. In traditional Marxist

terminology, capital extracted "absolute surplus value" from the workforce by prolonging the workday. Any value the capitalist could realize beyond production and labor costs, he could pocket as surplus value. If the capitalist could force workers to work more hours than would be required to repay their own wage and the costs of machinery, energy consumption, and resources, the value generated during these extra hours was free surplus value for capital. The political action of unions and socialist parties, however, put pressure on capitalists' ability to prolong the workday and, thereby, extract absolute surplus value. Through many decades of struggle, labor relations moved slowly to the norm of a nine-to-five job, five days a week. Workers were relatively successful in shortening the workday and establishing a fairly strict boundary between labor time and free time. Nonetheless, some Marxists in the 1960s and 1970s argued that this distinction was an illusion, since free time had been rendered serviceable to capital as well. According to Tronti, "when the factory extends its control over the whole of society—all of social production is turned into industrial production—the specific traits of the factory are lost amid the generic traits of society."[9] Frankfurt School thinkers like Adorno, for instance, complained that mass consumerism in the form of advertising or pop music extended the stultified mind of the assembly line worker to the social and cultural sphere.[10] Critics like Braverman, on the other hand, argued that mass production commodified many previously noncapitalist, leisurely activities, making people increasingly dependent on the world market.[11] Once people, for instance, stopped cultivating their own vegetables in their gardens, they depended on the capitalist production of food for their subsistence. The official workday might hence have shrunken down compared to the nineteenth century, but more and more free time had by the 1970s been incorporated in the cycle of capital accumulation.

(3) If the workday cannot be prolonged, capitalists must increase labor productivity to secure surplus value. They employ technology to increase the intensity of the work pace. The labor process thereby shifts from absolute to relative surplus value: by making workers more productive in the same amount of time, less labor-time is required to repay production costs and more surplus remains. The same amount of labor, subsequently, generates more value. One significant advantage of industrial machinery, in this regard, was that the centralized planning offices could predetermine production speeds. The assembly line set the pace of work, and workers had to follow. Slacking was not punished by the foremen but by the heavy machinery that mercilessly kept running. Since one cannot reason with a machine, technological innovations like the assembly line surreptitiously undermined working-class resistance. Production speeds were not determined through personal decisions but were embedded in the architecture of the production process itself. Management enforced higher productivity through automated means.

Still, the Fordist equilibrium between labor and capital, mediated by factory technology, was unstable. The technical composition of capital steadily created its own gravediggers in the form of working-class revolts during the 1960s and 1970s. According to Tronti, the political and technical integration of workers into the capitalist production process also posed a danger to capitalism itself:

> When the total labour agrees to participate reasonably in the general development, it ends up functioning as just another part of total social capital. The only thing to be attained along this path is the most balanced and rational development of capital. It is at this point that the working class must instead consciously organize itself as an *irrational* element within the specific rationality of capitalist production. The growing rationalisation of modern capital must find an insurmountable limit in the growing irrationality of the organised workers.[12]

By weaving a tightly knit production process of workers and machines, capital rendered itself vulnerable to working-class resistance. The main obstacle to the Taylorist rationalization of production remained a recalcitrant workforce embedded at the heart of industrial production. The factory gathered many workers in a concentrated space and forced them to cooperate intensely to manage the workflow of mass production. Small moments of disruption in the production cycle could, hence, create major ripple effects all over the factory system, as the example of *autoriduzione* from the previous chapter shows. The Fordist social compromise attempted to alleviate this pressure by "buying workers off" with high wages, social benefits, unions, and so forth, but these measures only made workers desire for more. "An insubordinate use of integration then becomes possible," according to Tronti.[13] The working class could use capital's means of political integration to incessantly increase its demands until they eventually threatened industrial profitability itself. At a certain threshold, wages and benefits became so expensive that the sustenance of capitalism was simply no longer worth the investment, pushing capitalism into a deep crisis.[14]

Simultaneously, new social movements extended the sense of crisis beyond the factory. In the workerist tradition, feminism especially transported working-class struggle into society as a whole. Fordist capitalism was premised on the inclusion of workers via waged labor, but it simultaneously pushed women out by consigning them to domestic labor. In the idealized "male-breadwinner model" of the twentieth century, the husband worked in large-scale industry while the wife stayed at home to do housework. The industrial production process, in other words, relied on an increasingly feminized system of social reproduction. The men produced commodities in the factory while the women reproduced labor-power at home. They fed their husbands, birthed future workers, and raised their children to become docile employees. Since domestic labor was, however, represented as essentially female work, it went largely unremunerated. It made hard work look like a personal service performed out of love. "Our role as women is to be the unwaged but happy and most of all loving servants of 'the working class,'" Federici laments.[15] The sustenance of capitalism hence extensively relied on a mass of unwaged labor to sustain the labor-power of workers. The 1970s, hence, saw a surge in feminist activity. Italian and American activists like Federici, Dalla Costa, and James, for instance, launched a "Wages for Housework" campaign claiming that, if domestic labor sustains capital accumulation, it should also be remunerated as such. Their aim was obviously not to merely negotiate wages for housewives but to radically question what it meant to be a woman in a capitalist society and to ripen the social imaginary for a postcapitalist future. "In the sociality of struggle women discover and exercise a power that effectively gives them a new identity. The new identity is and can only be a new degree of social power."[16]

2. THE AGE OF POST-FORDISM

Both inside and outside the factory, the Fordist social machine had run out of steam by the 1970s. Workers demanded more autonomy and higher wages, while women rejected their relegation to housework, but investors were also displeased with the downturn in industrial profits, the inflation crisis depressed mass consumers' purchasing power, etc. What came after is usually designated as "post-Fordism," but this term has caused a lot of confusion. Post-workerists characterize post-Fordism as an age dominated by "immaterial labor."[17] "The tasks of a worker or of a clerk no longer involve the completion of a single particular assignment, but the changing and intensifying of social cooperation."[18] Instead of imposing rigid conformity, immaterial labor regimes demand flexible, cooperative, and creative workers. Instead of executing centrally predetermined production targets, workers are left free to use their personal "virtuosity" in whatever way they see fit. The commodities produced are also no longer standardized material goods but immaterial or intangible goods like information, affects, knowledge, and so on. The post-workerists imagine work typified by highly educated knowledge workers, tech-savvy creatives, and manipulators of human affects. Put so crudely, the "immaterial labor" thesis is obviously an exaggeration. Script reading in a call center might deal with immaterial goods like communication, but it can hardly be called "virtuosic"; transporting food for Deliveroo is highly technological, but the goods delivered are very material; apart from the digital gadgets they carry, the order pickers in Amazon's fulfilment centers have not escaped Taylorism at all.[19] One should, furthermore, not forget that the factories of large-scale industry have not disappeared. They have merely moved to low-cost countries.

The crude presentations of immaterial labor from the early days of post-workerism did not fully account for the role of technology in post-Fordism. Post-workerists discussed this phenomenon under the heading of "the general intellect" (i.e., the common repertoire of communications, affects, or knowledges, externalized in machines, software, communicative networks, personal relationships, etc.)[20] Technology embodied the social cooperation of the multitude in material form. Post-workerists, however, subsequently focused only on either jobs that were largely unaffected by technological innovation, like care work, or newly created high-skill jobs in sectors like marketing, scientific research, or consultancy. They neglected the digitally mediated proliferation of deskilled jobs in the transportation sector, call centers, distribution chains, and so on. Hardt and Negri, for instance, briefly acknowledge deskilling in *Empire* discerning "a corresponding growth of low-value and low-skill routine symbol manipulation, such as data entry and word processing,"[21] but they only give a detailed account of contemporary "digital Taylorism" in their 2017 book *Assembly*.[22] That analysis is still a mere three pages long. To give a more complete description of the technical composition of capital today, I propose to first look at the social machine in which today's digital technologies are implemented. Just as the assembly line only made sense within the factory society, we must understand the digital gig economy within the social machine that created it.

A helpful starting statement is a remark from Deleuze's "postscript on the societies of control": "In a society of control, the corporation has replaced the factory, and the corporation is a spirit, a gas."[23] A factory is a solid mass held together with predetermined disciplinary molds that gather workers around the production of material commodities. Post-Fordist corporations like Amazon, Walmart, Apple, or Uber, on the other hand, disseminate their operations around the globe like a gas. The corporation splits itself up into an ephemeral conglomerate of parent company and innumerable subsidiaries. Apple, for instance, has its corporate headquarters in Cupertino, California, but also resides over supposedly independent factories in China like Foxconn, shell companies in tax havens, Apple Store franchises in commercial city centers, and so on. In management parlance, the parent company focuses on "core competences" but offshores or outsources its nonessential competences.[24] The parent company predominantly concentrates not on producing commodities but on marketing and brand management. According to Lazzarato,

> The post-industrial enterprise and economy are founded on the manipulation of information. Rather than ensuring (as nineteenth-century enterprises did) the

surveillance of the inner workings of the production process and the supervision of the markets of raw materials (labour included), business is focused on the terrain outside of the production process: sales and the relationship with the consumer. It always leans more toward commercialisation and financing than toward production.[25]

Post-Fordist parent companies manipulate affects and information that commercialize commodities corporate subsidiaries produce elsewhere, which requires continuous and meticulous interaction with the public. This is the realm of the highly skilled virtuosic jobs predicted by the "immaterial labor" thesis. Instead of first producing commodities and afterward advertising them to consumers, post-Fordist corporations try to enlist their consumers beforehand in the production process to avoid offering commodities nobody wants. Digital media has especially allowed corporations to directly access consumer desires before the first commodity is produced. Companies, for instance, launch co-creation projects where they ask consumers to suggest and comment on product designs for anything is built; or they extract data from internet searches to buy targeted ad space; or they have social media accounts to follow real-time feedback on their own products and readjust the latter accordingly. These endeavors necessitate an army of data specialists to gather and process consumer data, and marketeers to manipulate the "public conversation" about specific products.

The immaterial labor performed at the parent company produces not mere lines of communication with consumers but builds entire worlds for consumers to inhabit. The aim is to capture and enlist social cooperation "in the wild." Just like the factory performed a real subsumption of labor under capital by making workers conform to the logic of capital, the post-Fordist corporation enacts a real subsumption of public desires to make them fit its business strategies. The public ought to desire what capital has to offer. Major clothing lines, for instance, search the web for new trends, enlist social media influencers with particular public profiles to promote their brand, or cooperate with Hollywood celebrities to attract attention. All these efforts are meant to create an inviting community around their products so that consumers do not just buy a piece of clothing but enact a form of life through buying that product. As Lazzarato writes, "consumption is irreducible to the act of buying or 'depleting' a service or a product, like political economists and their critics argue. It means rather belonging to a world, fitting into a universe."[26] This form of immaterial labor entails the construction of worlds as market niches according to the logic of capital accumulation. Corporations, hence, establish a conversation with their consumers, not to democratize the use of goods but to voluntarily enlist the public in its own business model. Immaterial labor is in this sense, a political enterprise. If the ancient Greeks still distinguished between economy as the realm of survival and politics as the realm of the good life, the post-Fordist corporation obliterates the border. "The boundaries between pure intellectual activity, political action, and labour has dissolved," Virno states.[27] The production of worlds in post-Fordist marketing makes people literally buy into a particular conception of the good life. Where the coordination of public life used to be the task of politicians making representative claims that gather a public around the same symbols, rituals, and discourses, today's big brands perform this role in search of profits. They invent and commercialize ways of life and, afterwards, the public votes not on the ballot but with their wallet.

From the production side, the big advantage of the post-Fordist social machine is that it allows for "just-in-time production" or "lean manufacturing."[28] Instead of immediately mass-producing particular commodities, corporations first explore market demand and then place orders with their affiliated subsidiaries to respond to this demand. This avoids the problem not only of overstocking unsellable goods but also of overstocking redundant workers. Corporations like Apple or Walmart employ a minimal amount of core staff working in marketing and brand management, while their subsidiaries hire the workers producing and distributing the actual commodities. Apple, for example, merely sets up a production contract for iPhones with Foxconn, and the latter subsequently hires or fires the exact number of workers needed for that batch of products. Given that the workers are now employed by myriad smaller companies in predominantly low-cost countries, working-class political organization is scattered. There are fewer labor protections and lower wages in these countries, and parent companies carry less responsibility for the scandals inflicted by their subsidiaries. Sometimes stories of extreme working conditions in Bangladeshi sweatshops or Chinese megafactories reach Western media and damage the parent company's public image, but usually these scandals pass by unnoticed.

For workers around the globe, the emergence of post-Fordism means more precarious labor conditions. Instead of being concentrated in a single factory owned by the core company, they are scattered across multiple facilities each managed by a subsidiary receiving orders from elsewhere. The subsidiaries also have less strict employment regulations leading to a proliferation of freelance, temporary, and piece-rate work. People are employed on a "just-in-time" basis and discarded after use. Just like the corporation itself, also the working class is transformed into a gas. Nonstandard employment contracts have spread through outsourcing. Nonessential activities like cleaning, transportation, or menial data management are subcontracted to minor, subsidiary firms that, thanks to their small size, avoid the labor laws dating from the Fordist age. These companies can almost hire and fire at will and go bankrupt without making a sound. If Walmart itself closes a center, leaving many workers without a job, it is frontpage news. When one of its subsidiaries closes its doors, the media attention is more subdued, even if the effects on the workforce are identical. Platform businesses have especially mastered this technique of self-gasification. Companies like Uber employ a minimal number of staff and present their platforms as services to "independent contractors." Uber drivers are supposedly self-employed individuals who use the platform to access clients. This allows the companies to offer services like cheap rides without employing any drivers. Platform businesses have thereby outsourced the actual services they deliver, while their own workers focus on "core competences" like brand management, marketing, and lobbying. Though such outsourced jobs do not live up to the glamorous image of immaterial labor, they are the other side of the coin of the post-Fordist social machine. Underneath the surface of highly skilled, tech-savvy cognitive labor are masses of deskilled and precarious "independent contractors." This dark underbelly of post-Fordism forms our main research area.

3. THE ROLE OF DIGITAL TECHNOLOGY IN THE POST-FORDIST CORPORATION

The post-Fordist corporation is a very different terrain than the nineteenth-century factory of Marx' days. Still, from a Marxist perspective, one can expect digital technology to operate as 'supplying capital with weapons against the revolts of the working class." The aim is to integrate living labor into the cycle of capital accumulation in a way that capital, not labor itself, determines the modalities of the labor process. Digital technology is, in that sense, a new weapon for the psycho-physical adaptation of workers. It represents a new version of the real subsumption of labor under capital replacing the bureaucratic system of foremen and planners with automatized tracking apps, machine learning, and push notifications. To understand this digital psycho-physical adaptation, I first introduce Lazzarato's distinction between (A) social subjection and (B) machinic subjugation, suggesting that digital technologies predominantly employ the latter. Afterward I explain how digital machinic subjugation creates new forms of deskilling, prolonging the workday, and intensifying labor productivity.

(A) When it comes to explaining how power-relations construct particular subjectivities, Lazzarato argues that most critical theorists focus on the level of social subjection. Institutions supposedly spread discourses and images—what Lazzarato calls "signifying semiotics"[29]—that assign particular identities to subjects with which these individuals can subsequently consciously identify. They circulate the languages that give meaning to our universe and that thereby help individuals position themselves in the world. The major feminist critique of gendered language is, for instance, that it interpelates people to perform a particular gender identity and the social roles that accompany it. Gendered signifying semiotics imposes on people the vocation to see their world and themselves through a male or female gaze. In the case of platform companies, we can observe social subjection in the ways these companies address their workers as independent entrepreneurs. Fiverr, an online freelance platform, launched an ad campaign in 2017 to attract new freelancers with the slogan, "In doers we trust" on posters depicting young successful millennials.[30] By hailing its freelancers as romanticized "doers," Fiverr invites these people to self-identify as glamorous entrepreneurs of their own little business. They are purportedly not workers following orders from a boss but "doers" who can be trusted to take care of themselves. The signifying semiotics of self-employment and passionate work are mobilized to make conscious individuals relate to their own conditions of existence as entrepreneurs instead of workers. When, for instance, Fiverr's payment schemes change, freelancers-as-doers should allegedly not organize and form a union but react to the new market conditions like the lean entrepreneurs they supposedly are. These marketing interpelations have real effects on how people behave in everyday circumstances. On the level of social subjection, the technological infrastructure of the app itself is allegedly a mere neutral instrument. Decisions are made on the level of individual consciousness and technical machines are mere tools for those conscious subjects.

Social subjection in capitalism is, however, nothing new. Digital technology might play an increasing role in disseminating this signifying semiotics via social media or targeted ads, but the key tenets have not changed significantly since the nineteenth century. In those days, major manufacturers would, for instance, align themselves with the Catholic Church to cultivate discursive legitimacy. By hailing workers as sinners in need of redemption and the world as good because it was created by a good God, nineteenth-century institutions justified workers' material conditions of existence as willed by God and condemned resistance as an expression of sin. Instead of considering their lives through the lens of exploitation and alienation, workers would see their work and their submission to capital as a divinely administered vocation. As Marx wrote, "religion is the general theory of this world, its encyclopedic compendium, its logic in popular form, its spiritual *point d'honneur*, its enthusiasm, its moral sanction, its solemn complement and its universal basis of consolation and justification."[31] Nineteenth-century religion incorporated workers into capitalist society by spreading the signifying semiotics of sin and redemption as an ideological inversion for workers' material conditions of existence. Today's platform companies have substituted the creed of entrepreneurship for religion, but the basic operations of social subjection have not changed.

(B) To discern the specificity of digital technologies in the psycho-physical adaptation of workers, Lazzarato introduces a second form of subjectification: machinic subjugation, with its own instrument, "asignifying semiotics."[32] According to Lazzarato, some languages are not meant to produce meaning through which human beings can consciously interpret the world. They rather operate as "power-signs"[33] that command the circulation of things without the interference of human consciousness. The ones and zeros of binary code do not communicate any particular meaning but manage flows of electricity. Through a network of binary operations, computer code can subsequently translate magnetic strips on a microchip into flows of information and light on a screen. The flashy colors, buzzers, and sounds of a pinball machine, likewise, do not transport a clear message to the conscious individual, but puts the player preconsciously in a state of alertness and excitement. They highjack the player's brain through flows of neurological stimulation until the human and the machine recombine into a functional human-machine assemblage. Lazzarato explains this preconscious alteration of human conduct with the example of driving a car:

> When we drive, we activate subjectivity and a multiplicity of partial consciousnesses connected to the car's technological mechanisms. There is no "individuated subject" that says "you must push this button, you must press this pedal." If one knows how to drive, one acts without thinking about it, without engaging reflexive consciousness, without speaking or representing what one does. We are guided by the car's machinic assemblage. Our actions and subjective components (memory, attention, perception, etc.) are "automatised," a part of the machinic, hydraulic, electronic, etc., apparatuses, constituting like mechanical (non-human) components, parts of the assemblage.[34]

Driving a car entails reacting automatically to the lights and signals that the car and the street emit to govern the driver's actions. Ultimately, the car, the street, and the driver form a single human-machine assemblage of smoothly interacting electronic, hydraulic, nervous, and muscular flows governed by the car's asignifying semiotic of lights and sounds. Machinic subjugation succeeds insofar as it can automate these interactions without human consciousness interrupting or slowing down the exchange of commands. On this level, any hierarchy between the human subject and the technical object is cancelled: agency resides on the level of the entire human-machine assemblage. The driver drives the car as much as the car drives the driver.

From Lazzarato's perspective, what constitutes the novelty of digital technology today is that the post-Fordist corporation uses algorithmic control to increase the real subsumption of labor under capital. Post-Fordist corporations use digital means to integrate and adapt the workforce to the quest for private profit. Apps like Uber and Deliveroo, but also more classical companies like Walmart or Amazon, extract streams of data from their workers to subsequently modify their conduct through subtle, machinic nudges. These companies build connective data networks to manage workflows in real time for optimal efficiency. The Uber app, for instance, collects GPS-locations, average driving speeds, traffic information, customer satisfaction rates, and much more, to link potential drivers to consumers. Every worker is disassembled into streams of data that compare her to other workers present in Uber's database. The app's algorithm subsequently weighs the pros and cons of every possible combination of drivers and clients to construct the optimal connective network of supply and demand. Through digital means, Uber maintains "abstract cooperation" among strangers who do not explicitly communicate with each other.[35] The app augments overall efficiency by disassembling and reassembling workers into equivalent atoms of abstract labor time that can be re-arranged according to present or future market requirements. The corporation determines what tasks workers have to perform and how, whereas workers are expected to adapt to this algorithmically automatized allocation system. In the platform sector, according to Berardi, "[c]apital no longer recruits people, but buys packets of time, separated from their interchangeable and occasional bearers."[36]

These same apps subsequently employ the techniques of machinic subjugation to preconsciously integrate workers into the connective network the corporation's algorithms have calculated. Contemporary businesses "declare their right to modify others' behaviour for profit according to methods *that bypass human awareness*, individual decision rights, and the entire complex of self-regulatory processes that we summarize with terms such as autonomy and self-determination."[37] Some apps, for instance, establish a choice architecture that exploits workers' psychological biases for company profits.[38] Uber's forward dispatching system, for example, copies Netflix' automatic queuing system that spontaneously suggests and plays the next episode of a series to keep the viewer glued to the screen.[39] Netflix uses the human brain's inertia against itself to maximize the time spent watching Netflix' content and, thereby, boost its own profits. The automatic queuing system bypasses human consciousness to construct a human-machine assemblage that spontaneously increases viewing revenues. The Uber app similarly suggests new rides automatically even before the driver has completed the previous task, aiming to mobilize the power of neurological inertia to maximize drivers' labor time. The forward dispatching system allows drivers to smoothly flow from one task to another like an inert object in a vacuum. The app and the driver are expected to slowly morph into a human-machine assemblage that drives customers from one part of town to another so long as it generates profits for Uber. Human beings are slowly transformed into automatized nodes in an assemblage of cars, customers, and traffic, governed by the platform's algorithms.

Though the mode of psycho-physical adaptation in the post-Fordist corporation differs significantly from the methods employed in large-scale industry, the effects are remarkably similar. The three tactics Marx described in the industrial factory—deskilling, prolonging the workday, and intensifying labor productivity—return in the machinic subjugation performed by platform companies. Allow me to discuss all three separately.

(1) Just like deskilling in the factory led to an increase in competition among workers for fewer and simpler jobs, the platform economy undermines workers' rights by minimizing job vacancies and maximizing competition. Whereas a traditional cab company, for instance, requires its workers to possess a series of certificates proving their driving skills, Uber only demands workers to have a driver's license and own a car. Even when drivers do not own a car, Uber is more than willing to lease a vehicle for a significant interest rate.[40] Cab driving expertise is subsequently rendered redundant. Uber is not an isolated case. Amazon Mechanical Turk (AMT), for example, attracts workers from all around the globe to perform small digital tasks for a few cents per task. The platform relies heavily on cheap Asian freelancers and unemployed Americans, but also on workers ostracized in the traditional labor market like the mentally ill or transgender individuals. The effect is clear: while this benefits disadvantaged workers previously excluded from Western labor markets, it also minimizes overall opportunities for steady employment, while the globalization of the labor supply also undermines Western workers' bargaining position leading to a race-to-the-bottom in jobs, wages, and social benefits.[41] Digitalization not only opens up labor opportunities for increasingly deskilled masses of workers, but it also makes these workers compete for a shrinking number of jobs. Whenever workers mount resistance to their working conditions, by organizing strikes or forming unions, companies can easily fire and replace them with more docile substitutes from the global reserve army of the unemployed. Data analytics enables firms to exactly determine how many workers the company needs at any hour of the day, effectively minimizing the number of jobs companies have to offer. Why would Starbucks hire three full-time employees in one of its franchises when it only needs three in the early morning and one in the afternoon? Why keep the recalcitrant unionized worker if there are many waiting in line to replace her? By tracking sales numbers in its different franchises, Starbucks can generate a detailed prediction of how many workers are required at any time of the day, so the company will only hire the minimal amount of labor-time necessary.[42] Big data determines the minimal number of staff required for any particular task with great precision, eliminating superfluous workers from the balance sheets.

(2) Platform technology also prolongs the workday, which increases the extraction of absolute surplus value. Techniques of machinic subjugation, like the aforementioned forward dispatching systems, keep workers longer on the platform than they would have originally intended. They thereby earn more revenue not only for themselves but also for the platform. Uber uses surreptitious "means of behavioural modification"[43] to bypass human awareness and directly connect the human brain to the app. Another striking example is its tactical use of push notifications that posit arbitrary daily goals to encourage drivers to work longer hours. Uber knows that simply communicating a target poses a challenge to people that they subsequently try to meet, even if the challenge is meaningless. Uber preys on the feeling of gratification we experience from meeting just any target. Exploiting psychological biases is, however, not the only way platform companies use digital technology to incentivize people to work more. Airbnb, for instance, launched in 2016 a "superhost system" where it would award a select group of hosts privileged status.[44] If they reached a specific set of targets, Airbnb promised to put the superhosts higher on the search results lists for incoming guests. If a host secured minimally 10 stays a year, responded to guests quickly, maintained a 90 percent response rate or higher, had at least 80 percent five-star reviews, and honored confirmed reservations, Airbnb promised to increase their chances of future gigs. Airbnb hosts secure better income by taking on more work. They are encouraged to increase their work for the platform in their own self-interest, but mostly in the interest of Airbnb itself.

(3) Work is not only prolonged, but also intensified to generate more relative surplus value. Digital technologies boost workers' productivity so that they produce more surplus value in less time. Different forms of tracking devices, for instance, render surveillance more mobile and flexible. Amazon in its fulfilment centers sets productivity standards for their workers, which it measures through automatic tracking algorithms.[45] If workers pause too long or take too long to go to the bathroom, the tracker goes in alert and warns the worker for her decreasing productivity. If workers do not listen to this call, they risk automated dismissal. Amazon even patented a wristband that would track workers' hand movements and buzz whenever their hand moved "inefficiently."[46]

The digital techniques to boost labor productivity are not always as explicitly diabolical. Uber, for instance, composes safe-driving reports about its drivers by tracking their brake and acceleration speeds.[47] Drivers receive messages from the app like "Several harsh breaks detected" or "Great work." Drivers, hence, suspect that Uber is collecting much more information than it communicates. Like prisoners in Bentham's panopticon, workers do not know how or when their data is being tracked, so they internalize the surveillance mechanism and act as if they are always being watched. This leads to a potentially infinite feedback loop of self-improvement: there is always a new metric to control and optimize. Drivers have no access to the exact internal machinations of Uber's algorithms, so they engage in trial-and-error experiments to optimize their reputation vis-à-vis the algorithm. To secure future gigs, they try to unravel what the optimal driver constitutes for Uber's algorithm. Tracking apps like Uber's thereby establish a "mental subsumption"[48] incentivizing workers to internalize the platform's profit motive. The material subsumption of the factory primarily disciplined workers' unruly bodies to conform to the standards of the assembly line, but opaque tracking apps go further. They infiltrate the very minds of workers to such an extent that workers become their own disciplining officer. "Obligations [become] internalized and social control [is] exercised through a voluntary, albeit inevitable, subjugation to chains of automatisms."[49]

4. CONCLUSION

In this chapter, I explained how the real subsumption of the workforce into the capitalist production process has changed from the factory-society to today's post-Fordist corporations, of which the platform companies that fuel the digital gig economy are exemplary cases. Large-scale industrial factories depended on the successful psycho-physical adaptation of workers to the assembly line. This required not only a bureaucratic system of disciplinary controls and production targets but also political compromises in the form of high wages, social benefits, and so forth. Factory technology acted as a weapon in the hands of capital putting pressure on the political self-organization of the working class. It deskilled labor, leading to fewer jobs and more competition among workers; it prolonged the workday, maximizing absolute surplus value; and it intensified the workforce's productivity increasing relative surplus value. This system was, however, unstable, leading to revolts inside and outside the factory in the 1970s.

The post-Fordist corporation that succeeded large-scale industry split itself up into a gasified conglomerate of parent and subsidiary companies across the globe. The parent company focuses on "core competences": they hire immaterial, cognitive workers to construct consumer worlds through meticulous conversations with the public. Marketing and brand management performs the political function of imagining and implementing the good life according to what the corporation can offer. The less glamorous parts of the knowledge economy are outsourced or offshored to the subsidiary firms. The latter employ an army of freelance and temporary workers to produce commodities, transport them to consumers, fix bugs, and so on. Thanks to their smaller size, their unclear legal status, basing in low-cost countries, and so forth, the subsidiaries evade traditional labor protections from the Fordist factory. The working class, thereby, loses much of its collective bargaining power.

Digital technology is the post-Fordist way of psycho-physically integrating workers into this new social machine. Platform apps or logistical software disassemble workers into streams of data that they can subsequently reassemble according to market demand in real-time. Algorithms calculate exactly how much labor-time must be mobilized where at which time. The asignifying semiotics of machinic subjugation subsequently bypass human consciousness to stimulate workers to obey the algorithms. Different kinds of preconscious nudging integrate human beings into digital connective networks until both form a smoothly operating human-machine assemblage geared toward the maximization of profit. However, as the aforementioned example of driving a car shows, there is nothing inherently wrong with machinic subjugation. Human beings perform automatic, preconscious actions all the time. The problem is rather that machinic subjugation is here used as a weapon to extract control over the labor process from workers themselves. The post-Fordist corporation divests its workers through digital means from controlling and disrupting the cycle of capital accumulation.

In the next three chapter, I show how this loss of workers' autonomy over the labor process leads to three political problems: exploitation, alienation, and fatigue.

NOTES

1. Maurizio Lazzarato, *Governing by Debt*, trans. Joshua David Jordan (South Pasadena, CA: Semiotext(e), 2015), 203.

2. Karl Marx and Friedrich Engels, *Capital: Vol. 1*, Collected Works 35 (London: Lawrence & Wishart, 1996), 349.

3. Marx and Engels, 425–526.

4. Antonio Gramsci, *Selections from the Prison Notebooks of Antonio Gramsci*, trans. Quintin Hoare and Geoffrey Nowell-Smith (London: Lawrence & Wishart, 1971), 298.

5. See Harry Braverman, *Labor and Monopoly Capital: The Degradation of Work in the Twentieth Century* (New York: Monthly Review Press, 1975), 59–85.

6. Gramsci, *Selections from the Prison Notebooks of Antonio Gramsci*, 286.

7. For an insightful discussion of the concept of real subsumption, see Sandro Mezzadra, *In the Marxian Workshops: Producing Subjects* (London: Rowman & Littlefield International, 2018), 57–66.

8. Marx and Engels, *Capital*, 397–420.

9. Mario Tronti, *Workers and Capital*, trans. David Broder (London: Verso, 2019), 27.

10. Theodor W. Adorno, *The Culture Industry Selected Essays on Mass Culture* (London: Routledge, 2001).

11. Braverman, *Labor and Monopoly Capital*, 188–96.

12. Tronti, *Workers and Capital*, 61.

13. Tronti, *Workers and Capital*, 62.

14. George Caffentzis, *In Letters of Blood and Fire: Work, Machines, and the Crisis of Capitalism* (Oakland, CA: PM Press, 2013), 31.

15. Silvia Federici, *Revolution at Point Zero: Housework, Reproduction, and Feminist Struggle* (London: PM Press, 2012), 17.

16. Mariarosa Dalla Costa, *Women and the Subversion of the Community: A Mariarosa Dalla Costa Reader*, trans. Camille Barbagallo (Oakland, CA: PM Press, 2019), 31.

17. See, among others, Maurizio Lazzarato, "Immaterial Labor," in *Radical Thought in Italy: A Potential Politics*, ed. Michael Hardt and Paolo Virno (Minneapolis: University of Minnesota Press, 1996), 133–47. Michael Hardt and Antonio Negri, *Empire* (Cambridge, Mass: Harvard University Press, 2000), 280–303.

18. Paolo Virno, *A Grammar of the Multitude: For an Analysis of Contemporary Forms of Life*, trans. Isabella Bertoletti, James Cascaito, and Andrea Casson (Cambridge, MA: Semiotext(e), 2003), 62.

19. Angela McRobbie, "Fashion's Click and Collect: A Labor Perspective," *Verso Blogs* (blog), 13 February 2020, https://www.versobooks.com/blogs/4566-fashion-s-click-and-collect-a-labour-perspective.

20. The term originates in Marx' *Grundrisse,* where it designated "organs of the human brain, created by the human hand; the power of knowledge, objectified. The development of fixed capital indicates to what degree general social knowledge has become a direct force of production, and to what degree, hence, the conditions of social life itself have come under the control of the general intellect and been transformed in accordance with it." (Karl Marx, *Grundrisse: Foundations of the Critique of Political Economy*, 2005, 706).

21. Hardt and Negri, *Empire,* 292.

22. Michael Hardt and Antonio Negri, *Assembly* (New York: Oxford University Press, 2017), 131–33.

23. Gilles Deleuze, "Postscript on the Societies of Control," *October* 59, no. Winter (1992): 3–7, 4.

24. See, among others, Béatrice Appay, "Economic Concentration and the Externalization of Labor," *Economic and Industrial Democracy* 19 (1998): 161–84; Christian Marazzi, *Capital and Affects: The Politics of the Language Economy*, trans. Giuseppina Mecchia (Los Angeles, CA: Semiotext(e), 2011); David Weil, *The Fissured Workplace: Why Work Became so Bad for so Many and What Can Be Done to Improve It* (Cambridge, MA: Harvard University Press, 2014).

25. Lazzarato, "Immaterial Labor," 141.

26. Maurizio Lazzarato, *Les Révolutions du Capitalisme* (Paris: Empêcheurs de Penser en Rond, 2004), 96 (my translation).

27. Virno, *A Grammar of the Multitude,* 50.

28. Marazzi, *Capital and Affects*, 19.

29. Maurizio Lazzarato, *Signs and Machines: Capitalism and the Production of Subjectivity*, trans. Joshua David Jordan (Los Angeles, CA: Semiotext(e), 2014), 39. Lazzarato relies on Louis Althusser's theory of interpellation, see Louis Althusser, *On the Reproduction of Capitalism: Ideology and Ideological State Apparatuses*, trans. G.M. Goshgarian (London: Verso Books, 2014).

30. Alex Rosenblat, *Uberland: How Algorithms Are Rewriting the Rules of Work* (Oakland: University of California Press, 2018), 35–37.

31. Karl Marx, *Early Writings*, trans. Rodney Livingstone and Gregor Benton (London: Penguin Books, 2005), 244.

32. Lazzarato, *Signs and Machines*, 39.

33. Lazzarato, 84.

34. Lazzarato, 89.

35. Antonio Negri, *From the Factory to the Metropolis*, trans. Ed Emery, English edition (Cambridge, UK: Polity Press, 2018), 143.

36. Franco Berardi Bifo, *After the Future*, trans. Gary Genosko and Nicholas Thoburn (Oakland, CA: AK Press, 2011), 90.

37. Shoshana Zuboff, *The Age of Surveillance Capitalism: The Fight for the Future at the New Frontier of Power* (London: Profile Books, 2019), 297.

38. Rosenblat, *Uberland*, 135.

39. Nicolas Scheiber, "How Uber Pushes Drivers' Buttons," *New York Times*, 3 April 2017, https://www.nytimes.com/interactive/2017/04/02/technology/uber-drivers-psychological-tricks.html.

40. Rosenblat, *Uberland*, 65–68.

41. Gavin Mueller, *Breaking Things at Work: The Luddites Are Right about Why You Hate Your Job* (London: Verso Books, 2021), 119.

42. Cathy O'Neil, *Weapons of Math Destruction: How Big Data Increases Inequality and Threatens Democracy* (London: Penguin Books, 2017), 125–26.

43. Zuboff, *The Age of Surveillance Capitalism*, 8.

44. AirBNB, "How Do I Become a Superhost?," AirBNB Help Centre, accessed 19 May 2020, https://www.airbnb.co.uk/help/article/829/how-do-i-become-a-superhost?_set_bev_on_new_domain=1589896655_NWQ4YzAzMzE2ZTJm.

45. Colin Lecher, "How Amazon Automatically Tracks and Fires Warehouse Workers for 'Productivity,'" The Verge, 25 April 2019, https://www.theverge.com/2019/4/25/18516004/amazon-warehouse-fulfillment-centers-productivity-firing-terminations.

46. Thuy Ong, "Amazon Patents Wristbands That Track Warehouse Employees' Hands in Real Time," The Verge, 1 February 2018, https://www.theverge.com/2018/2/1/16958918/amazon-patents-trackable-wristband-warehouse-employees.

47. Rosenblat, *Uberland*, 139.

48. Franco Berardi Bifo, *Futurability: The Age of Impotence and the Horizon of Possibility* (London: Verso, 2017), 106.

49. Berardi Bifo, *After the Future*, 35.

Chapter 3

Exploitation and the Digital Capture of Social Cooperation

A major complaint about the digital gig economy concerns its propensity to exploit labor. Wages are remarkably low in this sector, especially among those who depend on digital platforms for their day-to-day subsistence. For the most part, the digital gig economy is not very different from other low-level jobs. Badly paid, precarious work is unfortunately not unique but part of the larger trend toward outsourcing, as mentioned in the previous chapter. Companies like Uber have, in fact, reintroduced the old putting-out system: just like eighteenth-century workers would work from home and be paid per produced commodity rather than receiving an hourly wage, gig workers today are very often independent contractors paid per completed service.[1] This externalizes the costs of inactive downtime to workers. Whereas a Fordist company would be forced to pay out wages even when there was no work for its employees, post-Fordist platforms cut labor costs by only paying for time actually worked. However, this business model only partly explains the platform businesses' financial success. Companies like Uber, Deliveroo, or Care.com provide services for which there already exist markets. By underpaying workers and avoiding labor regulations, they might be able to perform these services at a slightly cheaper price, but that does not suffice to explain their global rise to fame. Uber, for example, would not have attracted billions in venture capital and stock purchases if it were nothing but a marginally more efficient taxi company. The core of its business model concerns the ownership over data assets about people's transportation. In contrast to a traditional taxi business, Uber also collects, owns, and analyzes data about people's mobility, and it is this assetization of social life that makes Uber a lauded financial investment opportunity.

Using Uber as my main example, I explain in this chapter how platforms in the digital gig economy produce value through the digital capture of social cooperation, or what Negri calls "the common."[2] The latter names the wealth generated by spontaneous social interaction in the multitude. Whereas Fordist capitalism generated economic value by making workers produce commodities to be sold at a profit, post-Fordist capitalism transforms noncommodified social interactions into private property. By, for example, tracking data about people's transportation habits, Uber valorizes social interactions that were previously located outside the capitalist economy. People have been moving around since the dawn of time, but Uber has found a way to collect information about people's mobility and appropriate this information as a privately owned asset. In a first move, Uber does not sell any of its data, but collects it to optimize its services, build partnerships with tourism-related companies, or subsidize innovations like self-driving cars. This is what Birch and Cochrane call "enclave rent": Uber hoards data to subsequently build an enclave of services it can rent out.[3] In a second move, Uber uses its data assets as leverage to attract financial investments. It cultivates a good reputation among venture capitalists and financial investors to garner financial rent. In both cases of enclave and financial rentiership, Uber creates value by owning an infrastructure of data about social interactions that were previously held in common. Uber's success derives from its capacity to transform this common into an enclosed asset that it leverages to support an enclave of services and a good financial reputation. With this intellectual property on its books, Uber can sell advertisement access to tourists, finance innovative projects, or impress investors.

Before explaining Uber's mode of value production, however, I will first lay out the post-workerist theory of exploitation as the becoming-rent of profit. In the previous paragraph, it is not immediately clear why Uber's model would *exploit* anyone. The firm transforms its data ownership into income, but workers and consumers agreed to hand over their data when they accepted the app's terms and conditions. So, what would be the problem? One response is that digital interactions constitute "free labor" for digital companies. As the old saying goes, "if you are not paying for the product, you are the product." By accepting the terms and conditions, people would allegedly consent to working for Uber for free every time they use the app. However, authors like Negri, Vercellone, Marazzi, and Moulier Boutang claim that digital platforms do not exploit users by making them work for free. Rather, they first encourage the multitude to engage in social cooperation and afterward expropriate the multitude from the products of the common. Platform companies privatize social cooperation and live off the rent. Value is not accumulated through exploited unwaged labor but through dispossessed social cooperation. After clarifying this alternative theory of exploitation, I return to Uber's business model built on enclave and financial rentiership.

1. AGAINST THE "FREE LABOR" THESIS

The rise of digital mass media in the early 2000s triggered a first exploration into how economic value is produced on the internet. Large parts of the internet are under private ownership and Big Tech corporations are among the highest grossing companies in the world. This raises the question of how online communication can be a profitable line of business, especially if digital services are often free. Companies like Google, Facebook, Uber, or Amazon provide access to their platforms at no financial cost to consumers, so where is the money coming from? Tiziana Terranova gave a seminal answer in a 2000 article,[4] which has influenced not only critical media studies[5] but also some critics of platform capitalism.[6] The convincingness of her thesis lies in its simplicity: if, according to Marx' labor theory of value, capitalist profit derives from exploited surplus labor, and digital companies generate profit from users' online activities without paying them, then all online activity must be exploited surplus labor. To quote Terranova herself,

> In the overdeveloped countries, the end of the factory has spelled out the obsolescence of the old working class, but it has also produced generations of workers who have been repeatedly addressed as active consumers of meaningful [online] commodities. Free labour is the moment where this knowledgeable consumption of culture is translated into productive activities that are pleasurably embraced and at the same time often shamelessly exploited.[7]

According to Terranova, the internet offers fun activities as if they were a service in themselves, whereas in reality these activities are just gamified labor for platform companies. A clear illustration of Terranova's "free labor" thesis comes from social media research.[8] Platforms like Facebook or YouTube build online worlds but abstain from filling those worlds with their own creations. They encourage users to upload and share content of their own. As Terranova observes, "users keep a site alive through their labor, the cumulative hours of accessing the site (thus generating advertising), writing messages, participating in conversations, and sometimes making the jump to collaborators."[9] Through their content creation and consumption, users cultivate an ecology of social interactions that ultimately serve the company that owns the platform. People's online activity constitutes labor that produces the commodity of "audience attention" in the form of data.[10] Platform companies subsequently sell this data for a profit without paying users for their "click work." This is where Terranova locates online exploitation: online labor generates data for which users are not remunerated, but which is sold at a profit.

Arvidsson and Colleoni correctly observe that the "free labor" thesis is a fairly orthodox update to the classical labor theory of value.[11] The latter has been the subject of impressively elaborate studies, but in this chapter, I will stick to a simplified version. The theory locates the source of value production in exploited labor. According to Marx, labor-power is a unique commodity because it generates more value than it is itself worth on the labor market.[12] Workers produce more value than they receive in terms of wages. By hiring labor-power, capitalist enterprises can thus transform raw materials into commodities worth much more than the original input. A shoe manufacturer, for example, can buy three dollars' worth of leather and hire seven dollars' worth of human labor to produce twenty-dollar shoes.[13] After the capitalist subtracts costs, he is left with ten dollars of surplus value. In response to the question where these ten dollars come from, the simplified labor theory of value identifies it as the product of labor's value-generating efforts. By laboring on the original material, workers have upgraded three dollars of leather into twenty dollars of shoe. However, workers do not receive the full seventeen dollars as compensation for their labor. Their wages depend on the supply of and demand for workers on the labor market, which implies that workers tend to be paid less. Capitalists have an interest in keeping wages low to secure profits, and workers have to compete against each other for scarce jobs, so wages tend to fall to subsistence levels. The difference between generated value and wages establishes, for Marx, the rate of exploitation. If our worker needs one hour to produce a twenty-dollar pair of shoes out of three dollars of leather, in exchange for a seven-dollar wage, then the worker spends 7/17 of an hour on earning his wage—a little bit over twenty minutes—and 10/17 on generating surplus value for the capitalist—almost forty minutes. The latter is exploited surplus labor.

The "free labor" thesis in social media studies applies the same equation to online labor. If Facebook makes x dollars on advertisement revenues thanks to y hours of people's online activities, while paying nothing in return, then all y hours are surplus labor time. All online activity is exploited from this point of view. One could make a similar case for the digital gig economy. Here, workers might get paid for the service they provide to customers, but they are not remunerated for the data they produce during their work. Insofar as theirs and consumers' clicks keep the app alive and profitable, their work is unpaid. If one would thus subtract from overall profits the fees platforms in the gig economy pay to workers for their services, one would be able to calculate the surplus value exploited click work has generated for the company as free labor.

However, I would caution against this revival of the labor theory of value for three reasons. (1) Using the Facebook example, Arvidsson and Colleoni calculated the actual rate of exploitation for the providers of "free labor" with anticlimactic results.[14] According to the "free labor" thesis, Facebook derives surplus value from selling audience attention to advertisers. In 2010, its advertising revenues reached $355 million dollars. This seems impressive, but if Arvidsson and Colleoni divide it by the approximately 500 million users Facebook had at that time, the net outcome is an average yearly exploitation of 0.7 dollars per user. Put in this way, the "free labor" thesis sounds underwhelming. Many Facebook users would happily consent to being exploited for less than a dollar a year if they get their favorite social media platform in return. Even sillier calculations can be made for the digital gig economy. Many of these companies do not make profits at all. They rely on outside investors to keep themselves financially afloat (see *infra*). Here, the numbers would suggest the rate of exploitation to be negative. Users' click work would be subtracting value from digital platforms rather than producing valuable data commodities. Every time someone ordered an Uber, the company would lose value. This leads not only to strange conclusions about exploitation, but it also makes it impossible to explain how companies like Uber can find investors or why their market capitalization is so high. Why would people want to invest in firms that lose value every time their services are used?

(2) The "free labor" thesis, secondly, does not give a good description what platform companies actually do. It, for instance, identifies Facebook's business model with selling "datafied" audience attention as a commodity to advertisers, but Facebook rarely sells any of its data.[15] It rather auctions off advertisement space to other companies. Facebook uses the consumer database as leverage to charge companies more for advertising their products, because Facebook can guarantee that it will show the ads to the specific demographics most likely to click on them.[16] Christophers makes a helpful comparison between social media and shopping malls: a shopping mall does not "sell customers" to shops, but it rents out space in an area where it guarantees significant consumer traffic, increasing shops' chances of attracting potential customers.[17] In the same way, social media companies make money from licensing ad space in online areas with lots of consumer traffic. The same can be said about labor platforms like Uber. They do not often directly monetize and sell data about their users, but they own a digital platform to which people need access for acquiring social goods, like transportation. Uber licenses this access by charging a fee for every transaction conducted on its platform, similarly to how a shopping mall could ask shops to pay a fee every time they sold something. Any evaluation of labor exploitation in the digital gig economy should thus focus on infrastructural rent rather than the sale of commodities at a value higher than workers' wages.

(3) Lastly, Srnicek even doubts whether, in a strict application of the labor theory of value, most services offered by platform companies would actually count as "labor" according to orthodox Marxist criteria.[18] Traditionally, Marxists distinguish between exploitable, productive labor and nonexploitable, unproductive labor. The former is labor mobilized in the production

of commodities sold at a profit. Here, labor is exploited *only* insofar as it generates more value than it receives in the form of wages. Many occupations, however, do not generate value because they do not produce sellable commodities. Some of these jobs are, from Marx' perspective, purely consumptive, as when a capitalist hires a private chef to prepare diner. The chef is not exploited while preparing the food, because the latter is never sold but immediately consumed by the capitalist. The capitalist does not mobilize the chef's labor to accumulate capital, but to enjoy spending the capital he already has. Other occupations are concerned with *realizing* value rather than *producing* it. Returning to the example of the shoe manufacturer, workers might produce twenty-dollar pairs of shoes, but this value will never be turned into actual money until the capitalist employs truck drivers to bring the shoes to his shops, advertisers to attract people's attention, shop assistants to advise customers, and so on. These people do not produce value-holding commodities but secure the transition from abstract value to actual revenue. If one now turns to platform companies, one sees that most of their services fall in the category of unproductive rather than productive labor. Care.com, for example, provides at-home nursing services, which is a pure expenditure of capital that does not lead to the production of value-holding commodities. It is a way of spending rather than accumulating capital. Uber, on the other hand, offers cheap transportation, meaning it either helps realize value—when drivers, for example, bring productive workers to the workplace—or is a pure expenditure of value—when, for instance, tourists book an Uber to visit Brussels. In none of these scenarios do Uber drivers produce commodities that can subsequently be sold at a profit. As mentioned, the data they produce with their services hardly counts. This data is seldomly put out for sale, but is rather used to extract rent.

These minute discussions of the labor theory of value might look like unnecessary esoteric nitpicking, but they have utility beyond the dusty Marxist metaphysics of labor. Rather than pleading for strict theoretical orthodoxy, my aim is to question the utility of reviving the labor theory of value with the "free labor" thesis. Most forms of immaterial labor are, in a traditionalist sense, unproductive. People working in advertisement, research and development, care, or transportation, are all unproductive in the labor theory of value, but these sectors form the motor of the post-Fordist economy, as we discussed in chapter 2. If one thus applies a theory of exploitation that derives value from the production of material commodities, one is stuck with a theory blind to major changes in the global economy since the 1970s. The labor theory of value is no longer adequate to capture the heart of post-Fordism, so there is a need to rethink how exploitation and value operate today. This is why many post-workerists have abandoned the notion of exploitation rooted in the classic labor theory of value in favor of a theory of exploitation based on the becoming-rent of profit.

2. THE BECOMING-RENT OF PROFIT

According to many post-workerists, "conventional notions of exploitation fail to capture vast swathes of activity expropriated by capital."[19] Instead of applying the traditional concept of exploitation to digital platforms, these thinkers prefer to link digital forms of exploitation to "extraction,"[20] "accumulation-by-dispossession,"[21] or "primitive accumulation."[22] As Negri and Hardt phrase it,

> exploitation under the hegemony of immaterial labour is no longer primarily the expropriation of value measured by individual or collective labour-time but rather the capture of value that is produced by cooperative labour and that becomes increasingly common through its circulation in social networks.[23]

To see the difference between these two modes of accumulation, I start from Moulier Boutang's distinction between exploitation at degree 1 and degree 2.[24] Exploitation at degree 1 is the traditional form of exploitation in industrial commodity-production discussed in the previous section, where the production of value in excess of labor costs constitute exploited surplus labor. Exploitation at degree 2, however, is more relevant to post-Fordist capitalism. Capital does not directly mobilize labor to produce commodities for profit but encourages the multitude to establish spontaneous networks of common, social cooperation. Afterwards, capital captures and privatizes this "cooperation of brains"[25] to extract value from it.[26] Social media, for instance, encourage people to conduct their social conversations and friendships online, but subsequently transform these noncommodified social relations into data owned exclusively by the platform. Only the social media company has access to and owns the code to analyze people's data. Afterward, it uses this exclusive knowledge of people's personal networks and desires as leverage to attract advertisers. The company's value comes from rendering a potentially abundant common—the multitude's social relations and desires—scarce and renting it out for profit.[27] Surplus value comes not from the unequal exchange between labor-power and the wage, but through the exclusive ownership of data assets and the renting out of digital infrastructure on the basis of these assets. So, to increase the generation of value, social media companies add features that encourage users to spend more of their time on the platform and that translate more of this social interaction into legible data. Facebook's programmers, for instance, developed the Like-button to guide user behavior into generating more social interactions that can be reformatted as extractable data.[28] Linguistic conversation is hard to interpret on a massive scale, but the Like-button has a universally established unambiguous meaning. It allows Facebook to estimate users' interests and preferences without having to ask them directly. By adding this option, Facebook formats human interactions according to metrics legible to and extractable by its algorithms, allowing the company to collect more information about users' potential desires. This makes the ad space it rents out potentially more lucrative to interested advertisers. The more of the multitude's sociability can be translated into privatized data, the better Facebook's opportunity to rent out its knowhow about users' desires.

Vercellone calls this exploitation-through-expropriation of the common "the becoming-rent of profit." According to Vercellone, the clear division between profit and rent has been evaporating since the 1970s with firms turning to rent extracted from immaterial goods rather than the production material of commodities as their main source of profit. Moreno Zacarés puts it succinctly: "accumulation is now less about *making anything* and more about simply *owning something*" to which others need access.[29] For Vercellone, the turn to immaterial labor has instigated a shift toward capturing social cooperation and artificially making it scarce. This has, in turn, caused a crisis in the labor theory of value.[30] To return to the example of the shoe manufacturer, if a company sells sneakers at 200 dollars, chances are that most of the value does not come from exploited labor-time. Making a 200-dollar pair of shoes rarely requires significantly more work than making a 20-dollar pair. The labor theory of value is not very informative in explaining the value difference. The extra value probably comes from social communications that establish the sneakers' brand.[31] Post-Fordist corporations focus on the production of worlds consumers would like to inhabit, as I argued in chapter 2. The shoe manufacturer counts on people instituting affective bonds with each other around the brand. If, for instance, youth subculture makes sneakers part of its constructed identity, the sneakers become an instrument to cultivate one's youth identity. By owning the brand, the shoe manufacturer subsequently monopolizes access to this identity. The profits made consequently do not derive from surplus labor exerted by shoe factory workers but from the spontaneous social cooperation that has made the sneakers part of a world to which consumers desire to belong. The manufacturer grants access to this world by selling the sneakers but charges a fee for entrance to this desired identity. This "entrance fee" explains the sneakers' high price. The manufacturer has successfully claimed private and exclusive ownership over a marker of cultural identity.

In sum, in a regime of the becoming-rent of profit, "the source of the wealth of nations rests on a productive cooperation that is external to the company grounds."[32] Social cooperation in the multitude outside capitalist markets is absorbed by post-Fordist companies and turned into a privately owned asset. By dispossessing the multitude from these common social relations, firms are making potentially abundant resources artificially scarce. Shoe manufacturers turn youth culture into a privately owned brand, social media transform social interactions into consumer data, or software developers turn open-source software into intellectual property. In all these cases, companies make profit by extracting rent from the common. Once privatization has succeeded, owners can charge rent for accessing the former common.[33] In what follows, I will apply this theory of exploitation-through-dispossessing-the-common to Uber's business model. Two forms of capture lead to two forms of rent: Uber first captures data about people's transportation habits, leading to enclave rent, and it afterwards uses this rentier position to make itself attractive to venture capitalists and financial investors, leading to financial rent.

3. DIGITAL CAPTURE AND ENCLAVE RENT

In their typology of rent, Birch and Cochrane identify "enclave rent" as a crucial form of rent ubiquitous among platform companies. They define it as "the revenues Big Tech collects by controlling (1) an ecosystem of devices, apps, platforms, and other products; (2) the data that users generate through participation in the ecosystem; (3) the rules they set for users, developers, and others; (4) enforcement of the standards in the ecosystems."[34] Platform companies establish an ecosystem of apparatuses of which they are the sole owner and authority. Digital platforms insert themselves in noncommodified social relations as a presumably facilitating middleman, but meanwhile they make their intermediation indispensable for the continuation of these social relations. They effectively enclose and monopolies a part of common life. The reason behind this invasion in social life is that a single piece of data is in itself worthless without correlations to other data in a large database.[35] Its value increases with every meaningful connection, and even then, astronomical datasets are of no value if the platform company does not find a profitable use for it. The most strategic course of action is thus to first acquire as much and as detailed data as possible and afterward worry about how this data can be put to use. For this business model to succeed, digital platforms must try to colonize all of social life.

Dating platforms, for example, have become so widespread that face-to-face, analogue flirting is increasingly regarded as invasive and desperate. By gradually displacing nondigital human interaction, these platforms build an "enclave" or "ecosystem" in the social field, where they set the rules and own the data.[36] By achieving "platform lock-in,"[37] platform companies induce people to become increasingly dependent on platform services for the sustenance of their everyday lives.[38] Uber attempts, in a similar way, to enclose the social realm of urban transportation.[39] Cities provide many transportation options, but walking, cycling, or owning a private car can be either unsafe, impractical, or too expensive for the average city dweller. This trend explains the popularity of taxi services and public transport, and Uber tries to monopolize this field every time it enters a new city. So, though Uber predominantly uses its data extraction and analysis capacities to monitor its drivers, *only* this activity cannot be the basis for a viable business model.[40] Uber would be nothing more than a slightly more efficient taxi company by stringently coordinating their workers' conduct via algorithmic management and labor law evasion. The digital capture of social relations serves other purposes as well and these form Uber's long-term business strategy. Allow me to mention three ways Uber plans to extract enclave rent from its platform: (1) total monopolization, (2) promotional partnerships, and (3) function creep.

(1) As just mentioned, Uber bets on acquiring a monopoly on urban transportation. To be profitable, Uber needs to dominate the personal transportation sector in its entirety. It has become the only publicly accessible means of urban transportation, so that every individual moving through any city needs to book an Uber to move around. The company thus uses aggressive tactics to outcompete not only traditional taxi companies, but also public transport.[41] It even accepts temporarily running its business at significant losses to conquer the market and undermine genuinely profitable competitors.[42] Uber is infamous for lobbying for Uber-friendly government regulations and temporarily paying higher wages to redirect taxi drivers to its platform; it makes fares artificially cheap for consumers and convinces drivers to politically mobilize on its behalf vis-à-vis local governments.[43] Once a total monopoly is established, prices go up and drivers' fees go down, leaving a larger cut of on-platform transactions to Uber. Because Uber has outcompeted taxis and has dismantled public transportation, drivers and consumers have nowhere else to go. This allows Uber to charge monopoly prices with substandard workers' pay. For example, Uber has reduced drivers' fare per mile in New York between 2014 and 2018, when it had firmly embedded itself in the transportation market, from $3 to $1.75, an almost 50 percent reduction.[44]

Uber's total monopoly on the extraction and analysis of transportation data also grants it opportunities never available to traditional taxi companies, even where they had a monopoly. The latter could somewhat adjust prices to their own benefit, but Uber can use big data analytics to minutely calculate the best price for each transaction individually. It estimates how much each individual consumer is willing to pay and how low fees can go for any individual worker by mining its database for information about individuals' willingness to pay. In standard economic literature, this practice is called "price discrimination."[45] Vis-à-vis consumers, Uber breaks up a city's transportation market to charge every individual exactly the maximum price that this person is ready to pay according to algorithmic predictions. It can, for instance, look for data that suggest drunkenness because drunk passengers tend to think less critically about prices. The same tactic also works against drivers: Uber likewise calculates the lowest acceptable fee for every specific class of drivers, again leaving a bigger cut for Uber itself.

(2) A second strategy for Uber is to leverage its data enclave as a means to establish promotional partnerships with other companies interested in advertising to Uber's consumer base. Here, Uber most resembles social media companies: it licenses targeted access to its users for promotional purposes. As Birch and Cochrane write,

> Access to the enclave is valuable to outsiders like advertisers, software developers, and hardware manufacturers. Both the concentration of users and the collection of their data make access a near-necessity for the operations of other digital technology firms. Simultaneously, Big Tech firms augment their ecosystems through integrating these outsiders.[46]

If companies want access to this particular consumer base, they have to go through Uber and pay the platform rent to use its infrastructure. In 2015, for example, Pepsi launched a PR campaign where it paid Uber to add an exclusive add-on to its London app with which people could request free rides with the Delorean from the 1984 film, *Back to the Future*.[47] Pepsi created a promotional stunt by relying on Uber's easy access to everyone looking for transportation in the London area. It profited from targeting one gateway to access to an entire city. In 2016, Uber partnered with Starwood Hotels for a mutually beneficial campaign.[48] By providing tourists membership points in the hotel chain in exchange for kilometers driven with Uber, the companies encouraged tourists to engage with both as a one-package deal. Uber users would be incentivized to book Starwood rooms and *vice versa*. Ultimately, Uber builds a "super-platform"[49] where all services provided during a holiday are in one way or another delivered through the same network. Tourists can travel in an entirely Uber-made space, moving across the world without ever leaving the platform.

(3) A final tactic in Uber's playbook is repurposing data gathered for coordinating drivers to expand the Uber enclave in the social realm, a practice ominously called "function creep": data collected for the purpose of monitoring drivers' conduct is reused for new functions beyond workers' control.[50] Uber has, for example, been active in the development of self-driving cars.[51] For this venture, the company repurposes workers' data as training data for its algorithms. Drivers' datafied conduct becomes input to artificial intelligence

(AI) systems that subsequently operate cars that no longer need a human driver. Uber's monopoly on urban transportation data thereby becomes a launch pad for new businesses with potentially astronomical profits. If Uber were to succeed in acquiring a data pool and algorithms capable of automating cars entirely, it would expand its enclave to *all* forms of car-based transportation.[52] Uber drivers today are, in other words, unwittingly working themselves out of a job. With every piece of data Uber collects about their driving style, it teaches its algorithms to better mimic human driving until they no longer need a human behind the wheel.[53] This mechanism entails that drivers are performing double work during their shifts: they are simultaneously providing a transportation service to passengers and producing training data for Uber's self-driving AI.

4. DIGITAL CAPTURE AND FINANCIAL RENT

A large part of Uber's capacity for extracting enclave rent turns out be a promise for the distant future rather than a reality today. Uber has not yet introduced self-driving cars, and it rarely achieves a total monopoly in any particular city, let alone for urban transportation in general. For now, its (modest) revenues derive primarily from the transportation services Uber provides—no different from a traditional taxi company's business—and the almost-monopoly it has acquired for this service in some cities. The enclave rent hypothesis mainly explains Uber's future financial capacities, but not the company's current financial success. For the latter, Van Doorn and Badger correctly stress that the acquisition of data assets is a vehicle for attracting investment capital.[54] Uber thereby exemplifies a strategy typical of the digital sector: growth before profit.[55] Enclave rent only becomes profitable once the database becomes sufficiently large and once the company has acquired a total monopoly over the social cooperation generating this data. In the meantime, digital companies must rely on investors to grow to sufficient size. Platform companies count on investors rather than immediate profit to finance the early stages of development, while they build their digital capture techniques and experiment with ways to transform these data assets into profitable resources.

To keep itself afloat for long enough to reach this tipping point, Uber also relies in the first instance on venture capital. The latter names a series of funds that provide capital to start-up companies in exchange for shares and a cut of future profits.[56] This is a high-risk/high-rewards market where investors gamble on a series of promising companies in the hopes that some of them become the new Amazon or Google. Venture capital invests for longer periods of time than regular financial markets, but the operative logic is similar. They typically make ten-year contracts with start-ups, which gives the latter the time to grow without having to garner short-term profits.[57] Venture capitalists bet that, in a diverse portfolio of start-ups, many might fail but some will become so powerful that they will make astronomical profits.[58] In the case of Uber, "the hope is that the low margin business of taxis will eventually pay off once Uber has gained a monopoly position."[59] Once these companies are bought by larger players—as when Facebook bought WhatsApp in 2014—or once they go public on the financial markets, venture capitalists are reimbursed. The latter have invested cheap in successful start-ups and can subsequently sell their shares at multiple times the original value.

One could apply Lazzarato's theory of financial markets as quasi-Leibnizian gods to the role of venture capital in this ecosystem.[60] Lazzarato argues that financial markets exert power over populations by deciding which projects are worthy of investment and which are not. Every few months, corporations publish their performance projections in quarterly reports. On this basis, investors choose which companies' shares they would like to buy. As a result, the survival of corporations depends on their creditworthiness in the eyes of financial markets. According to Lazzarato, this logic mimics Leibniz' description of divine creation. According to Leibniz, God first imagined all possible worlds at the beginning of time. He saw their potential and subsequently created only the world that he expected to be "the best of all possible worlds." In his omniscience, God foresaw all potential futures and chose the configuration of the world that guaranteed the course of history in conformity to his plan. For Lazzarato, financial markets have today acquired a similarly powerful role in the neoliberal economy. Investors first acquire information about the future performance of economic ventures, and they subsequently select those that look most promising.[61] Finance is thus a selection machine that reconfigures the world in accordance with the interests of capital. Only those possible worlds that promise good returns on investment are allowed to survive. In the digital sector however, companies cannot make short-term profits, which makes it difficult for traditional financial investors to decide which firms are part of the best of all possible worlds. Venture capital, on the other hand, specializes in long-term investments, which makes it better suited to the digital sector. The operative logic is, however, fairly similar: companies still vie for the favor of the gods of capital in order to receive the funding they need to succeed. The main difference is whether the promised returns on investment are delivered in the short or long run. The importance of reputation remains, however, unchanged. As Moulier Boutang describes,

> For the company, the formation of a common opinion among shareholders via the means of communication and the accumulation of "confidence" are critical variables [sic], since they determine the market capitalisation and hence the

amount of borrowing that is possible. One could even argue that one of the main activities of cognitive capitalism is the production of different kinds of publics, of which the stock market public [or venture capital public] is not the least.[62]

Venture capital assesses its confidence in a diverse set of start-up and, on the basis of their faith, companies are given a chance at acquiring the monopoly they need to actually become profitable businesses. With their upfront financing, venture capitalists hence create the future that serves the accumulation of their capital.

In this particular ecosystem, platform companies aspire to the reputation of the ideal investee.[63] They make a temporal loop in which they leverage the prospect of future monopolies to access credit today. In other words, they pay upfront for their current expenses with the future rent they will extract once their business has succeeded. In this way, they make a merely potential but costly future a reality thanks to the credit provided by venture capital. To give one example, Uber—which made the transition from venture capital to financial markets in 2019—successfully lobbied for Proposition 22 to pass in a Californian referendum in 2020. The proposition allowed Uber to continue to classify its workers as "independent contractors" instead of employees. One effect of this referendum was a sudden spike in Uber's stock price. Because its chances at establishing total monopoly in California increased with the new law, Uber improved its reputation among potential investors. The latter consequently bought more shares in Uber for higher prices, effectively providing Uber with the cash-flow it needed to establish its total monopoly. Since investors were expecting Uber to succeed, they were injecting the capital into Uber that made this expectation a self-fulfilling prophecy. According to Moulier Boutang, this dynamic relies on a temporality that is neither present nor future but virtual:

> The virtual is neither the real (what is tangible) nor the possible (what does not yet exist), but that which, because of the fact of a publicly agreed representation of the future, becomes present and active in the present and at the same time modifies it. The virtual is effective in the formation of a common opinion on future values. Confidence in the future creates wealth immediately, just as lack of confidence in the future of a bank [or start-up], even if unfounded, puts it straight into bankruptcy.[64]

As quasi-Leibnizian gods, investors have the power to create with their portfolio the worlds they imagine. Their financial expectations provide the initial funding for companies to make their business plans a reality.

It is thus important for platform companies to properly manage their financial reputation as investees and the common opinion among potential investors. Their continuous cashflow depends more on the credit worthiness they publicly project than on the actual profits they make. The latter are merely doubtful promises start-ups make to attract as much venture capital as possible. But, in contrast to Leibniz' infallible God, venture capitalists are not omniscient higher beings who can see the future with absolute clarity. They rely on narratives, stories, and mimicking each other's conduct to justify their decisions.[65] In the initial phase of development, platform companies like Uber are thus more interested in developing a good image among investors than in the actual underlying business model and its prospects for profit. Their first income comes from the confidence they inspire among venture capitalists. This explains the ubiquity of legendary stories about "ruthless entrepreneurship from one's garage" and "disruptive technology" among Silicon Valley start-ups.[66] Start-up companies create hype around their brand by putting forward extravagant CEOs like Travis Kalanick (Uber), Elon Musk (PayPal and Tesla), or Adam Neumann (WeWork). The attention these people demand performatively embodies the revolutionary image they want to endow to the company. As Arvidsson highlights, Silicon Valley houses an entire consultancy sector devoted to coaching aspirational entrepreneurs into building successful start-ups. The business idea and its money-making potential are just one facet of this project. More important in the initial phases are the CEO's public persona, a convincing pitch, personal contacts in the venture capital bubble, and so on.

For outsiders, this might look like a big Ponzi scheme, and for many start-ups it is.[67] Both Uber's and Deliveroo's initial public offerings on financial markets were disastrous because financial investors did not have the same confidence in these companies' profitability as venture capitalists.[68] Nonetheless, this strategy has worked for companies like Amazon, Google, and Facebook. If platform companies succeed in due time at acquiring a total monopoly on a part of the social realm to extract enclave rent *and* they can live off financial rent in the meantime, they can become among the highest grossing firms in the world. Amazon had to rely on financial rent for almost ten years before its business could run independently at a profit, but it is now among the most powerful companies worldwide. Profits—or the lack thereof—today is thus no reliable indicator of platform companies' success in the future. Uber, for example, might be in a difficult spot today due to the threat of regulation or its disappointing revenues, but it can still become a powerhouse tomorrow. If its strategy for the extraction of enclave rent succeeds and it can rely for long enough on financial rent, it could become the Amazon or Google of the transportation sector.

5. CONCLUSION

One of the major questions in the political economy of Big Tech is how these companies actually make money. Most digital platforms provide free access to consumers, but they extract data from people's online interactions. The latter are the crucial ingredient for the Big Tech business model. Some argue that the datafication of human conduct entails that people's online social interactions constitute unpaid, exploited labor. If individuals perform "click work" that subsequently generates profit for private companies, then the latter must have exploited internet users, so the argument goes. I have criticized this description in favor of a more complex theory of the becoming-rent of profit and the assetisation of human conduct as data. Platform companies do not exploit individuals as if they were unpaid factory workers from Marx' days. They rather commodify previously noncommodified social interactions and subsequently extract rent from market agents that wish to access these social interactions. Uber, for instance, tries to monopolize urban transportation habits so that it can, in the future, charge monopoly prices to consumers and drivers for its services, charge rent to companies looking to advertise through its platform, and expand its business to new fields, like self-driving cars. These forms of rent extraction, however, do not suffice to explain the continued existence of the digital gig economy today. Most of these platform companies do not garner sustainable profits. They rather rely on venture capital investments to support themselves until they reach the monopoly status that makes the aforementioned forms of rent extraction possible.

NOTES

1. Caffentzis, *In Letters of Blood and Fire*, 113; Jones, *Work without the Worker*, 47.
2. Negri, *Reflections on Empire*, 183.
3. Kean Birch and D. T. Cochrane, "Big Tech: Four Emerging Forms of Digital Rentiership," *Science as Culture*, 2021, 1–15.
4. Tiziana Terranova, "Free Labor: Producing Culture for the Digital Economy," *Social Text* 18, no. 2 (2000): 33–58.
5. Christian Fuchs, "Labor in Informational Capitalism and on the Internet," *The Information Society* 26, no. 3 (2010): 179–96. Fuchs seems to have moved away from this position, however, since it no longer appears in more recent publications. See, e.g., Fuchs, *Rereading Marx in the Age of Digital Capitalism*.
6. Scholz, *Uberworked and Underpaid*; Evangelos Papadimitropoulos, "Platform Capitalism, Platform Cooperativism, and the Commons," *Rethinking Marxism* 33, no. 2 (2021): 246–62; Eduard Müller, "Putting the Habitus to Work: Digital Prosumption, Surveillance and Distinction," in *Augmented Exploitation*, ed. Phoebe Moore and Jamie Woodcock (London: Pluto Press, 2021), 50–61.

7. Terranova, "Free Labor," 37.

8. Adam Arvidsson and Elanor Colleoni, "Value in Informational Capitalism and on the Internet," *The Information Society* 28, no. 3 (2012): 136.

9. Terranova, "Free Labor," 49.

10. Christian Fuchs, "Dallas Smythe Today - The Audience Commodity, the Digital Labour Debate, Marxist Political Economy and Critical Theory," *TripleC: Communication, Capitalism & Critique* 10, no. 2 (2012): 692–740.

11. Arvidsson and Colleoni, "Value in Informational Capitalism," 135.

12. Marx' seminal expression of the theory of wages, capital, and exploitation can be found in Karl Marx, *Wage-Labour and Capital & Value, Price, and Profit* (New York: International Publishers, 1976).

13. For simplicity's sake, I ignore fixed capital costs in this example. In reality, however, the manufacturer would also have to invest in maintaining a factory, buying machinery, etc.

14. Arvidsson and Colleoni, "Value in Informational Capitalism," 138. Fuchs has responded to this criticism by arguing that Arvidsson and Colleoni ignore the difference between value and price. It is not because Facebook sells the audience commodity at the price of 0.7 dollars a year that this is also the value of each user's click work. Facebook might have had to undersell its product for lack of demand. This explanation, however, leaves the question of why Facebook—and all other internet giants—are so bad at marketing their products. See Christian Fuchs, "With or Without Marx? With or Without Capitalism? A Rejoinder to Adam Arvidsson and Eleanor Colleoni," *TripleC: Communication, Capitalism & Critique* 10, no. 2 (2012): 633–45.

15. Brett Christophers, *Rentier Capitalism: Who Owns the Economy, and Who Pays for It?* (London: Verso Books, 2020), 195.

16. Srnicek, *Platform Capitalism*, 52. For a counter-argument, see Donald MacKenzie, "Cookies, Pixels and Fingerprints," *London Review of Books* 43, no. 7 (2021).

17. Christophers, *Rentier Capitalism*, 181.

18. Srnicek, *Platform Capitalism*, 55–56. See also Smith, *Smart Machines and Service Work*, 92–113.

19. Crawford Spence and David Carter, "Accounting for the General Intellect: Immaterial Labour and the Social Factory," *Critical Perspectives on Accounting* 22, no. 3 (2011): 307. See also Lazzarato, *Les Révolutions du Capitalisme*, 79.

20. Sandro Mezzadra and Brett Neilson, "Extraction, Logistics, Finance: Global Crisis and the Politics of Operations," *Radical Philosophy* 178, no. 2 (2013): 9; Srnicek, *Platform Capitalism*, 48; Hardt and Negri, *Assembly*, 168.

21. Negri and Hardt, "Empire, Twenty Years On," 80.

22. Carlo Vercellone, "The Crisis of the Law of Value and the Becoming-Rent of Profit," in *Crisis in the Global Economy*, ed. Andrea Fumagalli and Sandro Mezzadra (Los Angeles, CA: Semiotext(e), 2010), 94; Yann Moulier Boutang, *Cognitive Capitalism*, trans. Ed Emery (Cambridge, UK: Polity Press, 2011), 104.

23. Michael Hardt and Antonio Negri, *Multitude: War and Democracy in the Age of Empire* (New York: Penguin Books, 2005), 113.

24. Moulier Boutang, *Cognitive Capitalism*, 92–98.

25. Moulier Boutang, 57.

26. Arvidsson and Colleoni, "Value in Informational Capitalism," 140; Negri, *From the Factory to the Metropolis*, 15; Massimiliano Nicoli and Luca Paltrinieri, "Platform Cooperativism: Some Notes on the Becoming 'Common' of the Firm," *South Atlantic Quarterly* 118, no. 4 (2019): 810.

27. Data always requires particular software to make it legible and platform companies keep secret the algorithms that translate social relations into data. As a result, platform companies are monopsonists vis-à-vis individual users and the data they provide, which allows them to push the price of data down to zero (Couldry and Mejias, *The Costs of Connection*, 43–45; Christophers, *Rentier Capitalism*, 211–12.). No one but this individual platform company can read the data people produce, meaning users cannot prosper from competition among platform companies for their data. This monopsony power explains how platform companies can easily dispossess users of their data with the latter having only a limited capacity to fight back.

28. Armin Beverungen, Steffen Böhm, and Chris Land, "Free Labour, Social Media, Management: Challenging Marxist Organization Studies," *Organization Studies* 36, no. 4 (2015): 483.

29. Javier Moreno Zacarés, "Euphoria of the Rentier?," *New Left Review* 129, no. 3 (2021): 48.

30. Carlo Vercellone, "The Becoming Rent of Profit? The New Articulation of Wage, Rent and Profit," *Knowledge Cultures* 1, no. 2 (2013): 195.

31. Moulier Boutang, *Cognitive Capitalism*, 32; Arvidsson and Colleoni, "Value in Informational Capitalism," 142.

32. Vercellone, "The Crisis of the Law of Value," 105.

33. Vercellone argues that post-Fordist companies that rely on rent ultimately parasitize on the welfare state and its sustenance of the multitude's social cooperation, which makes the becoming-rent of profit an unstable regime of accumulation. Post-Fordist companies privatize the common but give nothing in return to reproduce it. On the contrary, by monopolizing the platforms where this social cooperation takes place, they potentially stifle the very resource they need for their own growth. Social cooperation fares best when it is completely unhindered, but post-Fordist capital must introduce obstacle to the free circulation of knowledge, affects, and communication to secure its own profits (see Vercellone, 92; Moulier Boutang, *Cognitive Capitalism*, 116–17). It subsequently counts on the welfare state to sponsor the sustenance of social cooperation. It relies on the state funding education, healthcare, social security, and so forth, to make high-quality social cooperation possible. In sum, post-Fordist capital parasitizes on welfare institutions to reproduce the multitude, whose wealth capital subsequently expropriates. See Carlo Vercellone, "From the Crisis to the 'Welfare of the Common' as a New Mode of Production," *Theory, Culture & Society* 32, no. 7–8 (2015): 85–99.

34. Birch and Cochrane, "Big Tech," 5.

35. Jathan Sadowski, "When Data Is Capital: Datafication, Accumulation, and Extraction," *Big Data & Society* 6, no. 1 (2019): 8; Jathan Sadowski, "The Internet of Landlords: Digital Platforms and New Mechanisms of Rentier Capitalism," *Antipode* 52, no. 2 (2020): 571.

36. Couldry and Mejias, *The Costs of Connection*, 129; Kean Birch, "Technoscience Rent: Toward a Theory of Rentiership for Technoscientific Capitalism," *Science, Technology, and Human Values* 45, no. 1 (2020): 9; Sadowski, "The Internet of Landlords," 568.

37. Massimiliano Nuccio and Marco Guerzoni, "Big Data: Hell or Heaven? Digital Platforms and Market Power in the Data-Driven Economy," *Competition & Change* 23, no. 3 (2019): 319.

38. Tim Christiaens, "Convivial Autonomy and Platform Capitalism," in *Autonomy: Interdisciplinary Perspectives*, ed. Oliver Davis and Chris Watkin (London: Routledge, 2022).

39. Srnicek, *Platform Capitalism*, 44; Couldry and Mejias, *The Costs of Connection*, 115.

40. Srnicek, *Platform Capitalism*, 87.

41. Schor, *After the Gig*, 117.

42. Woodcock and Graham, *The Gig Economy*, 8; Schor, *After the Gig*, 35.

43. Especially the work of Kathleen Thelen and Alex Rosenblat succinctly documents the political tactics of platform companies like Uber. See Rosenblat, *Uberland*; Rahman and Thelen, "The Rise of the Platform Business Model and the Transformation of Twenty-First-Century Capitalism"; Pepper Culpepper and Kathleen Thelen, "Are We All Amazon Primed? Consumers and the Politics of Platform Power," *Comparative Political Studies* 53, no. 2 (2020): 288–318.

44. Ravenelle, *Hustle and Gig*, 75.

45. Rosenblat, *Uberland*, 110; Nuccio and Guerzoni, "Big Data: Hell or Heaven?," 320–21.

46. Birch and Cochrane, "Big Tech," 6.

47. Uber, "Fancy a Ride to the Future?," Uber Newsroom, 2015, https://www.uber.com/en-GB/newsroom/fancy-a-ride-to-the-future/.

48. Nour Ahmadein, "Revving up Rider Rewards with Starwood Hotels," Uber Newsroom, 2016, https://www.uber.com/en-EG/newsroom/revving-up-rider-rewards-with-starwood-hotels/.

49. Schor, *After the Gig*, 151.

50. Couldry and Mejias, *The Costs of Connection*, 133.

51. Rosenblat, *Uberland*, 179; Schor, *After the Gig*, 151; Woodcock and Graham, *The Gig Economy*, 66.

52. Uber's sale of its self-driving car program to the start-up Aurora, however, indicates that it might not have faith in the short-term achievability of the effort. On the other hand, Uber still owns a significant part of Aurora's shares and the start-up combines people from Uber and Google's self-driving cars program, so the sale could also be furthering the "cooperation of brains" to make the project succeed.

53. Phoebe Moore, "AI Trainers: Who Is the Smart Worker Today?," in *Augmented Exploitation*, ed. Phoebe Moore and Jamie Woodcock (London: Pluto Press, 2021), 17.

54. Niels Van Doorn and Adam Badger, "Platform Capitalism's Hidden Abode: Producing Data Assets in the Gig Economy," *Antipode* 52, no. 5 (2020): 1480.

55. Srnicek, *Platform Capitalism*, 75; Christophers, *Rentier Capitalism*, 221.

56. Paul Langley and Andrew Leyshon, "Platform Capitalism: The Intermediation and Capitalisation of Digital Economic Circulation," *Finance & Society* 3, no. 1 (2017): 11–31; Scholz, *Uberworked and Underpaid*, 46; Rosenblat, *Uberland*, 28; Rahman and Thelen, "The Rise of the Platform Business Model and the Transformation of Twenty-First-Century Capitalism," 183–84.

57. Robyn Klingler-Vidra, "When Venture Capital Is Patient Capital: Seed Funding as a Source of Patient Capital for High-Growth Companies," *Socio-Economic Review* 14, no. 4 (2016): 691–708.

58. Langley and Leyshon, "Platform Capitalism," 14.

59. Srnicek, *Platform Capitalism*, 87.

60. Lazzarato, *Les Révolutions du Capitalisme*, 95. See also Tim Christiaens, "Neoliberalism and the Right to Be Lazy: Inactivity as Resistance in Lazzarato and Agamben," *Rethinking Marxism* 30, no. 2 (3 April 2018): 256–74.

61. See also Moulier Boutang, *Cognitive Capitalism*, 136; Negri, *From the Factory to the Metropolis*, 172.

62. Moulier Boutang, *Cognitive Capitalism*, 145.

63. Michel Feher, *Rated Agency: Investee Politics in a Speculative Age*, trans. Gregory Elliott (New York: Zone Books, 2018). See also Josh Bowsher, "Credit/Debt and Human Capital: Financialized Neoliberalism and the Production of Subjectivity," *European Journal of Social Theory* 22, no. 4 (2019): 513–32; Tim Christiaens, "Performing Agency Theory and the Neoliberalization of the State," *Critical Sociology* 46, no. 3 (2020): 393–411.

64. Moulier Boutang, *Cognitive Capitalism*, 180–81.

65. Lazzarato, *Les Révolutions du Capitalisme*, 112–13; Marazzi, *Capital and Affects*, 93.

66. Arvidsson, *Changemakers*, 83.

67. Arvidsson, 91.

68. Schor, *After the Gig*, 37.

Chapter 4

Alienation in the Platform Economy

I am selling my smile for a five-star rating.

—Freddy, a young Uber driver[1]

One of the most alarming aspects of digital platforms is the predominance of digital rating systems. Platforms like Airbnb, Yelp, or Uber allow customers to rate their service providers with a score between zero and five stars. The official *raison d'être* of this metric is to establish and measure trustworthiness among strangers.[2] In the case of Airbnb, for example, tourists might refrain from booking an Airbnb because they fear being duped by hosts promising far more on the internet than they offer in practice. Online reputation systems are a handy tool to put guests' minds at ease and guarantee quality services. It punishes dishonest practices and rewards trustworthy individuals. Popular representations of the rating system, however, reveal a darker side. The *South Park* episode "You're Not Yelping," for instance, shows the local bully, Eric Cartman, terrorizing the town's restaurants with his outrageous demands in exchange for good Yelp reviews. The *Black Mirror* episode "Nosedive," on the other hand, depicts a dystopian future where people constantly rate each other, and online reputation has become the main currency—even displacing money. One's digital reputation determines in what neighborhoods one can afford to live, where one can work, and even with whom one can be friends. As a side-effect, people are constantly on their best behavior to avoid public scrutiny. The smiles are fake, the personalities inoffensive yet one-dimensional. Genuine human connection has been buried under a stream of data.

As with most dystopian fiction, these stories exaggerate a tendency already present today. Platform users already report worrying levels of alienation caused by constant digital surveillance. In order to retain one's digital reputation, people on Airbnb or Uber have to continuously hide behind a mask of complacent pleasantness. Anything unexpected could trigger a downgrade; and, since platform workers depend on their ratings for their incomes, such downgrades could prove detrimental to one's revenues. People are under pressure to perform a likeable version of themselves, which undercuts the potential for genuine human contact. Instead of acting like themselves, workers act like extensions of the algorithms that monitor their conduct. If, for example, Airbnb asks guests to review hosts on the matters of overall experience, cleanliness, accuracy, check-in, communication skills, location, value, and amenities, one can expect hosts will modulate their behavior to fit exactly those criteria.[3] Not workers but the algorithms screening their conduct determine whether they will clean the guestroom, smile to a guest, or show people the way to the city center.

In this chapter, I discuss this digital variant of alienation with Paolo Virno's ambivalent appreciation of the general intellect, using Airbnb as my main example. The choice for Airbnb comes with specific advantages and disadvantages.[4] Compared to companies like Uber and Deliveroo, one hears less about workers' complaints vis-à-vis Airbnb. Many of its hosts are either speculating real-estate investors who buy entire streets in metropolitan city centers to list them on Airbnb or so-called "supplemental earners" (i.e., people who have a secure income from other sources and merely sublet a room on Airbnb as a supplement to their main income source).[5] The average Airbnb host is wealthier and more privileged than their counterparts on the bottom of the platform hierarchy—they own or can rent housing with at least one extra room. Their subsistence seldomly hinges on a single bad review. Since these people are less dependent on Airbnb and its algorithmic management, they are under diminished pressure to conform to its standards. Experiences are consequently more positive than with other platforms. Nonetheless, compared to, for instance, Deliveroo, social contact with the consumer is more sustained and more intense on Airbnb, rendering it an ideal case for the study of emotional labor and its alienating effects. This chapter, hence, focuses primarily on the relatively small section of Airbnb hosts that are vitally dependent on this income.

To clarify the issue of alienation among Airbnb hosts, I will start with how Marx introduced the concept of "general intellect" to denote the increasingly entanglement of humans and machines in capitalist production.[6] The concept encapsulates the machines, scientific data, electric infrastructures, and so forth, mobilized in capitalist production. Digital platforms embody in an exemplary fashion the general intellect today: they extract data from human conduct and use these data to subsequently steer human conduct in a profitable direction. Human social cooperation is absorbed into algorithms and congealed into a quantum of reputational stars that connote the worker's value to the production process. Whereas most post-workerists emphasize the emancipatory potential of the general intellect, Virno stresses its political ambivalence. He agrees with Negri and the others that digital technology and automation create an opportunity for the inauguration of a post-work society where technology liberates us from the toils of labor, but he also notices the surreptitious ways in which human workers are subjugated to their digital machinery. Once human beings become mere data-carriers in a self-managing digital system, the latter can surreptitiously enforce commands on its human users. Through the digital extraction process, workers are alienated from their own conduct. They become mere bystanders to algorithmic processes beyond their control. According to Virno, this imbalance nurtures negative emotions of fear, opportunism, and cynicism.

1. THE AMBIVALENCE OF THE GENERAL INTELLECT

Marx briefly entertains the notion of a "general intellect" in the *Grundrisse* in what has later become known as "The Fragment on Machines."[7] It refers to the assemblage of machines, software, communication networks, and so on, that coordinate the industrial production process. According to Marx, machines are no longer mere "means of labour,"[8] but the moving force of capitalist production. This tremendously increases labor productivity, but it also entails that workers have to adapt to the machinic self-propelling system.

> It is the machine which possesses skill and strength in place of the worker, is itself the virtuoso, with a soul of its own in the mechanical laws acting through it . . . The science which compels the inanimate limbs of the machinery, by their construction, to act purposefully, as an automaton, does not exist in the worker's consciousness, but rather acts upon him through the machine as an alien power, as the power of the machine itself.[9]

The entanglement of humans and machines entails that the latter absorb human social knowledge that is subsequently used to coordinate human conduct. The more the general intellect extracts practical knowhow and scientific knowledge into mathematical equations, the more meticulously it can enforce the capitalist profit motive in the production process. Technology is, hence, for Marx, not a neutral tool for human labor, but an arena of class struggle. Capitalist control over the form and development of the general intellect leads to a particularly capital-friendly organization of machines, software, human labor, and so forth.

The one-sided, optimistic understanding of the general intellect popular among many contemporary post-workerists and those they have inspired, is thus misplaced.[10] In their view, technological advancement is an unambiguously positive step toward cyborg communism. The general intellect purportedly embodies an emancipatory potential that will only be truly unleashed under a form of communism that fully embraces technological innovation. They argue that workers must only "reappropriate the general intellect," seize the means of production, in order to autonomously take control over their future.[11] Marx himself does not entirely disagree with this strategy. He argues that the creation of real wealth depends less and less on the exploitation of actual workers, so that the opportunity arises for the production process to govern itself with the worker stepping aside as a mere "watchman and regulator."[12] Because the general intellect automates large parts of the production process, Marx and some post-workerists dream that one day, human labor will become entirely superfluous. The production process will manage itself leaving humankind with an abundance of free time to enjoy. As Virno summarizes, "abstract knowledge . . . moves toward becoming nothing less than the principal productive force, relegating parceled and repetitive labor to a residual position."[13] According to Marx, capitalism "works toward its own dissolution as the form dominating production"[14] without even the need for a violent revolution.[15]

Marx, however, redacted most of his optimistic dreams of an electric future from subsequent writings. As noted in chapter 2, Marx' diagnosis of the role of technology in *Capital: Volume I* is significantly more pessimistic. Automation does not necessarily lead to and might even actively impede human emancipation. As Virno states, "what is striking now is the complete factual realization of the tendency described in the 'Fragment' without any emancipatory or even conflictual outcome."[16] Three factors explain why cyborg communism has not yet reached our shores more than 150 years after Marx wrote the *Grundrisse*: (1) the ideology of work, (2) the imperfections of automation, and (3) the ambivalence of an inherently capitalist general intellect.

(1) When anthropologists call Western societies "work-centered," they mean that these communities predominantly distribute social recognition through employment. One acquires recognition as a productive member of society on the basis of the job one holds. Employment is, in capitalist modernity, a key source of personal identity. The extent to which this sociological insight rings true can be gauged by the frequency with which people introduce themselves with their name and occupation during casual conversations. If one quickly wants to know who someone is, modern capitalist societies require to state one's name and one's employment status. Moreover, the better the job is paid, the more value an individual is presumed to contribute. However, if people's social value is measured through employment, automation does not translate into free time but unemployment.[17] This is not just a

matter of ideology or discourse but is inscribed into the core operations of social organization itself. As noted in chapter 1, capitalism is built on the antagonism between living labor and its commodification of labor-power. Workers can only survive insofar as they sell their labor-power in exchange for a wage. The latter grants them access to goods and services necessary for their sustenance. The legal framework that governs people's livelihoods, for instance, is built around the employment status. Only those with full-time employment are paid a full wage and employment is, in many legal systems, also the primary gateway for social security services like health insurance, unemployment benefits, or pension savings. This legal order consolidates the central place of employment, even if automation steadily undermines the availability of jobs. Through labor and social security law, the ideology of work has some efficacy of its own that cannot be directly reduced to economic factors. If the automation of the general intellect, then, reduces the overall demand for human labor-power, the outcome is not free time but idle labor-power. Society is left with an excess stock of labor-power. Only by decoupling human survival from wage-labor does one allow for a post-work future, but this directly contradicts the tenets of capitalism itself. This would require fundamental changes to the legal order, like a shortening of the workweek or the introduction of a basic income.[18]

(2) Not all labor processes can be automated with the tools currently at our disposal.[19] Though industrial labor has been extremely amenable to automation, the same cannot be asserted about service work. This is especially troubling because labor statistics suggest that automation in the industrial sector since the 1970s is one of the key causes for the increase in service jobs in recent decades. Once manufactured goods have become cheaper thanks to technological innovation, people spend more of their disposable income on services like restaurant food, taxi rides, holidays, and so on. Jobs that entail person-to-person interaction, however, rely on tacit knowledge that resists automation. A service worker must understand implicit social norms, adequately respond to small visual and auditory cues, process emotions, and so forth. Automated machinery, on the contrary, only outperforms humankind in singular and straightforward tasks. That explains why machines can easily replace workers in a Tailorized factory but are unable to perform supposedly "simple" tasks like making soup or smiling appropriately. Automation in the service sector consequently does not replace workers, but rather it optimizes labor-process coordination by integrating them in digital platforms. Digital technology does not replace taxi drivers, hotel managers, or nurses, but monitors their performance through apps like Uber, Airbnb, or Care.com. These businesses can only automate the matching process that connects workers to clients, but they cannot (yet) replace the workers themselves.

One further reason for the lack of automation in the service sector concerns labor cost: some services are cheaper in their analogue variant.[20] Many of the emotional and care skills required in the service sector are acquired in nonmarket settings. They are labelled as "women's work" and, to that extent, they remained unpaid. From capital's point of view, this means that the skills demanded in the service sector require little investment, since they occur spontaneously in society through unpaid shadow work. Given the free supply of emotional intelligence, there is no financial incentive to invest in automation research. Artificial intelligence can be relatively expensive if compared to the wages some workers receive for their labor. In those cases, businesses' cost/benefit analyses point toward the deployment of human labor. As long as there is an oversupply of workers in the service sector and their skills are underappreciated, the wages are too low to incentivize companies to invest in labor automation.

(3) Within capitalist modernity, the general intellect can function as a double-edged sword. Most of the general intellect's components—its software, algorithms, design, and so on—have been developed with the profit motive in mind. The current general intellect at our disposal is hence of a particularly capitalist bent. Until now, most technology has been invented to cut on labor costs or increase productivity independently of workers' well-being. A society with different values would have created other technologies, so it is unclear whether the technologies at our disposal today are really well-suited for a post-work society. Digital platforms like Uber and Deliveroo, for instance, constantly send push notifications to their workers. If they refuse to respond, they risk being downgraded. Smartphone technology makes this possible, but the practice hinders human emancipation from work. Even if workers have more free time than ever before, technologies like push notifications and e-mails make workers feel *as if* they are constantly available for work. Even if people are not actually working, they cannot escape the *feeling* of work during their free time. Their subjugation to wage labor is written into the design itself of apps like Uber's or Deliveroo's. Such technologies cannot be simply repurposed for cyborg communism without a thorough revision of their constitution. In the case of emails and push notifications, for instance, a start could be made with Trebor Scholz' "right to log off": workers should have the right not to respond to digital messages from work during their free time without punishment (see chapter 8).[21] Reappropriating the general intellect is, in other words, not a mere transfer of ownership from the capitalist to the working class; it reshapes the very core of what machines we allow into our society. Current technologies have been designed to make workers dance to the "algo-rhythm" of their smartphones. A reappropriated general intellect ought to emancipate people from the pressures of work by politicizing and democratizing the design of the general intellect itself.

In what follows, I would like to focus on this last remark. A capitalist general intellect is not immediately suited to a post-work, cyborg communism, but to generating profit. Digital platforms and the digital gig economy reveal a general intellect particularly apt at subjugating workers to an algorithmically imposed labor process. In the remainder of the chapter, I use Airbnb's digital rating system as my primary illustration. Airbnb asks its hosts and guests to rate each other with stars on metrics like cleanliness, communication skills, amenities, and so on. With these reviews, Airbnb users build an online reputation to access future transactions. Potential guests are more likely to get future rooms if they have good reputations, while hosts need good ratings to appear on the top of the list of suggestions clients view when they visit the Airbnb website. The higher they are on the list, the greater the chance they will acquire more and better guests in the future. Digitalizing reputation has both (a) extended and (b) deepened the domination of capital over labor.

(a) Extension. If one looks carefully into the specific characteristics that Airbnb asks its users to review, it becomes obvious that more areas of people's private lives are becoming part of the general intellect's database. Through the reputation system, the company holds meticulous records about how clean hosts' rooms are, how kindly hosts help tourists to get to know the city, whether they provide amenities like free wi-fi or bottled water, or how comfortable the beds are. It trusts its users to provide reliable information on these aspects of workers' private lives and subsequently stores this information in digital databases. Even in the housing market, these metrics were previously never recorded with such care and precision. Whereas traditional factories would restrict surveillance to the workspace, Airbnb must extend surveillance into the household to ensure its profits. Hosts must voluntarily submit to being monitored in their own homes in order to procure an income. Parts of life that have before never been part of capitalist surveillance are now, due to the general intellect, captured into the labor process. People's cleanliness, their easy-goingness with strangers, or their knowledge of local tourist attractions have now become Airbnb assets. The digital reputation system is, therefore, more than simply a device to build trust among strangers; it is a surveillance technique that tracks parts of human conduct that previously evaded capitalist control.

(b) Deepening. The digital rating system not only captures more parts of people's private lives in digital databases but does so more meticulously as well. It delves deeper into the individual's privacy to optimize capitalist control over the labor process. If Airbnb hosts were to have a human supervisor, the latter would only have been able to inspect the rooms sporadically. Airbnb has, however, outsourced quality controls to consumers. Airbnb hosts must consequently internalize guests' expectations in the way Airbnb measures

them through its review system. Hosts must spontaneously enact the behavior that guests expect during their visit. Airbnb promises tourists a comfortable and adventurous travel experience, but these qualities depend largely on hosts' emotional labor. Guests feel comfortable if they are well-received in their new room. Hosts must, thus, voluntarily engage in human conversation and manage their guests' emotions to produce the "Airbnb experience." Their emotions and communication skills become an asset mobilized in Airbnb's business model. The imperative for emotional labor entails that hosts maintain a certain level of performed, yet spontaneous professionalism whenever there are guests around. The entire experience must be filled with positive emotions and fond memories if hosts expect to receive good ratings, but "communication loses its character of gratuitous, pleasurable and erotic contact, becoming an economic necessity, a joyless fiction."[22] Tourists do not want to be bothered with their hosts' private troubles, so certain "shameful" dimensions of private live must be hidden from view. A host cannot burst into tears when a guest arrives, nor complain about his marital problems or STDs. Hosts must have their life in order if they want to survive on Airbnb's platform. Failure results in negative reviews and thus a loss of potential income.[23]

2. ALIENATION AND THE GENERAL INTELLECT

In the idiom of the young Marx, the problem I have highlighted appears under the rubric of "alienation": with their behavior, workers produce data that is subsequently collected and used to dominate the workforce. Especially in the *Economic and Philosophical Manuscripts of 1844,* Marx already argues that the capitalist technical composition of humans and machines puts workers in the paradoxical position that, the more they produce, the less control they exert over their own conduct.

> The worker is related to the product of his labor as to an alien object. For it is clear that, according to this premise, the more the worker exerts himself [sic] in his work, the more powerful the alien, objective world becomes which he brings into being over and against himself, the poorer he and his inner world become, and the less they belong to him. [. . .] The worker places his life in the object; but now it no longer belongs to him, but to the object.[24]

With their labor, workers produce value that the capitalist subsequently sells for a profit. This profit goes to the latter's stock of capital, which he reinvests in order to acquire even more profit. As noted in chapter 2, this additional surplus value comes from exerting increasing managerial control over the labor process, either by prolonging the workday (absolute surplus value) or by increasing labor productivity (relative surplus value). Either way, the capitalist uses his capital—which comes from workers' surplus labor—to improve the managerial coordination of the production process. So, the more value workers produce, the more capital managers possess to make workers produce even more future value.

From this perspective, today's digital general intellect appears as a sedimentation of past labor solidified into a digital infrastructure designed to control living labor today. Platforms extract information from a population's conduct to govern these conducts in ways that suit the platform itself. The algorithmic commands workers receive *appear* like alien powers subjugating workers, but they *are*, in fact, the products of their labor reflected back at them through a technological façade. Airbnb, for instance, collects data about hosts' past performances to meticulously monitor and coordinate hosts' work. The digital reputation metric gathers information about workers' performance in a single metric in order to maximize control over future work. Hosts are subsequently governed by forces of their own making, perversely reflected back at them as a haunting number of stars. Workers in the digital gig economy are ultimately reduced to powerless cogs in a gigantic digital machine of their own creation . . . and with every piece of data they produce, they hand over a little bit more of their autonomy.

Marx unsurprisingly suggests that this dynamic fosters feelings of despair, despondency, and frustration among workers. The latter feel like it is the machines operating them, as if they themselves had no agency in the labor process. Their living and breathing bodies are apparently reduced to mere moments in capital's own cycle of self-reproduction. A "mentally and physically dehumanised man"[25] no longer recognizes himself in his own conduct; capital is ultimately pulling the strings. The labor process manifests itself as a self-governing system ruled by natural laws over which workers exert no control.

> Estrangement appears not only in the fact that the means of *my* life belong to *another* and that *my* desire is the inaccessible possession of *another*, but also in the fact that all things are *other* than themselves, that my activity is *other* than itself, and that finally . . . an *inhuman power* rules over everything.[26]

Digital platforms today both extend and deepen this grip of capital on human life. With the rise of a digital general intellect, alienation thus reaches a new apex. Airbnb's rating system, for instance, integrates details about people's private lives in order to use those data against hosts.[27] It profits from streamlining hosts' behavior down to the smallest detail. For the hosts, on the other hand, a bad rating will result in fewer guests. They, thus, have to focus on maintaining "good data." And with every piece of data the produce, the platform's all-seeing eye becomes more powerful.

A particularly ugly side-effect of this *modus operandi* is that digital platforms detect people's racial and gender biases and present them as neutral facts in hosts' reputation scores.[28] Guests might not always judge their hosts fairly, especially when the hosts have bodies that are in some way considered undesirable. A black man's lower score on "cleanliness" might thus not be a truthful reflection of his sloppiness, but a technologically obscured expression of racial prejudice. Online ratings might seem objective facts, but they are, in reality, aggregations of subjective judgments. They constitute "opinions embedded into mathematics."[29] Biases widespread in society will thus show up in the numbers. Since the reputation system measures trustworthiness, and biased guests tend to distrust nonwhite races, for example, nonwhites have to perform extra well to merit the same score as a mediocre white host. The alienation predominant in the digital gig economy thus intersects with other social divisions along the lines of race, gender, disability, and so forth. Though the reputation number might look like a politically neutral metric, it reflects political divides in society. Those with bodies considered "abnormal" are especially vulnerable to the disciplining force of Airbnb's algorithms. The company justifies their exclusion from lucrative opportunities on the basis of digital ratings that "whitewash" popular prejudice.

The feelings of frustration and powerlessness that Marx observed in nineteenth-century factories thus return in the digital gig economy. The more data digital platforms collect and use to discipline human behavior, the more digital users become exiles to their own behavior.[30] Airbnb hosts, for instance, report feeling displaced in their own homes.[31] They can no longer be themselves because they constantly have to conform to guests' expectations. They perform the role of the perfect host: they clean their house, are nice to visitors, study local tourist guides, not because they want to, but because the algorithm expects them to perform these tasks. Airbnb's algorithm has penetrated their minds to such an extent that it seems like the company acts *through* its workers. Even the most outrageous demands must be met with a smile to avoid a downgrade. In 2016, for example, a Sydney host found her apartment ransacked after a group of drug addicts booked her place.[32] The damages went up to 10,000 dollars. Of course, not all Airbnb encounters go so horribly wrong, but guests wrecking their room, doing drugs, or stealing from their hosts, are not out of the ordinary. However, when guests misbehave, hosts have little tools to defend themselves.[33] They can give their guests a bad rating, but since Airbnb privileges consumers over its own workers, guests usually get the benefit of the doubt. The general intellect is designed in consumers' favor. Hosts cannot count on the same level of trust. Virno summarizes the phenomenology of this contemporary form of alienation with three emotions: (1) fear, (2) opportunism, and (3) cynicism.[34]

(1) According to Virno, the primary emotion of post-Fordist capitalism is fear, more specifically the fear of being left behind in an economy that continuously races forward. Given that employment under post-Fordism is becoming more precarious, individual workers are more vulnerable to changes in the labor market than before. The digital gig economy has emerged specifically in response to the decline of protections in traditional economic sectors. Once collective bargaining opportunities dwindle, factories move abroad, and welfare state institutions are dismantled, many workers have nowhere to turn but to digital platforms. These platforms, however, rely on precariousness to keep workers from protesting their alienating working conditions. As Virno states, "the post-Fordist undertaking puts to good use this practice of not having routines, this training in precariousness and variability."[35] On Airbnb, even a 0.1 difference in one's digital reputation can mean the difference between a reliably high income and no income at all. Even the slightest negative remark can put hosts back for months until they have reearned their former rating. A small slip-up can have major repercussions in terms of income.

It comes as no surprise that Airbnb hosts live in fear of offending their guests, which leads to constant self-policing. In order to avoid retaliation from the platform's algorithm, hosts already discipline themselves to avoid future setbacks. Kyle Chayka, for instance, observes that Airbnb hosts tend to copy the same "airspace" aesthetic to attract potential guests.[36] Since the latter choose their lodgings on the basis of first impressions on the Airbnb website, the main aim for hosts is to be as inoffensive as possible. This leads to the same interior design techniques of innocuous colors and minimalist furniture replicated across the globe. Whoever has browsed through Airbnb's offerings for any city will have noticed lots of white walls, beige leather sofas, black and white pillows, and cheap yet reasonably trendy Ikea furniture. Rooms are designed with the aim of showing nothing that could be considered "off-putting." Anything that could be considered "unique" is subsequently a risk. The ironic outcome is that, although Airbnb promises tourists to be immersed in vastly different cultures with real people and authenticity, all Airbnb rooms look approximately the same. Hosts spontaneously internalize a particular Airbnb aesthetic that fits the propensities of the platform's algorithm.

(2) As the example of airspace already suggests, opportunism is a crucial survival tactic in post-Fordist capitalism. According to Virno, "the opportunist confronts a flux of interchangeable possibilities, keeping open as many as possible, turning to the closest and swerving unpredictably from one to the other."[37] This character encounters the world as a series of opportunities jumping from one to the other in search of even more opportunities. Airbnb

hosts, for instance, start working for Airbnb because they learn to see their own housing as a financial opportunity rather than a home. The home is reinterpreted from a quasi-sacred private space into a financial asset waiting to be maximally monetized. Hosting is a side-hustle to make money out of property homeowners already possess. To succeed in converting their lodgings into money, they must be attentive to the inner workings of the general intellect. They must see their home like a hedge fund manager sees her assets: they have to skillfully and experimentally balance risks and investments to maximize future returns. This results in endless attempts to "game the system" by slightly optimizing their online profiles: Will I get better gigs if I respond to messages more quickly? Should I put an extra water bottle in the room to get a higher "amenities" score? Should I update my profile picture to come across as more likeable? The list goes on indefinitely. Instead of authentically presenting oneself to others, the opportunist experiments with his self-presentation until he has found the most marketable version of himself.

Beyond Airbnb's rating system itself, the labor market for the digital gig economy is so volatile that workers can hardly survive without hustling opportunistically.[38] Even hobbies are monetized as side-hustles rather than experienced as genuine relaxation. Many digital workers do not confine themselves to just one platform. They combine several platform gigs to maximize their opportunities at every turn. Airbnb hosts regularly also drive for Uber, act as a courier for Deliveroo, do some tasks on Amazon Mechanical Turk once in a while, and so on. These people incessantly chase down opportunities and adapt their skillsets, desires, and attitudes to fit the profile. As a result, one does not build a stable work identity but hops from one gig to the next acquiring myriad skills along the way. One could sum this up by arguing that the ideal post-Fordist worker resembles the polyvalent functionality of a smartphone.[39] The latter is, at heart, a blank canvas capable of the most divergent functions. It possesses a certain "omnipotentiality"[40] in the sense that the device possesses myriad potentialities not yet geared toward a specific actualization. The smartphone has the potential to become a phone, a social media device, a heart monitor, or wi-fi hotspot, but it coincides with none of these functionalities entirely. It is always capable of much more than what it actually does. Consumers use their smartphones to order food, call their friends, measure distances, monitor their heart rate, and so much more. In itself, the smartphone is an empty set of potentialities that can yet be actualized in many different ways. Likewise, workers in the digital gig economy are just empty stocks of labor-power. They can drive cars for Uber, guide tourists for Airbnb, fill out questionnaires on AMT, depending on what sells at any particular instant. They are omnipotential devices to be inserted in an algorithm's operations at whatever point suits the moment. "Our presentation of self has to demonstrate just the right mix of servility and rebellion, strategically tailored to fit not only the expectations of the job market, but also those of friends and thousands of other viewers."[41] Whoever becomes rigid, is left behind.

(3) After a while, it becomes obvious to workers that this quest for opportunities ultimately leads nowhere.[42] The worker has to self-adapt with every new gig, but there is no final trajectory leading somewhere. Likewise, the Airbnb host refines her emotional performance with every new guest, but with no destination in sight. After the guest has left, a new one arrives and the whole performance starts all over again. Once workers learn that their opportunistic pursuit of opportunities is endless with no salvation in sight, they tend to become cynics. One resigns to one's fate and learns to abide by the rules of the general intellect in the full knowledge that they regularly change without notice. Airbnb sometimes alters its algorithm so that some metrics gain more weight while others become less important. Hosts must adapt accordingly to survive. In 2018, for example, Airbnb introduced Airbnb Plus for luxury lodgings. To qualify for this program, hosts had to implement strict rules on the design of their rooms, the pictures they post on their online profiles, their room descriptions, and so on. Airbnb examined hosts' profiles to check whether they fitted the Airbnb Plus requirements and made suggestions accordingly. The company, however, monitored compliance with dysfunctional software, leading to numerous mistakes.[43] It, for instance, misinterpreted shadows on the floor as carpet stains and obliged hosts to remove the nonexistent stains before being granted Airbnb Plus status. It also ordered hosts to put up extra water bottles in rooms, simply because Airbnb's software was unable to identify the bottles already present. Profile pictures and descriptions were also regularly butchered for the sake of compliance to abstract rules. Many hosts simply implemented all the suggested changes—even if they were ridiculous—simply because explaining Airbnb why the suggestions were wrong, was too tiring. There is no sense in arguing with an opaque and nonaccountable machine that does not know any better. The best thing to do was to resign themselves to their fate and move on. Such workers take on a detached stance vis-à-vis their own labor. They no longer care whether they can express themselves in their work as long as Airbnb's algorithm does not bother them too much.

3. CONCLUSION

The digital gig economy puts pressure on human autonomy from three perspectives: exploitation, alienation, and fatigue. In this chapter, we have looked at the second problem. The digital gig economy is the latest instalment of the capitalist general intellect that Marx already discerned in nineteenth-century capitalism. It deploys an assemblage of algorithms to discipline workers into following the profit motive in their personal conduct. Airbnb, for example, introduced a digital rating system not just to guarantee the trustworthiness of hosts and their offers to potential tourists; it also uses this system to maximize its control over the way individual hosts manage their business. The digitalization of the general intellect extends and deepens the control capital exerts of the labor process in the gig economy. Not only are more aspects of private life captured within the general intellect's operations, but they are also monitored more intensely. This produces a situation that the young Marx called "alienation": the more data workers produce, the more information digital platforms possess to coordinate the labor process. Workers are, in other words, creating their own private panopticon by providing platforms with their data. Living under such conditions produces negative emotions like fear, opportunism, and cynicism. One is continuously exposed to precarious labor conditions, and the only viable response is opportunistically hopping from one gig to the next. Eventually, the ideal worker in the digital gig economy is an omnipotential being that can adapt to whatever quality is currently in demand. The worker is reduced to a blank canvas of potentialities that can be filled in at random depending on what the situation requires.

NOTES

1. See Rabih Jamil, "Uber and the Making of an Algopticon—Insights from the Daily Life of Montreal Drivers," *Capital & Class* 44, no. 2 (June 2020): 11.

2. Schor, *After the Gig*, 7.

3. Airbnb, "How Do Star Ratings Work for Stays?," Airbnb Help Centre, accessed 1 December 2020, https://www.airbnb.co.uk/help/article/1257/how-do-star-ratings-work-for-stays?_set_bev_on_new_domain=1589896655_NWQ4YzAzMzE2ZTJm.

4. One issue to which I will not pay attention is that of gentrification. Because cheap tourist lodgings in many global cities are in high demand, investors have flocked to the housing markets of cities like Barcelona, New York City, and Lisbon, in order to cheaply buy real estate and subsequently let it on Airbnb. This might be vastly profitable for these individual firms, but it displaces local residents from their neighborhoods. City centers increasingly become Disneyfied theme parks for rich tourists, while poorer residents can no longer afford to live in their ancestral homes. For more on this topic, see Sarah Gainsforth, *Airbnb città merce: storie di resistenza alla gentrificazione digitale* (Roma: DeriveApprodi, 2019); Agustin Cocola-Gant and Ana Gago, "Airbnb, Buy-to-Let Investment and Tourism-Driven Displacement: A Case Study in Lisbon," *Environment and Planning A: Economy and Space*, 19 August 2019.

5. Schor, *After the Gig*, 49.

6. Marx, *Grundrisse*, 706.

7. Marx, 690–712. Marx had not intended his "Fragment on Machines" as a separate text. It is rather a pastiche from his notebooks first published as an independent text by Renato Solmi and Raniero Panzieri in a 1964 issue of the *Quaderni Rossi*. The latter was one of the main journals for the workerist movement in the 1960s. It is from the Italian translation that the philological tradition of the "Fragment" arose. See Mario Tronti, "Italy," in *Karl Marx' Grundrisse: Foundations of the Critique of Political Economy 150 Years Later*, ed. Marcello Musto (London: Routledge, 2008), 229–35.

8. Marx, *Grundrisse*, 692.

9. Marx, 693.

10. For a detailed reading of the optimistic and pessimistic arguments in Marx' Fragment on Machines, see Tim Christiaens, "General Intellect, Conscious Organs: Marx' Aristotelian Theory of Alienation in the Machine Fragment," *Shift: International Journal of Philosophical Studies*, 2022.

11. Michael Hardt and Antonio Negri, *Assembly* (New York: Oxford University Press, 2017), 119; Antonio Negri, *From the Factory to the Metropolis*, trans. Ed Emery, English edition (Cambridge, UK: Polity Press, 2018), 171.

12. Marx, *Grundrisse*, 705.

13. Virno, *Grammar of the Multitude*, 100.

14. Marx, *Grundrisse*, 700.

15. Some post-workerists, like Hardt and Negri, combine this dream of fully automated luxury communism with the belief that human biology is supposed to be surpassed by transhumanist experimentations with our own embodiment. They argue that the general intellect allows us to become fully immersed in a cyborg future where the distinction between human and machine becomes entirely obsolete. See Michael Hardt and Antonio Negri, *Empire* (Cambridge, MA: Harvard University Press, 2000), 214–18; Helen Hester, *Xenofeminism* (Cambridge: Polity Press, 2018); Aaron Bastani, *Fully Automated Luxury Communism: A Manifesto* (London: Verso, 2020).

16. Paolo Virno, "The Ambivalence of Disenchantment," in *Radical Thought in Italy: A Potential Politics*, ed. Paolo Virno and Michael Hardt (Minneapolis: University of Minnesota Press, 1996), 23.

17. For critiques of the ideology of work, see, among others, Kathi Weeks, *The Problem with Work: Feminism, Marxism, Antiwork Politics, and Postwork Imaginaries* (Durham, NC: Duke University Press, 2011); Paul Lafargue, *The Right to Be Lazy*, trans. Charles H Kerr (Auckland: The Floating Press, 2012); Nick Srnicek and Alex Williams, *Inventing the Future: Postcapitalism and a World without Work* (London: Verso, 2016).

18. I will here not deal with the proposals that are often grouped under the rubric of the post-work society. Good introductions to these topics are Srnicek and Williams, *Inventing the Future*; Weeks, *The Problem with Work*; Hester and Stronge, *After Work*.

19. Benanav, *Automation and the Future of Work*; Smith, *Smart Machines and Service Work*.

20. See Smith, *Smart Machines and Service Work*, 120–26.

21. Scholz, *Uberworked and Underpaid*, 183–84.

22. Berardi Bifo, *The Soul at Work*, 87.

23. Ravenelle, *Hustle and Gig*, 13.
24. Marx, *Early Writings*, 324.
25. Marx, 336.
26. Marx, 366.
27. Roelofson and Minca add that Airbnb tracks more than just guest reviews. It measures, for instance, the "response rate" (i.e., if and how fast hosts respond to potential guests' online queries), and the "commitment rate," which is the rate of acceptance or annulation of reservations. See Maartje Roelofsen and Claudio Minca, "The Superhost. Biopolitics, Home and Community in the Airbnb Dream-World of Global Hospitality," *Geoforum* 91 (May 2018): 176.
28. See especially Virginia Eubanks, *Automating Inequality: How High-Tech Tools Profile, Police, and Punish the Poor* (New York: St. Martin's Press, 2017); Benjamin Edelman, Michael Luca, and Dan Svirsky, "Racial Discrimination in the Sharing Economy: Evidence from a Field Experiment," *American Economic Journal: Applied Economics* 9, no. 2 (1 April 2017): 1–22.
29. O'Neil, *Weapons of Math Destruction*, 21.
30. Zuboff, *The Age of Surveillance Capitalism*, 100.
31. Gainsforth, *Airbnb città merce*, 188–89.
32. Liam Mannix, "Airbnb Horror Story: Guests Trash Sydney Apartment, Turn It into a "Junkie Den,"" *Sydney Morning Herald*, 4 September 2016, https://www.smh.com.au/national/airbnb-horror-story-guests-trash-sydney-apartment-turn-it-into-a-junkie-den-20160902-gr7ej9.html. For more examples, see Ravenelle, *Hustle and Gig*, 45–47.
33. Gainsforth, *Airbnb città merce*, 183.
34. Virno, "The Ambivalence of Disenchantment," 13–34; Virno, *Grammar of the Multitude*, 84–93. See also Massimo De Carolis, "Toward a Phenomenology of Opportunism," in *Radical Thought in Italy: A Potential Politics*, ed. Paolo Virno and Michael Hardt (Minneapolis: University of Minnesota Press, 1996), 37–51; Frédéric Lordon, *Capitalisme, Désir et Servitude: Marx et Spinoza* (Paris: La Fabrique, 2010).
35. Virno, *Grammar of the Multitude*, 85.
36. Kyle Chayka, "Welcome to Airspace," The Verge, accessed 3 December 2020, https://www.theverge.com/2016/8/3/12325104/airbnb-aesthetic-global-minimalism-startup-gentrification.
37. Virno, "The Ambivalence of Disenchantment," 16.
38. Ravenelle, *Hustle and Gig*, 4.
39. See Christiaens, "Neoliberalism and the Right to Be Lazy."
40. Stefano Micali, "The Capitalistic Cult of Performance':, *Philosophy Today* 54, no. 4 (2010): 379–91.
41. Scholz, *Uberworked and Underpaid*, 69.
42. De Carolis, "Toward a Phenomenology of Opportunism," 50.
43. Gainsforth, *Airbnb città merce*, 151–52.

Chapter 5

The Human Limits to Growth

> *As Mengele discovered, you can work a human to death in a few minutes, but you won't be able to do anything with the scraps except perhaps art deco lampshades and inefficient fertilizer.*
>
> —George Caffentzis

Ken Loach's recent film *Sorry We Missed You* (2019) tells the story of Ricky, a self-employed delivery driver in the UK's emerging gig economy. After being unemployed in the wake of the Global Financial Crisis, Ricky finds work in the gig economy to support his family and keep track of their mortgage payments. To start as a delivery driver, however, he has to sell the family car and lease a company-licensed van from his supplier. The story starts with debt and it only gets downhill from there. Throughout the film, the audience witnesses the gradual breakdown of the family. Both Ricky and his wife spend increasing amounts of time working simply to stay financially afloat, while the neglected children start acting out. We see Ricky physically and mentally succumbing to the company's constant harassment, costumers' unsympathetic demands, and the family's demise. Every day he cannot work, Ricky has to pay a fine to his supplier. At the end of the film, some local thugs have beaten him into the hospital, but the driver returns to his van for another shift while his wife and children beg him to stop. With that harrowing scene, the screen fades to black, the theater lights turn back on, and the audience is left in silence mourning for these fictional characters.

Tragic stories like Ricky's are sadly based on real-life experiences in the gig economy. In 2018, Don Lane, a British diabetic courier driver for DPD, tragically died after DPD discouraged him from getting proper treatment by fining him 150 pounds per day he could not find a replacement.[1] Physical and mental exhaustion are rampant among workers in platform companies: Uber drivers fall asleep behind the wheel, Deliveroo couriers lose limbs in traffic accidents, and Amazon Mechanical Turk workers suffer from chronic sleep deprivation.² The realities of the digital gig economy starkly contrast with the optimistic picture of the multitude's infinite potential promised by Hardt and Negri. They argue that, once the post-Fordist economy unleashed the creative potential of the general intellect, the latter would be an unstoppable force. In reality, the multitude seems worn out, burnt out, and depressed. According to Berardi, the cognitive transformation of production "was a deception, because even if the general intellect is infinitely productive, the limits to growth are inscribed in the affective body of cognitive work: limits of attention, of psychic energy, of sensibility."³ Today's information economy requires workers to pay constant attention to computer and smartphone screens, leading to generalized exhaustion. Though the general intellect as a totality can constitute a tremendously productive growth engine, the human beings that supposedly sustain this machine cannot keep up with it. Digital acceleration imposes too severe burdens on finite human bodies and mind, according to Berardi. He hence predicts that 'the coming European insurrection will not be an insurrection of energy, but an insurrection of slowness, withdrawal, and exhaustion."⁴

The disposability of the gig economy's workforce has become particularly clear during the COVID-19 pandemic.⁵ Middle- and upper-class workers predominantly stayed at home and practiced social distancing, while the working class lost jobs or continued to work in unsafe conditions despite health risks and increasing deaths. Especially at Amazon, harsh struggles were waged over workers' protections.⁶ By Amazon's own admission, 19,816 workers had contracted COVID-19 over the summer of 2020.⁷ On the one hand, the pandemic had increased demand for at-home deliveries. Since people were working from home and could not go shopping, they bought commodities online. On the other hand, Amazon fought all attempts at unionisation or to guarantee workers' health and safety.⁸ On the contrary, it increased the pace of work, demanded people to work longer hours, and undermined attempts at unionisation. At one point, the Amazon board even cynically applauded that the media took the fired worker and activist Chris Smalls as the spokesperson for disgruntled workers, because Smalls was "not smart or articulate."⁹ Due to the availability of a reserve army of unemployed workers, companies like Amazon did not have to invest in the adequate reproduction of its workforce, resulting in excess mortality among working-class people during the pandemic.¹⁰

In this chapter, I argue that, beyond the traditional Marxist criticisms of exploitation and alienation, there is also a Marxian tradition worried about the problem of fatigue among workers. Capitalism tends to impose unsustainable working conditions on finite bodies and minds. It depletes human energy faster than it regenerates labor-power. By structurally exhausting the labor-power capital needs to persist, capitalist economies cut the branch they are sitting on. Marx himself particularly focuses on the problem of fatigue in chapter XV of *Capital: Volume I*. He criticizes large-scale industry for imposing a machinic system on the workforce that accelerates the work rhythm beyond what workers can handle. Since capitalist management could count on an industrial reserve army of unemployed workers, it was under no obligation to slow the pace of work down to more humane levels. Relying on Berardi's critique of digital media in post-Fordist capitalism and the workerist-feminist theory of social reproduction, I highlight two ways in which this nineteenth-century problem of workers' fatigue returns in the digital gig economy. First, because digital platforms abstract from human embodiment, their algorithms are blind to the limits of what a body can do. Platform companies rely on an oversupply of available workers as well, so there is no incentive to render the work pace sustainable in the long run. Second, the reproduction of labor-power requires leisure time during which workers can regenerate the depleted energy spent in their labor. By annulling the distinction between work and free time with smartphone technology and by dismantling institutions like the family and the welfare state, post-Fordist working conditions neglect the reproductive conditions of possibility for a functional capitalist economy. In sum, the digital gig economy induces fatigue by excessively straining workers during their labor and denying them adequate leisure time to regenerate their labor-power.

1. MARX AND THE PROBLEM OF FATIGUE

During Marx' lifetime, German scientific sentiment shifted gradually from Romanticism and Hegelianism toward positivism. Especially the emergence of thermodynamics made a tremendous impression on the German research community.[11] These physicists pictured a new vision of the universe as built out of a constant reserve of energy. Helmholtz even called this energy "labor-power" (*Arbeitskraft*).[12] The latter could take many different forms, but the general tendency was toward disorder and entropy. According to the second law of thermodynamics, the cosmos is an ordered structure doomed to follow the trajectory of entropy toward the heat death of the universe. Thermodynamics had a significant impact on social theory in the second half of the nineteenth century. Social reformers increasingly dismissed moral accounts of work based on ethical exhortations about the values of a good work ethic in favor of physiological studies of workers' bodies. Workers supposedly did not stop working because they were inherently lazy—as eighteenth-century liberal economists believed—but because the labor process was not adapted to their anatomical makeup. Social theorists' attention shifted toward how to optimally insert the body in the labor process and how to defer its entropic exhaustion. They subsequently advised capitalist managers to lighten the workload and ensure adequate resting time to keep workers' bodies healthy and operative. By regularly replenishing the reserve of labor-power and avoiding overexploitation, the threat of generalized fatigue in the workforce could be avoided.

Marx went through a similar shift of perspective, even if he never entirely abandoned his Hegelian heritage. In later writings, especially *Capital: Volume I*, he highlighted the difficult balance between the exertion and regeneration of labor-power as a central characteristic of the capitalist productive system. Marx conceptualized the working class as a reserve of labor-power that capital inserts in a self-propelling industrial system like cogs in a machine. Just like those machines need coal and steam power, they require manpower to keep them up and running. However, the philosopher was less optimistic than the social reformers about the possibilities for capitalism to avoid a general crisis of fatigue.[13] According to Marx, capitalism tends to burn through more labor-power than it regenerates. There is a fundamental contradiction at play between the labor workers are expected to perform and the labor workers' bodies can actually deliver. This problem becomes particularly obvious in chapter XV on "Machines and Large-Scale Industry," which elaborates a critique of capitalist industrialization in almost thermodynamic terminology. Marx depicts the condition of workers as one of insertion in a self-moving industrial machine in which labor-power is just one resource among others depleted in the name of commodity production:

> In handicrafts and manufacture, the workman makes use of a tool; in the factory the machine makes use of him. There the movements of the instrument of labour proceed from him; here it is the movements of the machine that he must follow. In manufacture the workmen are part of a living mechanism. In the factory we have a lifeless mechanism independent of the workman, who becomes its mere living appendage. . . . By means of its conversion into an automaton, the instrument of labour confronts the labourer, during the labour process, in the shape of capital, of dead labour, that dominates, and pumps dry, living labour-power.[14]

Earlier Marxian critiques of large-scale industry—particularly in the *1844 Manuscripts* and *The German Ideology*—articulated a predominantly moral account of industrial labor: capitalist working conditions were allegedly undignified vis-à-vis human-species-being, they undermined the human propensity for self-objectification in the world. In *Capital*, Marx emphasizes the physiological unsustainability of an industrial system that "pumps dry" living labor-power. Large-scale machinery purportedly imposes a stringent work rhythm on finite human beings well beyond what a human body can take. In chapter XV, Marx documents a litany of workplace accidents and deaths from overwork that result from the irresponsible acceleration of the labor process. According to Marx, the stress from overexertion in an unhealthy work environment leads to a general shortening of lifespans among the working class.[15] Even the senses are under constant assault:

> Every organ of sense is injured in an equal degree by artificial elevation of the temperature, by the dust-laden atmosphere, by the defeating noise, not to mention danger to life and limb among the thickly crowded machinery, which, with the regularity of the seasons, issues its list of the killed and wounded in the industrial battle.[16]

Marx' observations about the "systematic robbery of what is necessary for the life of the workman while he is at work"[17] lead him to a peculiar theory of resistance:

> In the first place, in the form of machinery, the implements of labour become automatic, things moving and working independent of the workman. They are henceforth an industrial *perpetuum mobile* that would go on producing forever, did it not meet with certain *natural obstructions in the weak bodies and the strong wills of its human attendants*. The automaton, as capital, and because it is capital, is endowed, in the person of the capitalist, with intelligence and will; it is therefore animated by the longing to reduce to a minimum *the resistance offered by that repellent yet elastic natural barrier, man*.[18]

Marx suggests large-scale industry would keep accelerating were it not for resistance from workers' weak bodies and strong wills. Most Marxists—including most workerists—emphasize the strong wills as "the demand for power, all power, to the workers."[19] However, the weak bodies are not to be underestimated as a force of friction. One should not forget that, historically, many advances in working-class struggle arose from spontaneous uprisings after workplace accidents. The first working-class victories in the domain of social security concerned accomplishments like the shortening of the working day, workplace safety regulations, and social insurance against workplace-related injuries. The body puts physiological limits on the industrial growth machine. Once a certain threshold of labor intensity is crossed, bodies break down and disrupt the productive rhythm of industry. The shape of resistance in this passage is more akin to the electrical resistance of conducting materials. Metal substances, for instance, somewhat resist the flow of electrical currents, generating heat as a by-product. Likewise, workers' bodies resist the conduct of the industrial *élan* of capitalist production. Bodily friction slows the production process down and generates the incendiary heat of revolt as a byproduct. The human body might possess some elasticity—it is frequently capable of much more than one usually imagines—but it remains a repellent natural barrier for capital's propensity to grow.[20]

The only way nineteenth-century capitalism was able to alleviate the contradiction between infinite growth and finite bodies was, according to Marx, by rapidly replacing worn-out workers with new blood. Capital depended on the availability of an industrial reserve army of unemployed workers who could step in whenever people started dropping out. According to Marx, "since the motion of the whole system does not proceed from the workman [sic], but from the machinery, a change of persons can take place at any time without an interruption of the work."[21] As long as this system of easy substitution remained in place, there was no incentive for capital to invest in more sustainable working conditions. It was cheaper to dispose of worn-out workers than to guarantee a healthy work environment that ensured a balance between workers' finite bodies and the requirements of profitable business. As Wendling observes, "many unhealthy and short-lived generations will suffice so long as they supplant one another's labour-power with sufficient continuity and rapidity."[22] However, by so quickly depleting the reserve of labor-power in the working class, capital rendered itself vulnerable to a general exhaustion of its resources. If the working class could not reproduce itself sufficiently fast, the capitalist motor of production would grind to a sudden halt. This tendency, according to Marx, put a looming risk of catastrophe at the heart of capitalist modernity. Capitalism would allegedly succumb to the industrial entropy of the working class.

2. PHYSICAL AND MENTAL FATIGUE IN THE DIGITAL GIG ECONOMY

Contrary to Marx' expectations however, the imminent heat death of the capitalist universe was averted in the twentieth century. Social reforms, labor regulations, and the emerging welfare state fostered a more balanced tension between capitalist growth and human finitude. Recent neoliberal deregulations and the dismantling of the welfare state have, however, signaled an uncanny return of the problem of fatigue. Sluggish job growth and the downgrading of social security services have created a new reserve army of un(der)employed workers, obstructing yet again the incentive for capitalist management to invest in sustainable working conditions.[23] Well-educated technical workers at the top of the post-Fordist labor market might be difficult to replace, but those at the bottom of the food chain compete for a decreasing number of jobs. As Alessandro Delfanti reports an Amazon warehouse worker saying,

They tell you "this is a complete meritocracy, if you are worth more than the next guy, quickly you will build a career for yourself." . . . But it's exactly the opposite: if you are faster, never call in sick with a backache, after a while your back is gone, you have carpal tunnel, psoriasis caused by stress . . . and those are the first they set aside.[24]

In the digital gig economy, underregulated digital technology has given momentum to the acceleration of work. As the plot of *Sorry We Missed You* and the horror stories on which it is based show, working conditions in the digital gig economy are becoming unsustainably severe, leading toward a general sense of exhaustion among workers. Nonetheless, diagnosing a simple return of the nineteenth century would be too haphazard. Digital platforms and post-Fordist immaterial labor have mostly displaced the physical labor of large-scale industry in the global North. But digitalization gives a particular inflexion to the problem of fatigue. It supersedes old forms of exhaustion and generates new ones: today's gig workers do not suffer from malnutrition or asbestos poisoning but are involved in car accidents or suffer from burnout. When working conditions become increasingly immaterial, digitally mediated acceleration also assaults the human body in new ways. The novelty of digital fatigue becomes clearer when studied through the lens of Franco "Bifo" Berardi's critique of digital capitalism.

Berardi argues that digital media coordinate human interactions through a grid of so-called "connections" as opposed to "conjunctions."[25] The latter are encounters that spontaneously and horizontally generate meaning without the need for a predetermined design. Berardi takes as his paradigm the orchid and the wasp from Gilles Deleuze's and Félix Guattari's *A Thousand Plateaus*.[26] The orchid and the wasp are both starkly different beings inhabiting different worlds. Yet in their encounter, both learn to benefit from each other. The wasp is looking for nutrition, while the orchid desires the transportation of its pollen. By gradually adapting to each other's mode of existence—the wasp's becoming-orchid and the orchid's becoming-wasp—they establish a symbiotic relation that strengthens both their chances of survival. They come to cooperate as if they were of the same substance without a higher being organizing their coordination from above. I do not claim that both beings experience some kind of "pure" or "immediate" presence to each other in conjunction. External factors always intervene in the mutual adaptation process. But there is room for variation and surprise that cannot be reduced to these external factors. How the interaction between the orchid and the wasp develops, is not set in stone and cannot be entirely predicted in advance. By mimetically responding to each other's bodily proximity, the orchid and the wasp enter into "conjunction" with each other. Berardi envisages social cooperation in the multitude along similar lines. Through bodily proximity and sensibility to each other's mode of existence, people can form a spontaneous and self-organizing multitude. The interaction between mother and child, for example, can institute a spontaneous symbiosis between the mother's becoming-child and the child's becoming-mother.[27] Communication between both is not a mere transfer of information; through mutual care and love, the mother learns to pick up microscopic signals from the child's bodily movements and the child learn to gauge its mother's state of being by the timbre of her voice and the gestures of her hands. Though mediating factors like language and culture prestructure these human conjunctions, such factors can never entirely eliminate the emergence of the new. These forms of mutual sensibility and horizontal coordination are quite common, even in politics. They explain the possibility of spontaneous cooperation in protesting crowds, mutual aid after natural disasters, or the rapid global dissemination of social movements. Human beings are mimetic creatures that autonomously adapt to each other's movements and thereby institute self-organizing collectives.

Berardi opposes conjunctive collectivities to digital connections. The latter supplant bodily proximity with a digital medium as the milieu for social cooperation. Such media limit the scope for spontaneous or creative elements of surprise that Berardi discerns in conjunctive sociality. Technological insertion implies that people no longer adapt directly to each other but to the digital infrastructure responsible for organizing social interaction, which sets limits to the scope of human potentialities. Algorithms format human decisions into precomputable arrangements to align human conducts.[28] Human users must learn to adapt their conduct not directly to each other but to the digital platforms they use. Their actions must be registered as legible input before the platform can connect users to each other. Algorithmic infrastructures determine who meets whom and under what conditions. The Tinder app, for instance, displaces spontaneous amorous encounters "in the flesh" with a predesigned system of digitally managed matches between people of similar backgrounds. The spontaneity of human encounters is rationalized in order to optimize efficiency and speed. Instead of the slow process of—often failed—seductions, people can opt for a platform that immediately connects singles ready to meet. Tinder efficiently streamlines this matching process by scoring individuals' attractiveness. It tracks how users evaluate each other and the algorithm weighs this data to form a general picture of how "valuable" every single profile is. Afterward, the algorithm ranks these profiles and connects those of matching attractiveness.[29] The cost of this rationalization entails the loss of spontaneous sensibility.[30] Once such apps become generally accepted, they push the practice of traditional face-to-face flirting into the background. The slow and laborious process of two bodies adapting to each other's imperceptible signals of attraction is reduced to a single swipe based on a few carefully curated photos. Success on Tinder does not require adapting to each other's physical presence, but insight into how Tinder's algorithm weighs the value of its profiles. Success is, in other words, conditional upon sufficient adaptive obedience to Tinder's digital infrastructure.[31]

Gig work apps like Uber's and Deliveroo's also establish a grid of connectivity to coordinate social cooperation. They curate a platform that matches workers to potential clients on the basis of algorithmic calculations. If workers want to garner success in such an environment, they must primarily adapt to the criteria of the platform. Although these companies promise flexible working hours and personal autonomy, digital commands intervene in this supposedly autonomous process to ensure the compatibility of the supply of labor and the demand for services. An individual Uber driver, for instance, might want to avoid working late afternoons to pick up his children from school. However, if Uber needs more drivers in that timeframe, his logging off can trigger a downgrade in his digital ranking. This will make it harder for him to attract profitable rides in the future. Drivers consequently learn, over time, to adapt their "self-chosen" flexible schedules to the algorithm's demands.[32] The algorithm operates as a capillary machine that surreptitiously structures the range of choices drivers can rationally make. This predetermined design nudges individuals into choices profitable for Uber, independently of whether they suit the drivers themselves. In sum, "the multitude does not manifest itself as autonomy at all, but rather as dependence from the automatisms that biopower builds and activates in everyday life."[33]

The smartphone is the ideal instrument to establish a connective grid.[34] It allows platform companies to call upon workers exactly when they need them and not pay them a single minute extra. Workers are available non-stop, day and night, and they can be activated at will by sending them push notifications. As Berardi observes, "cellular phones realize the dream of capital: that of absorbing every atom of time at the exact moment the productive cycle needs it. . . . Workers offer their entire day to capital and are paid only for the moments when their time is made cellular."[35] This automated system activates and deactivates workers to exactly mirror fluctuating market demand. It disassembles the workforce into a collection of time-atoms the algorithm can combine and recombine at its own convenience. Uber drivers are not considered full persons but are reduced to bundles of fragmented labor-time that the platform has permanently available but only pays for specific services. Digital connectivity thereby abstracts from the embodied conjunctions that make up the workforce. As long as individuals' brains are cognitively wired to the platform to work on its behalf, the algorithm does not care about the rest of the body or its psycho-physical limitations. As Berardi argues, "capital no longer recruits people, but buys packets of time, separated from their interchangeable and occasional bearers."[36] This neglect can lead to a desynchronization of rhythms that recalls Marx' critique of industrial fatigue: "although the productivity of the networked brain is potentially infinite, the limits to the intensification of brain activity remain inscribed in the affective body of the cognitive worker."[37] The rhythm of the platform closely tracks market demand, but this is not necessarily compatible to workers' life rhythms. It is impossible to arrange a somewhat reliable schedule if one's working hours are disassembled and rendered dependent on fickle consumer demand. Algorithms can consequently arbitrarily accelerate and decelerate the pace of work independently of what is livable for human beings.

Food delivery apps like Deliveroo's provide good examples of pathological desynchronization. The company presents its software as a nice opportunity to work out and have fun while making money, but workers quickly realize this advertisement is misleading.[38] There might not be a simple general tendency toward acceleration, as Berardi sometimes suggests, but the platform establishes an intricate web of accelerations and decelerations that make the work unsustainable. Moments of intense stress are combined with long periods of depressing downtime. Julie Chen and Ping Sun call this a "fragmented rush."[39] On the one hand, couriers must rush through traffic to keep the food warm at the time of delivery.[40] The algorithm tracks couriers' average speeds to calculate the ideal distance between couriers' positions and the delivery address, so the faster couriers cycle the further away will their destinations be and the faster they will have to keep cycling to earn a decent income.[41] The algorithm does not account for traffic, bad weather conditions, the state of the road, yet it pushes workers to deliver food as quickly as possible. The app promises consumers a certain time of delivery, but if the courier does not make it in time, only the courier bears the negative consequences in terms of bad reviews. Delivery couriers hence frequently report taking big risks in traffic to beat the clock.[42] However, Deliveroo refers to workers' status as "independent contractors" to avoid having to take responsibility for injuries from traffic accidents. On the other hand, Deliveroo couriers do not rush the whole day.[43] When demand is low, they wait aimlessly for the next order. This is not a time for relaxation or regeneration, but for anxious availability. Couriers' eyes are glued to their screens while they hope to move from unpaid idle time to paid working time. Even when these workers are entirely offline, they are still constantly plagued by the fear of missing out. Platform workers consequently state that 'you can get pretty obsessed with this . . . Instead of laying around the house, you feel guilty if you're not working."[44] Workers know that they *could* be making money by turning on their app, so any free time feels like a wasted opportunity to boost one's income.

The perverse outcome of Deliveroo's model of labor coordination is that a successful working day is marked by increasing acceleration. The more gigs a courier accomplishes, the more tasks he can acquire in the future. This makes an increase in rushed labor-time over idle downtime crucial to workers' income. There is an invisible hierarchy between the top workers who get most of the best gigs but must keep up their good performance to retain their income, and the lower ranks of workers who are fruitlessly waiting all day for the less-rewarding gigs. This system does not check the long-term sustainability of working conditions, since it pushes well-performing couriers to overexert themselves while making underperforming couriers stop out of frustration. Deliveroo also weaponizes the opaqueness of its evaluation criteria to pressure everyone to keep intensifying their work rhythm.[45] Individual couriers do not know exactly what gets them deactivated or downgraded, but they gradually learn it is harder to attract good gigs after rejecting orders or logging off without prior notice. They subsequently start guessing "what the algorithm wants" and adapt their conduct accordingly. They take on more orders than they would have intended to ensure their status for the algorithm. Because apps like Deliveroo can count on an oversupply of un(der)employed workers, there is no incentive to make the work pace more sustainable, even if it puts couriers in a continuous pendulum movement between burnout and bore-out. Frantic busyness and constant self-optimization are combined with dreadful waiting times, which explains the high labor turnover for apps like Deliveroo or Uber.[46] Workers cannot keep up with this rhythm for very long, so they usually quit after a few months. Only those who have no alternative stay. Ultimately, many workers crash—mentally or literally. Their "weak bodies," that repellent yet elastic natural barrier, can no longer keep up.

3. THE HIDDEN ABODE OF SOCIAL REPRODUCTION

A second contradiction less emphasized by Marx himself but very prominent among Marxist feminists, is the imbalance between the temporalities of production and reproduction.[47] Work under capitalism is not only too straining for finite human bodies, but capitalism also inhibits sufficient time and resources to regenerate or reproduce labor-power off work. It relies on feminized domestic labor to ensure the sustenance of labor-power because "to do without the reproductive part of the cycle is capitalist suicide."[48] Labor-power requires sleep, nourishment, and meaningful human contact to get through the day.[49] The interest of capital, however, is to maximize production time and minimize reproduction time or render it entirely functional to production. In Marx' days, the social reproduction of the working class was starkly deficient, leading to short and unhealthy lives. The existence of an industrial reserve army and the low work requirements in large-scale industry entailed that it was cheaper to replace workers than to invest in their reproduction. In the beginning of the twentieth century, social reformers and the emergent welfare state redirected capitalist strategy toward socially engineering the private sphere, family and leisure time, to serve the intensification of labor productivity.[50] Fordist capital agreed to invest in generous social services in exchange for a compliant and industrious working class. Its keystone was the Fordist family and its stable sexual division of labor: the male acted as a breadwinner in the sphere of production to secure the family's income, while the female stayed at home taking care of reproduction.[51] The housewife ensured the replenishment of her husband's labor-power and raised her children to become the future workforce.

During the 1960s and 1970s, the feminist movement protested against the required confinement and subordination of women in the household. In Italy, a Marxist-workerist version of this movement was espoused by activists like Leopoldina Fortunati, Mariarosa Dalla Costa, Carla Lonzi, or Silvia Federici.[52] They argued that, if women's domestic labor reproduced the labor-power responsible for the production of value, then domestic labor is in fact also productive labor, even if it is unremunerated.[53] Male workers produced commodities in the factory in exchange for a wage, while women produced the commodity labor-power without receiving a wage in return. Instead, an ideology of female identity and care interpellated women to see their domestic labor as immediate expressions of their female nature, the rewards for their labor being "self-actualisation as a woman."[54] Women were allegedly not working when they were cleaning the house, raising children, or feeding their husbands; they were rather realizing their God-given essence as women. According to Federici, this division of labor drove a political wedge within the working class. It promised working-class men a personal servant at home in exchange for submission in the productive sphere. "In fact, our role as women is to be the unwaged but happy and most of all loving servants of the 'working class' i.e., those strata of the proletariat to which capital was forced to grant more social power."[55] The ideology of femininity thus functioned as a smokescreen to sustain a precarious balance between production and reproduction in Fordist capitalism. Fordism was only sustainable as a social formation because it counted on the free labor of women. If women would subtract this domestic labor, the system would allegedly crumble.

In response to this injustice, workerist feminists called for "wages for housework" (*salario al lavoro domestico*) and care strikes. The goal was obviously not to merely increase women's financial income or to encourage them to move into the labor market like their husbands. According to Dalla Costa, "those who advocate that the liberation of the working-class woman lies in her getting a job outside the home are part of the problem not the solution. Slavery to an assembly line is not a liberation from slavery to a kitchen sink."[56] The demand for a wage was rather a rhetorical device to cut through the ideology of feminine care and reveal the exploitative nature of Fordist capitalism from women's point of view. Federici clarifies that "just to want wages for housework means to refuse that work *as an expression of our nature*, and therefore to refuse precisely the female role that capital has invented for us."[57] The campaign demystifies domestic labor as a socially enforced and historically contingent form of actual labor rather than a natural expression of womanhood. Historical ideological forces have constructed the Fordist housewife. By negating their vocation as unpaid care-workers, women would allegedly undermine the precarious balance between production and reproduction and would thereby undermine Fordist capitalism itself. Once women refused their role as reproductive workers, so the argument goes, capital would be forced to confront its defects on the reproductive front. In the words of Dalla Costa:

> To abandon the home is already a form of struggle, since the social services we provide would then cease to be carried out under these conditions, and all those who work out of the home would then demand that the burden carried by us until now should be thrown squarely where it belongs—onto the shoulders of capital.[58]

Given that capitalism is still around, it is fair to assume that this change of perspective never fully materialized. Nonetheless, gender relations shifted significantly in the last fifty years. As discussed in chapter 2, cultural and working-class struggles in the 1970s triggered a recomposition of capital toward post-Fordism and immaterial labor. The latter entailed a stratification of the working class in which some benefited from the rise of cognitive and communicative labor, while others suffered from outsourcing and offshoring. When women entered the workforce during the last fifty years, they positioned themselves on both ends of the immaterial labor spectrum. The "winners" of post-Fordism have indeed been able to emancipate themselves from a lot of housework. Well-educated women have joined men among the workforce in the many communication- and care-centered sectors of the reformed labor market. However, to compensate for the reduced female input in the sphere of reproduction, upper- and middle-class families have increasingly turned to cheap migrant workers (predominantly women) to serve as cleaning ladies, babysitters, cooks, and so on.[59] Thanks to their double income, these families have been able to outsource reproductive work. Since their time is financially more valuable than the time of less-educated migrants, they prefer to deflect the burden of reproduction unto lower-class workers. The gendering of domestic labor has thereby remained in place, but it has been commodified and often racialized.[60] Ironically, this means that women now do receive wages for housework, but not in the way workerist feminists intended.

Workers in the digital gig economy, however, obviously cannot afford houseworkers to take care of the reproduction of their labor-power. Deliveroo couriers or Uber drivers do not make enough money to hire nannies or cooks. Nonetheless, working for platforms like Uber or Deliveroo can be both physically and mentally straining. Their labor is easily replaceable and does not require a lot of training, which diminishes the incentive for capital to ensure the proper reproduction of its workforce. Any individual worker unable to keep up can be substituted for another worker from the reserve army of un(der)employed workers. At the bottom of the labor market, it is largely up to workers themselves to ensure they can sufficiently reproduce their labor-power. Especially at platform companies like Deliveroo and Uber, many workers are single males, which means that they cannot count on a female servant at home ensuring their sustenance.[61] Sara Sharma reports the following complaints from cab drivers' experiences, but the same could have been said by Uber drivers:

> Judy expresses frustration over a lack of adequate health insurance and benefits: "We have to do everything ourselves—I mean take care of ourselves. Many drivers don't do anything. They die from heart attacks." Judy explains how she makes time to work out at home in the morning before her shift with a Pilates DVD. Abraham . . . also reiterates Judy's stories of casualties in the driver's seat. They don't result from crashes, but rather strokes, heart attacks, and high blood pressure. Abraham feels that even a few years ago he could have had a little more time to take care of himself. He reminisces about playing soccer some days: "I used to be more active. You know, I'm pretty young. I'm thirty-five and I have trouble walking. I can hardly run. Now driving for years and living in the city, I basically sleep, drive the cab, eat. I don't exercise."[62]

At the bottom of the post-Fordist labor market, there is often insufficient time and energy to adequately ensure the reproduction of labor-power. As a result, workers often encounter health problems early in life. I am not arguing for a return to the Fordist breadwinner model with its gendered division of labor. I rather wish to highlight that, in today's digital gig economy, workers have been made responsible for their own reproduction, with detrimental results. Sleep deprivation is also rampant among workers in the digital gig economy.[63] Gig workers agree to long shifts to fit into algorithmic evaluation criteria, but this leaves them with less time to rest. They also take their smartphones to bed, resulting in a diminished quality of sleep because workers keep waking up to push notifications. Another major issue reported among gig workers is social isolation: workers conduct their jobs entirely on their own and because they work long hours at variable times, they encounter difficulties in maintaining a social life or a family.[64] Many gig workers end up alone alternating between their jobs and their lonely apartments. As Chen and Sun report, "when the riders were asked what they do on the weekend or other free time, the most frequent answers were sleeping or working overtime."[65]

The only way for full-time workers in the digital gig economy generally manage to survive in the long run is by relying on external "networks of care."[66] If they lack sufficient "off time" themselves to regenerate their labor-power, they must rely on support from others to keep them going. For some, the family, friends, and social welfare services constitute this safety net: gig workers ask their neighbors to prepare food, let older siblings babysit younger children, or count on unemployment benefits to get through the month. Gig workers also build spontaneous voluntary networks for advice and moral support. Mostly, these initiatives are not institutionalized, as when Deliveroo couriers talk to each other at restaurants or send each other advice through text messages. There are, however, also more institutionalized support networks like TurkerNation, an online forum for AMT-workers.[67] On this website workers mostly give each other tips about how to find work opportunities or signal untrustworthy clients, but the website also provides possibilities for moral support. AMT is an online platform that distributes small digital tasks to workers sitting at home in front of their computers, but some clients abuse this service to let workers do jobs akin to online content moderation without adequate preparation. They are, for instance, asked to label pictures to then suddenly be confronted with pictures of ISIS beheadings, child pornography, or animal cruelty.[68] In those cases, TurkerNation provides a helpful gateway for understanding and posttraumatic support. The question remains, however, whether mere online moral support suffices to keep work in the digital gig economy sustainable. In the long run, capital seems to be burning through its reserve of labor-power faster than it regenerates the workforce. As long as there are un(der)employed workers still looking for jobs, this mechanism can continue, but it is highly uncertain whether capital might not run out of labor-power at some point.[69]

4. CONCLUSION

Apart from exploitation and alienation, a major problem encountered in the gig economy is the tendency toward fatigue among workers. Marx had already observed in nineteenth-century, large-scale industry that the working class was pushed beyond the limits of what a human body can take, leading to workplace accidents and generalized exhaustion. They only way industrial capital could retain its growth rate is by relying on an industrial reserve army of unemployed workers, which made it possible to expel worn-out workers in favor of fresh labor input. Because there exists a similar oversupply of labor in the digital gig economy today, an analogous tendency toward overexertion of workers' bodies and minds reveal itself in this sector. Digital technology, however, gives a particular novel inflexion to this trend. On the one hand, digital platforms favor coordination of the labor process through so-called "connections," (i.e., predesigned communicative networks that format human conduct to fit the needs of algorithms. This grid of connectivity abstracts from workers' concrete bodies, reducing them into disassembled time fragments that can be composed and recomposed according to unstable market fluctuations. This leads to fatal desynchronizations between the biological and social rhythms of the human body and the accelerated rhythm of digital gig work. The latter imposes a time schedule on workers to which the latter cannot conform. On the other hand, the digital gig economy pays insufficient attention to the balance between productive and reproductive time. Instead of allowing workers sufficient time and resources to regenerate their labor-power, digital platforms cut workers off from social support networks, family life, and adequate sleeping patterns. Workers somewhat alleviate this tension by relying on and building their own networks of care, but these initiatives do not suffice to keep them afloat in the long run. As a result, one has to conclude that the digital gig economy provides an unsustainable model of work.

NOTES

1. Peter Fleming, Carl Rhodes, and Kyoung-Hee Yu, "On Why Uber Has Not Taken over the World," *Economy and Society* 48, no. 4 (2019): 500.

2. See, among others, Rosenblat, *Uberland*, 187; Kessler, *Gigged*, 75–76; Cant, *Riding for Deliveroo*, 54–58; Karen Gregory, "'My Life Is More Valuable than This': Understanding Risk among On-Demand Food Couriers in Edinburgh," *Work, Employment and Society*, no. Published online (2020): 1–16.

3. Berardi Bifo, *The Uprising*, 77.

4. Berardi Bifo, 68.

5. Stijn De Cauwer and Tim Christiaens, "The Multitude Divided: Biopolitical Production during the Coronavirus Pandemic," in *Pandemic and the Crisis of Capitalism*, ed. Vincent Lyon-Callo et al. (Brighton: ReMarx Books, 2020), 118–27.

6. Dania Rajendra, "The CEO Has No Clothes: Worker Leadership and Amazon's Failures during COVID-19," in *The Cost of Free Shipping: Amazon in the Global Economy*, ed. Jake Alimahomed-Wilson and Ellen Reese (London: Pluto Press, 2020), 238–49.

7. Jay Peters, "Amazon Says 19,816 Workers Have Contracted COVID-19," *The Verge*, 1 October 2020, https://www.theverge.com/2020/10/1/21497941/amazon-disclose-workers-contract-covid-19.

8. Delfanti, *Warehouse*, 145.

9. Paul Blest, "Leaked Amazon Memo Details Plan to Smear Fired Warehouse Organizer: 'He's Not Smart or Articulate,'" *Vice News*, 2 April 2020, https://www.vice.com/en/article/5dm8bx/leaked-amazon-memo-details-plan-to-smear-fired-warehouse-organizer-hes-not-smart-or-articulate.

10. Yea-Hung Chen et al., "Excess Mortality Associated with the COVID-19 Pandemic among Californians 18–65 Years of Age, by Occupational Sector and Occupation: March through October 2020," preprint (Occupational and Environmental Health, 2021), https://doi.org/10.1101/2021.01.21.21250266.

11. See Anson Rabinbach, *The Human Motor: Energy, Fatigue, and the Origins of Modernity* (Berkeley: University of California Press, 1992); Amy Wendling, *Karl Marx on Technology and Alienation* (Basingstoke: Palgrave Macmillan, 2009), 61–92; Caffentzis, *In Letters of Blood and Fire*, 11–57.

12. Rabinbach, *The Human Motor*, 46.
13. Rabinbach, 72; Wendling, *Karl Marx on Technology and Alienation*, 3–4.
14. Marx, *Capital*, 425–26.
15. David Harvey, *A Companion to Marx's Capital* (London: Verso, 2010), 143.
16. Marx, *Capital*, 428–29.
17. Marx, 429.
18. Marx, 406. Emphasis added.
19. Tronti, *Workers and Capital*, 258.
20. Wendling, *Karl Marx on Technology and Alienation*, 141.
21. Marx, *Capital*, 424.
22. Wendling, *Karl Marx on Technology and Alienation*, 86.
23. Niels van Doorn, "Platform Labor: On the Gendered and Racialized Exploitation of Low-Income Service Work in the 'On-Demand' Economy," *Information, Communication & Society* 20, no. 6 (2017): 904.
24. Alessandro Delfanti, "Machinic Dispossession and Augmented Despotism: Digital Work in an Amazon Warehouse," *New Media & Society* 23, no. 1 (2021): 50. For more on the problem of fatigue at Amazon, see Delfanti, *Warehouse*, 30–54.
25. Berardi Bifo, *The Uprising*, 123.
26. Berardi Bifo, 122. For the original description, see Gilles Deleuze and Félix Guattari, *A Thousand Plateaus: Capitalism and Schizophrenia*, trans. Brian Massumi (London: Continuum, 2011), 11.
27. Franco Berardi Bifo, *And: Phenomenology of the End: Sensibility and Connective Mutation* (South Pasadena, CA: Semiotext(e), 2015), 241.
28. Berardi Bifo, *The Soul at Work*, 192.
29. For a more elaborate discussion of online dating and emotional capitalism, see Eva Illouz, *Cold Intimacies: The Making of Emotional Capitalism* (Cambridge: Polity Press, 2007); Eva Illouz, *The End of Love: A Sociology of Negative Relations* (New York: Oxford University Press, 2019).
30. Berardi Bifo, *The Uprising*, 126–27.
31. Berardi Bifo, *Futurability*, 19.
32. Aaron Shapiro, "Between Autonomy and Control: Strategies of Arbitrage in the 'On-Demand' Economy," *New Media & Society* 20, no. 8 (2018): 2966.
33. Berardi Bifo, *The Soul at Work*, 194.
34. Franco Berardi Bifo, *Heroes: Mass Murder and Suicide* (London: Verso, 2015), 140.
35. Berardi Bifo, *The Soul at Work*, 90.
36. Berardi Bifo, *Heroes*, 139.

37. Berardi Bifo, 54.

38. Gregory, "My Life Is More Valuable than This," 4.

39. Julie Yulie Chen and Ping Sun, "Temporal Arbitrage, Fragmented Rush, and Opportunistic Behaviors: The Labor Politics of Time in the Platform Economy," *New Media & Society* 22, no. 9 (2020): 1567.

40. Cant, *Riding for Deliveroo*, 51.

41. Job Van Nieuwenhove, "Zo Is Het Om Te Werken Voor Deliveroo," VRT NWS, 20 November 2017, https://www.vrt.be/vrtnws/nl/2017/11/20/zo-is-het-werken-voor-deliveroo---hoe-sneller-ik-fiets--hoe-verd/.

42. Ping Sun, "Your Order, Their Labor: An Exploration of Algorithms and Laboring on Food Delivery Platforms in China," *Chinese Journal of Communication* 12, no. 3 (2019): 314; Cant, *Riding for Deliveroo*, 54.

43. Cant, *Riding for Deliveroo*, 57; Gregory, "My Life Is More Valuable than This," 2.

44. Schor, *After the Gig*, 41.

45. Gregory, "My Life Is More Valuable than This," 11.

46. Rosenblat, *Uberland*, 72.

47. See especially Tithi Bhattacharya, ed., *Social Reproduction Theory: Remapping Class, Recentering Oppression* (London: Pluto Press, 2017).

48. Caffentzis, *In Letters of Blood and Fire*, 45.

49. Ravenelle, *Hustle and Gig*, 16.

50. Nancy Fraser, "Crisis of Care? On the Social-Reproductive Contradictions of Contemporary Capitalism," in *Social Reproduction Theory: Remapping Class, Recentering Oppression*, ed. Tithi Bhattacharya (London: Pluto Press, 2017), 26.

51. Nancy Fraser, *Fortunes of Feminism: From State-Managed Capitalism to Neoliberal Crisis* (London: Verso, 2013), 123; Silvia Federici, *Genere e Capitale: Per Una Lettura Femminista Di Marx* (Roma: DeriveApprodi, 2020), 62.

52. For an historical overview, see Lumley, *States of Emergency*, 313–36; Dario Gentili, *Italian Theory: Dall'operaismo Alla Biopolitica* (Bologna: Il mulino, 2012), 129–43; Louise Toupin, *Wages for Housework: A History of an International Feminist Movement, 1972–77* (London: Pluto Press, 2018); Luca Paltrinieri, "Italian Theory and Feminist Materialism: A Reappraisal," *Italian Studies* 76, no. 2 (2021).

53. Dalla Costa, *Women and the Subversion of the Community*, 28; Federici, *Revolution at Point Zero*, 31.

54. Federici, *Revolution at Point Zero*, 16.

55. Federici, 17.

56. Dalla Costa, *Women and the Subversion of the Community*, 29.

57. Federici, *Revolution at Point Zero*, 18. Emphasis added.

58. Dalla Costa, *Women and the Subversion of the Community*, 34.

59. Federici, *Revolution at Point Zero*, 71; Fraser, "Crisis of Care?," 32–33; Dalla Costa, *Women and the Subversion of the Community*, 119. For more on the effects on migration, see Sandro Mezzadra and Brett Neilson, *Border as Method, or, the Multiplication of Labor* (Durham, NC: Duke University Press, 2013), 103–11; Sara R. Farris, *In the Name of Women's Rights: The Rise of Femonationalism* (Durham, NC: Duke University Press, 2017).

60. van Doorn, "Platform Labor," 905.

61. Cant, *Riding for Deliveroo*, 94–95.

62. Sarah Sharma, *In the Meantime: Temporality and Cultural Politics* (Durham, NC: Duke University Press, 2014), 69.

63. Scholz, *Uberworked and Underpaid*, 120; Rosenblat, *Uberland*, 67.

64. Alex J. Wood et al., "Good Gig, Bad Gig: Autonomy and Algorithmic Control in the Global Gig Economy," *Work, Employment and Society* 33, no. 1 (2019): 66.

65. Chen and Sun, "Temporal Arbitrage," 1574.

66. Scholz, *Uberworked and Underpaid*, 32. See also Heiner Heiland and Simon Schaupp, "Breaking Digital Atomisation: Resistant Cultures of Solidarity in Platform-Based Courier Work," in *Augmented Exploitation*, ed. Phoebe Moore and Jamie Woodcock (London: Pluto Press, 2021), 138–48; Joanna Bronowicka and Mirela Ivanova, "Resisting the Algorithmic Boss: Guessing, Gaming, Reframing and Contesting Rules in App-Based Management," in *Augmented Exploitation*, ed. Phoebe Moore and Jamie Woodcock (London: Pluto Press, 2021), 149–62.

67. Kessler, *Gigged*, 35.

68. Kessler, 113.

69. Fleming, Rhodes, and Yu, "On Why Uber Has Not Taken over the World," 12–13.

Chapter 6

Worker Autonomy as Collective Self-Valorization?

> "What, then? Do you act, or what? Are you preparing for action?" Bazarov made no answer. Something like a tremor passed over Pavel Petrovitch, but he at once regained control of himself. "Hm! . . . Action, destruction . . ." he went on. "But how destroy without even knowing why?" "We shall destroy, because we are a force," observed Arkady. Pavel Petrovitch looked at his nephew and laughed. "Yes, a force is not to be called to account," said Arkady, drawing himself up.
>
> —Ivan Turgenev

We have seen where the digital gig economy comes from and what obstacles it poses to workers' autonomy. Though platform companies promise workers flexible schedules, no boss, and entrepreneurial self-management, they deliver exploitation, alienation, and exhaustion. Under the auspices of capital, algorithmically tracked labor is not necessarily any more autonomous than what came before. In this chapter, I start the *pars construens* of this book's argument. To know what workers' autonomy in the digital gig economy should look like, one needs a working definition of "autonomy." What capabilities should workers retain vis-à-vis digital technologies to be considered autonomous? Though post-workerism is famous for its championing of worker's autonomy—it often goes by the name of "autonomist Marxism"—I argue that its conceptualization of autonomy is flawed. In his seminal *Marx beyond Marx,* Antonio Negri defines autonomy as collective self-valorization. The latter refers to "an alternative social structure of value that is founded not on the production of surplus value [in the service of capital] but on the collective needs and desires of the producing community."[1] Workers make autonomous use of their technologies, according to Negri, if they succeed at decoupling this use from technology's original purpose in the cycle of capital accumulation. As I argued in chapter 2, workplace technologies are originally designed as weapons of capital in the class struggle to encourage the creation of capitalist profit and diminish the potential for working-class resistance. According to Negri however, capitalism has reached a stage where capital itself has become obsolete for the further creation of wealth. Workers can thus take control over capitalist technologies, seize the means of production, and make the latter operate in their favor. Applied to the digital gig economy, this entails that, once gig workers have succeeded in taking control over their smartphones from Big Tech, they have acquired the capacity for self-valorization. They can use digital technology to generate values useful to themselves, rather than producing exchange value profitable for capital.

Negri's vision is tempting, but it runs into three problems. Negri, firstly, underestimates the embeddedness of capitalist imperatives in digital technology itself. A simple working-class takeover of the technological apparatus changes the ownership structure over technologies, but not the technologies themselves. If the latter are, however, predesigned to extract surplus value, it is considerably more difficult to repurpose digital technology as a working-class weapon. If we accept Virno's thesis about the ambivalence of the general intellect from chapter 4, we must admit that heteronomy is hardwired into digital platform design itself. Negri's notion of autonomy, secondly, exaggerates the importance of the struggle for autonomy relative to what this autonomy is supposed to be used for. He posits workers' autonomy as an end in itself, rather than as an instrumental value. If Negri explains workers' self-valorizing autonomy as workers' ability to act upon *their own values*, he has to explain what those values are to avoid autonomy becoming directionless. Negri, lastly, neglects the relational embeddedness of human autonomy. From a feminist perspective, Negri's suggestion is complicit in the patriarchal tradition of conceptualizing autonomy as a liberation from all relations of dependence, as if human beings would ever be capable of being their own supreme lawgiver. Human beings are always already enmeshed in relations of care and interdependence, so any notion of collective autonomy should consider how to combine collective autonomy with these primordial relations of care, a perspective lacking in Negri's writings.

1. AUTONOMY AS SELF-VALORIZATION

Post-workerists generally highlight workers' autonomy as the ultimate aim of communism. Pier Vittorio Aureli even names his history of the workerist movement "The Project of Autonomy."[2] Nonetheless, the meaning of "autonomy" is seldomly defined. A helpful gateway into its meaning is Antonio Negri's *Marx beyond Marx,* a lecture series in which the Italian defends his interpretation of the tenets of communism. This book provided the political backbone for Negri's later projects coauthored with Michael Hardt. Negri argues that capitalism obstructs workers' autonomy. Living labor is always capable of much more than for what it is mobilized in capitalist production. As many other Italian philosophers, Negri tends to distinguish here between potentiality (*potenza*) and power (*potere*).[3] Reality is ontologically constituted as an amalgamation of potentialities (i.e., embodied capacities to act in specific ways). Power, on the other hand, determines which of these potentialities can be actualized and which have to remain merely potential. In *Marx beyond Marx,* Negri argues that capital sets itself up as a power that determines the production process and marginalizes the excess of human potentialities that cannot fit into its business plans. Capital's prospects for profitable accumulation regulates which potentialities workers enact and how. Capital thus operates as a selection machine determining which the enactment and nonenactment of potentialities in the sphere of labor. Work is reduced to a mere moment in the self-propelling dynamic of capital accumulation with no agency of its own. It is forced to do the bidding of capital at the expense of its own desire to determine the cultivation of its potentialities.

In Negri's understanding, by refusing work (*rifiuto di lavoro*), living labor unleashes the human potentialities that the capital accumulation cycle was unable to integrate.[4] Work refusal allows workers to retake control over the passage from potentiality to act in their own conduct. Maurizio Lazzarato helpfully explains the Negrian concept of work refusal with reference to Paul Lafargue's plea for the right to be lazy. He argues that we need "a time of rupture, a time that arrests the 'general mobilization,' a time that suspends the apparatuses of exploitation and domination—an idle time."[5] Laziness or work refusal is not mere inaction but the rejection to devote one's time solely to what is deemed valuable by and for capital.[6] According to Lafargue, industrial capitalism in the nineteenth century had evolved to a level where the labor-time necessary for the production of goods required for human survival had dropped dramatically. If everyone were to work for just a few hours a week, society could allegedly easily subsist. This techno-utopian dream encouraged Lafargue to prophesize that newly acquired opportunities for free time would become an inexhaustible source of human wealth. Activities not immediately conducive to profit could be cultivated in this liberated time. So, contrary to some of the productivist tendencies of his father-in-law Karl Marx, Lafargue identified communism not with the general industrialization of society on proletarian terms, but with deindustrialization, hedonistic lazy living, and reducing the workload for all:

> If, uprooting from its heart the vice which dominates it and degrades its nature, the working class were to arise in its terrible strength, not to demand the Rights

of Man, which are but the rights of capitalist exploitation, not to demand the Right to Work which is but the right to misery, but to forge a brazen law forbidding any man to work more than three hours a day, the earth, the old earth, trembling with joy would feel a new universe leaping within her.[7]

By decoupling the time of everyday life from labor-time, workers would create a "new universe" in which they, and not capital, determined to which activities they devote their time and labor. The selection of potentialities would not be subjected to capital's prospects for exchange value, but to workers' own value judgments.

Negri makes a structurally analogous argument for contemporary post-Fordist capitalism. In his view, capitalism today has truly created the technical conditions for its own supersession. He writes, "liberation of the forces of production, what does that mean? It means that, at a certain level of capitalist development, capital's command is no longer necessary."[8] Automation allegedly allows for a significant reduction in necessary labor-time, while the turn to immaterial labor grants workers the capacity to organize their own work without the need for direct capitalist steering. The affective and virtuosic forms of labor typical to the post-Fordist age purportedly rely more on spontaneous social cooperation than on capitalist direct coordination. Work performance in sectors of immaterial labor is hardly encouraged with factory-style surveillance and oversight. Scientists, for example, produce innovative and valuable goods not by merely executing top-down orders but by horizontally cooperating with their peers and with creative thought. They experience management's direct meddling with their work as hindrance to performance rather than its condition of possibility. To give a second example, successful airline stewards probably perform emotional labor because they are genuinely good-humored, not out of contractual obligation. Authenticity is crucial to the performance of affective labor, but it cannot be coordinated by top-down command. Affective and cognitive cooperation in the post-Fordist multitude is immediate and self-sustaining. It does not require capital's direct command to generate wealth. Capital merely privatizes the value generated in social cooperation and expropriates the multitude from its own capabilities. It might look like capital is responsible for the mobilization of cognitive work and social affects, but in reality, these forms of interaction succeed *despite* rather than *because of* capital. The latter's role is to merely transform these forms of self-organizing cooperation into monetary profit. It, for instance, acquires intellectual property rights on scientific discoveries, but it generally abstains from micromanaging its employees; it might ask airline stewards to smile and be friendly to customers, but it knows this only follows if workers have good reasons to smile. Negri even believes that capital ultimately obstructs the further creation of multitudinal wealth.[9] It parasitizes on the common, feeds off the vitality of the multitude, and thereby saps it of some of its potentialities. Intellectual property rights, for instance, hinder the further dissemination of knowledge, and as long as smiling is a contractual obligation to affective workers, there is always the risk of alienating them from their activity. The success of direct social cooperation under post-Fordism is always under threat of being micromanaged by capital. The latter can hence hardly be considered a necessary factor in the creation of collective wealth. According to Negri, the wealth of the common would be better served without the bloodletting intermediation of capital. By "cutting out the middleman," the multitude would be able to foster genuine social cooperation more effectively. By allowing for the cross-pollination of immaterial labor across the multitude—without the obstructions coming from capital's need to monetize this productivity—even more wealth would be within reach.

Negri subsequently argues that the multitude must take control over the technological apparatus of post-Fordism to establish a novel, communist mode of production. By seizing the means of production in the age of automation and digitalization, the multitude can allegedly repurpose these technologies to working-class ends. There is purportedly even no need for a transitional stage of "real socialism" to move from capitalism to communism.[10] Since post-Fordist production relies on the spontaneous social cooperation of the multitude, once capitalist expropriation is abolished, the multitude can immediately produce the wealth it desires on its own terms. It is merely a matter of substituting a multitudinal for a capitalist selection machine without altering the labor process itself. Negri calls it a shift from capitalist valorization to multitudinal self-valorization: the values created in the production process are no longer functional to capital accumulation, but reflect the values the multitude itself desires.[11] Open-access research or online peer-to-peer networks like Wikipedia are just two examples of cooperative processes that perform the same immaterial labor as privatized scientific research, but without submitting to the profit imperative. For Negri, such initiatives establish a template for rethinking the entire global economy. Social cooperation is encouraged to flourish by making the exchange of knowledge easily accessible and free of charge. Such examples allow for a "collective planning" of the common.[12] They do not even require the state apparatus to take charge of economic planning, since the multitude can directly organize itself.

According to Negri, these practices of libertarian communism maximize the opportunities for workers' autonomy. For him, "communism is the negation of all measure, it is the affirmation of the most extensive plurality and creativity."[13] Unprofitable human potentialities dismissed in post-Fordist capitalism are now given free reign. Communism maximizes the range of possibilities for workers beyond what can immediately be put at the service of capital. The wild freedom of exploration and discovery that Lafargue associated with the new universe of laziness provides the basis for this communist form of life. The point is to enhance people's capacity for collective "self-determination" (*autodeterminazione*).[14] Which human potentialities are actualized or not depends not on the selection machine of capital but on the desires and decisions of workers themselves. To return to the example of Wikipedia, it is clear that profitability is not a benchmark for knowledge production on the website. It is rather Wikipedia contributors themselves that choose which pages are updated and how. The online multitude can cultivate those forms of social cooperation that it itself deems valuable rather than obeying capitalist command.

Negri's writings have inspired a whole literature on post-capitalist futures built on automation and direct multitudinal self-government.[15] Our contemporary right to be lazy could allegedly be substantiated by entrusting to machines the work necessary for social persistence. As Negri writes,

> The liberation of living labour increases its creative potentiality, the abolition of labour is its highest vivification. The content and programme of communism are a development of universal needs that were created according to the collective yet immiserating measure of the organisation of wage-labour, but that, in revolutionary fashion, lead toward the abolition and definitive death of labour.[16]

By making the technological apparatus underlying capitalist production work for the multitude, the latter can allegedly reduce necessary labor-time to its absolute minimum. Right now, capital purportedly blocks some of this potential for automation because it only invests in those technical innovations that guarantee immediate profit. It subordinates technical progress to the production of surplus value. Only technological advances that promise to increase profitability are implemented. However, techno-optimists with Negrian sympathies claim that "fully automated luxury communism" is on the horizon once the profit motive is left behind. They argue, for example, that important technical advancements in the field of gene editing and hormone therapy are today blocked because they would undermine the business model of post-Fordist capital.[17] Cheap DIY hormonal and genetic engineering would benefit trans and queer communities, but it is not a savvy business strategy for pharmaceutical companies. They prefer expansive treatments under specialist supervision. Collectivizing biotechnologies would purportedly allow trans and queer potentialities to flourish without the mediation of scarce treatments and surgeries. As Srnicek and Williams summarize,

> The full development of synthetic freedom therefore requires a reconfiguration of the material world in accordance with the drive to expand our capacities for

action. It demands experimentation with collective and technological augmentation, and a spirit that refuses to accept any barrier as natural or inevitable. Cyborg augmentations, artificial life, synthetic biology and technologically mediated reproduction are all examples of this elaboration.[18]

By dispossessing pharmaceutical capital of the production of biotechnology, the multitude can allegedly subject human biology to collective self-valorization. People could refurbish genes and hormones to reflect the multifarious desires and potentialities of the multitude in all its variety and diversity.

Applying this message of multitudinal autonomy as self-valorization to the digital gig economy would entail rekindling the original promise of the sharing economy. As mentioned in chapter 1, the digital gig economy originates in an ecology of internet platforms that enabled people to share goods and services for free.[19] It started among early internet enthusiasts who saw digital technologies as a means for revitalizing bottom-up voluntary association. Direct peer-to-peer coordination would allegedly cut out the middleman, independently of whether the latter was the state or capital. Instead of buying goods like cars or services like hotel stays, for example, car-sharing apps and couch surfing platforms would foster a genuinely democratic sharing culture.[20] Instead of letting idle resources wear out unused, the internet would be a place of communication and communal sharing. Insofar as these attempts at decommodifying the exchange of goods and services through online media still exist, they incarnate the kind of multitudinal planning of the common that Negri envisaged in *Marx beyond Marx*. Direct social cooperation through online communication channels in a tightly knit network of creative individuals allows for collective economic planning without capitalist intermediation. Platform users in the sharing economy can autonomously decide which values to cultivate insofar as these platforms are not subject to the imperatives of surplus value production. The injustices of the digital gig economy are, in this regard, the outcome of a broken promise in the sharing economy.[21] Capital has appropriated social cooperation on the net and repurposed it to fit the valorization process of capital itself. Negri's call for workers' autonomy thus implies that, in the digital gig economy, workers are to seize for themselves the digital technologies that coordinate the labor process. Once they have taken control over the technical apparatus of the gig economy, they can reinvigorate the project of online multitudinal self-valorization.

2. OBJECTIONS TO NEGRI'S NOTION OF WORKER AUTONOMY

The post-workerist theory of autonomy and technology revolves around two poles. On the one hand, workers ought to be independent from capital's selection machine and its determining force over human potentialities. By refusing work and decoupling the production of value from capital, workers allegedly become more autonomous. On the other hand, mere independence does not yet guarantee worker autonomy. The latter requires capabilities for collective self-determination. The power over the selection of potentialities must pass from capital to the multitude. Once the multitude has emancipated itself from capital, it should be able to determine for itself which forms of social cooperation it deems valuable. Tempting as this theory of autonomy seems, I will highlight three objections. First, it naively overestimates how easily capitalist technologies can be made to serve working-class needs. Second, by not specifying the goals of collective self-determination, post-workerists risk encouraging any and all liberations of human potentialities regardless of their quality for the good life. Third, the isolated emphasis on collective self-determination ignores the constitutive relationality and dependencies of the human condition.

(1) Negri's confident claim that the multitude could simply seize and repurpose digital technology is somewhat naïve. He forgets that capitalist forms of heteronomy are often ingrained in the fundamental design of digital technology. In chapter 4, we have already discussed the ambivalence of the general intellect in relation to digital reputation systems. Transforming privately owned platforms like Airbnb into genuine sharing economy apps does not necessarily end the alienating efficacy of digital reputation systems. Users would still have to conform to algorithmic expectations to access social goods and services. The mere abolition of private ownership over digital platforms is no automatic route to multitudinal self-valorization. "Taking back control over fixed capital,"[22] as Negri and Hardt suggest, might thus be harder than expected. That particular form of the general intellect today is the outcome of centuries of capitalist development. No sudden revolution can make that impact disappear overnight. As Kate Crawford writes, "to suggest that we democratize AI [or digital technology in general] to reduce asymmetries of power is a little like arguing for democratizing weapons manufacturing in the service of peace. As Audre Lorde reminds us, "the master's tools will never dismantle the master's house."[23]

Furthermore, one should recall the criticism of the "immaterial labor" thesis outlined in chapter 2. Negri and Hardt argue that the capitalist coordination of the labor process has become superfluous on the basis of examples that do not represent the full gambit of digitally mediated labor. They often focus on high-value cognitive labor in the IT-sector or emotional labor in sectors that have always been somewhat immaterial. There is only limited attention devoted to sectors that are still very similar to Taylorized factory labor or where digital technology has increased capitalist command rather than genuine social cooperation.[24] Lower down the food chain of the post-Fordist labor market, there are plenty of jobs that are far less virtuosic or self-organizing. The digital gig economy exemplifies this type of immaterial yet highly heteronomous labor. Uber drivers, Deliveroo couriers, or Amazon warehouse workers perform standardized, uncreative work that is nonetheless connected in vast social networks through digital technology. Their labor is part of the push toward immaterial labor, but it is also under tremendous pressures from capitalist surveillance and command. These workers' choices and movements are closely monitored and frequently disciplined to fit into the capitalist valorization process. To repurpose labor platforms like Uber's or Deliveroo's, more would be required than a simple change in ownership structures. The platforms' basic designs would need a complete overhaul to serve the aims of workers' autonomy.

(2) Though Negri and Hardt often stress that the post-workerist quest for autonomy is an affirmative political program, it is hard to substantiate its meaning beyond autonomy-*from*-capital. They leave the pole of collective self-determination too empty to discern the meaning of autonomy as a whole. Hardt, for instance, describes autonomy as self-valorization as follows:

> Self-valorisation was a principal concept that circulated in the [(post-)workerist] movements, referring to social forms and structures of value that were relatively autonomous from and posed an effective alternative to capitalist circuits of valorisation. Self-valorisation was thought of as the building block for constructing a new form of sociality, a new society.[25]

Hardt's definition is clear about what self-valorization is aimed to overcome, namely capitalist circuits of valorization, but not what it is supposed to achieve. It references vague visions of "new forms of sociality" and "a new society" in the unspecified future. This sounds eerily like a Marxist version of Yevgeny Bazarov from Ivan Turgenev's novel *Fathers and Sons,* who wants to annihilate the past and rebuild a supposedly better yet unspecified world from its ashes. Negri as well, in *Marx beyond Marx,* likens autonomy to merely the release of human potentialities from capitalist bondage, without specifying *which* potentialities are worth saving.[26] The self-determination Negri promises is identified with a mere multiplication of the courses of action workers can choose from. Negri defends work refusal because the latter decouples workers *from* capital and fosters free time. What workers are supposed to do with this assimilated new time is left unspoken. Self-determination seems to equate with more potentialities to choose from. Years later, in *Empire,* Negri and Hardt together move in the same direction. They identify the source of the multitude's resistance to capital in a "will to be against" and advise the multitude as "new barbarians [to] destroy with an affirmative violence and [to] trace new paths of life through their own material existence."[27] It remains unclear what is to be affirmed in violence or which new paths are worth pursuing. The point is rather to expand the scope of available potentialities for the multitude without any clear guidance as to which potentialities are worth having.

On first sight, Negri and Hardt have good reasons not to specify the content of multitudinal autonomy in advance. If the multitude is to be genuinely autonomous, philosophers should obviously not tell them what to do. As radical democrats, post-workerists believe the multitude itself should determine the use of noncapitalist free time. The ultimate goal is the capacity to negate the status quo, to flee from the constituted order, and to start anew and generate "greater possibilities for creation and liberation."[28] It should be determined through democratic decision making how free time is to be used and which human potentialities are to be cultivated. The only normative standard Negri and Hardt set in advance is that it should be the multitude—and not capital—that performs the selection over these potentialities.

Leaving the scope of collective autonomy strictly open, however, has a perverse side-effect. If post-workerists celebrate the multiplication of new potentialities and abstain from determining their quality in advance, then *any* multiplication of potentialities available to the multitude is *ipso facto* good. Any time workers refuse the mobilization of their time for the demands of capital and thereby liberate free time and alternative potential conducts, they have already enhanced workers' autonomy. From this perspective, the aforementioned will to be against indeed suffices to generate workers' autonomy. Independently of the quality of the liberated possibilities, any form of anticapitalistic struggle is allegedly a good in itself.[29] Radicalism and "exodus" are to be pursued for their own sake, independently of whether this grants workers better or happier lives. Universalizing access to gene editing or hormone therapies, for example, might enhance collective capabilities to modify our own biological constitution, but that does not necessarily make us happier or our lives more meaningful. Likewise, post-workerists can protest the welfare state or social security because the latter pacify workers' resistance against capital, but that does not make the abolition of these institutions any more emancipatory.[30]

According to Broder, this strategy leads to "revolutionary faddism": any supposedly trending form of radicalism that opposes the hold of capital over living labor is encouraged merely for its will to be against, independently of what it ultimately stands for.[31] Militancy and resistance are valued for their own sake. This makes post-workerism a flexible but also directionless political project.[32] Negri and Hardt have been able to connect to multiple disparate social movements, but their approach may also be *too* inclusive. The theory operates at such a high level of abstraction that one can map multiple mutually exclusive political project unto the same plane, which ultimately says very little about what politics post-workerism exactly endorses.[33] Negri, for instance, naively believed that merely stopping the French Yellow Vest movement of 2018 from turning into a hierarchical organization or a political party would suffice to purge its alt-right tendencies.[34] Some post-workerists have publicly endorsed the Italian Five Star Movement on the sole ground that its disruptive influence would destabilize Italian capitalism.[35] They ignored how irresponsible it was to jeopardize socialist accomplishments like the welfare state or social security merely to get a chance at resisting capital. And what to say about the terrorist actions of the Red Brigades, the infamous splinter faction of the workerist movement of which Negri was wrongly condemned to have been its political mastermind? Though Negri was not involved in its violent form of "revolutionary education," it is also not surprising that ideas about the will to be against can be taken in such a nihilistic direction.[36] In sum, not any action that destabilizes the status quo is *ipso facto* emancipatory.

What is missing from the post-workerist theory of autonomy is "anything like an equally detailed study of worker attempts to fill the time liberated by [struggles against work]," as Harry Cleaver attests.[37] This requires a theoretical strategy that determines which potentialities are valuable enough to liberate without telling workers directly what to do or how to live. What criterion or value would make the acquisition of free time in which we could autonomously determine our own conduct a desirable endeavor? For Negri and Hardt, workers should struggle for autonomy just to be autonomous, with no explanation as to why autonomy is worth having. Making autonomy an end in itself is thus ultimately self-referential—to dangerous political effect. It voids the project of autonomy of meaning. Ever since Tronti's *Workers and Capital*, it has been commonplace in workerist and post-workerist circles that "no worker who is fighting a boss is going to ask, 'And then what?' The fight against the boss is everything. The organisation of this struggle is everything. This constitutes a whole world."[38] However, today we should ask ourselves, "And then what?"

(3) From the 1960s onwards, Italian feminists have criticized Marxist notions of autonomy for being implicitly patriarchal.[39] The latter present a particularly masculine ideal of emancipation as complete collective independence and control over production. The working class or the multitude seemingly takes over from capital hierarchical control. This might substitute democratic for autocratic decision making, but the hierarchical selection

machine that *ex nihilo* decides which potentialities for human conduct are enacted and which are not, remains in place. The Marxist image of multitudinal decision making remains in the "realm of action," where an autarkic, albeit democratic, subject exhaustively determines its own fate and future.[40] Here, "the disavowal of dependency becomes the precondition of the autonomous thinking and acting political subject," as Judith Butler writes.[41] The collective "self" of multitudinal self-determination is still assumed to be a traditional modern subject that can master its own conduct independently of its relations with others. The only difference is that where capitalism or traditional liberalism allots this position to capital or the liberal individual, the post-workerists grant this role to the multitude as a collective subject.

Many parts of everyday life, however, do not conform to this power fantasy, according to feminists like Adriana Cavarero and Luisa Muraro.[42] Human beings are always already enmeshed in bonds of care and social relationships not of their own making. How they conduct their lives is never decided upon or selected by a single self-sufficient agent. It is the outcome of the social relationships into which individual subjects are always already thrown. The form of social cooperation in the multitude, even under communist conditions, is thus not entirely subject to the power of collective self-determination. We are always already dependent on others, and we always already have obligations of care toward others that we cannot simply self-determine out of existence. How we cultivate our liberated free time will hence partly depend on our embeddedness in social relationships rather than autonomous decision making. However, once one accepts that relationality and dependency are constitutive of the human condition, the notion of an autocratic subject becomes untenable.[43] It requires one to think of autonomy in a relational manner rather than as comprehensive self-determination *ex nihilo*.

This observation does not entail that autonomy is an entirely worthless project. We need free time and democratic autonomous governance to be able to devote ourselves to matters of care. And *vice versa,* we need a secure footing in relations of care to confidently feel and practice autonomy. We need to know we can fall back on networks of social support in order to take control of our lives. Autonomy and care, in other words, form a chiasmic bond: relations of care enable us to take responsibility for our lives and autonomy is a necessary condition to build our lives around what we care about. To cite Butler again,

> The life of the other, the life that is not our own, is also our life, since whatever sense "our" life has is derived precisely from this sociality, this being already, and from the start, dependent on a world of others, constituted in and by a social world. . . . To find that one's life is also the life of others, even as

this life is distinct and must be distinct, means that one's boundary is at once a limit and a site of adjacency, a mode of spatial and temporal nearness and even boundedness.[44]

What Butler calls "our life" as opposed to "my life" is not an autocratic collective subject that could govern itself through the imposition of an almost Rousseau-like general will. It is rather the interweaving of chains of dependency and care that animates everyday life. Social relationships simply "happen" well before they can be subjected to any procedure of collective will-formation. Even if the multitude were to succeed at repurposing the productive apparatus to serve self-valorization, this would not exempt the multitude from the obligations of "our life." We will still have to tend to the vulnerable, care for our children, show loyalty to our friends, and so forth. The post-work future will not be a Walhalla of autarkic self-determination.

We have already touched upon these matters of care in the previous chapter when dealing with social reproduction and domestic labor. Capitalism allegedly imposes housework and care labor disproportionally on women to keep the capitalist valorization machine running. Negri and Hardt agree with this feminist-Marxist analysis and claim that communism as workers' autonomy can solve this unjust gendered division of labor. They explicitly align themselves with feminist calls to refuse essentialism vis-à-vis women's identities.[45] Negri emphasizes the need for automation and the multitudinal capture of new technologies not just for worker autonomy, but also as a means toward women's liberation from housework:

> Think of what a house used to be—I am not saying one hundred years ago, but just fifty: a home with no machines, where everything was organised by people who took care of housework. Inside a house with no mechanical equipment, women were forced to heavy and repetitive daily labor, concealed under the appearance of love and affects. . . . Today the context has changed completely: there has been a process of liberation of women, a general machinic transformation, which thus should be viewed in its positive, progressive aspect. . . . Some material possibilities of liberation are nevertheless given in this process and pass through a feminine reappropriation of fixed capital in the home.[46]

Negri argues that a "feminine reappropriation" of new domestic technologies can liberate human time from its functionality to capitalist valorization analogously to how the multitudinal takeover of digital technologies can liberate social cooperation from capitalist control. This would liberate women from their functional role as housewives under the capitalist breadwinner model.

The empirical record, however, contradicts Negri's optimistic prediction. Automating household tasks or granting workers autonomous control over technologies has not immediately translated into women's liberation from housework so far. Domestic innovations like the dishwasher, the vacuum cleaner, or the microwave have not automatically emancipated women from their role as "loving servants of the working class," as Federici wrote.[47] These appliances have rather increased social expectations with regard to cleanliness and good parenting.[48] In the household, technologies that were marketed to save people time have actually increased time spent on housework. Time gained on one end thanks to technical progress has been lost on the other due to increasing housework demands on women. Simply replacing capitalist with workers' control over the technical apparatus does not suffice on its own to generate more free time for women. Liberating women from their social duties as supposedly natural caretakers requires a politics specifically tackling gendered social roles rather than the reappropriation of technology.[49]

An even more fundamental criticism from the feminist camp comes from the question whether one should really regard care work as exclusively a necessary evil that must be technologically overcome. Some might dream of entirely automating care labor with social robots, but those people are rare. Human flourishing requires more than independence and the power of self-determination. What often gets people through the day is not necessarily their own self-chosen projects, but the little obligations of "our life," picking up the children from school, helping grandma install her wi-fi, chatting with coworkers around the water dispenser, or helping a stranger find the bus stop. These caretaking relations, however, do not diminish one's quality of life but rather enhance them. They grant people something to *live for* and devote one's life and labor to. Our entanglement in chains of human dependencies often undermine the capacity for total self-determination, but this is a sacrifice many are willing to make.[50] Cavarero illustrates this phenomenon with the image of children playing on slides: "The euphoria children feel playing on slides is testimony that, in abandoning oneself to the laws of gravity, in asserting to descent without resistance, there is an intrinsic pleasure."[51] The experiences that often give most meaning to our lives, like falling in love or caring for one's children, often have to do with these forms of losing control and voluntarily abdicating the power of self-determination. That explains why we often struggle to acquire free time and autonomy exactly to devote it to the people and projects we care about. Many acquisitions of free time or reductions of the work week have, in the last decades, been motivated by workers' desire to spend more time taking care of loved ones, like children or older relatives, not to increase personal self-determination.

This is not to say that autonomous self-determination is irrelevant to the good life or that women should simply learn to identify with their socially imposed role as primary caretakers. The claim is not to naturalize the bourgeois family or neoconservative family values.[52] What exact cultural form relations of care take is secondary to the mere fact of their insuperable existence and importance. Even in communist multitudes there would be relations of care that evade the legislating powers of a self-determining constituent collective. Not all social relations are subject to the human will. If relations of care and dependency are truly markers of the human conditions as such—and not just of female identity—then the just cultivation of these relations of care entails an inexorable politics of gendered justice.[53] Collective autonomy as self-determination cannot be a sufficient condition for the good life if it does not consider these bonds of care or attempts to reduce them to objects of collective will formation. A third pole apart from independence and self-determination has to be added to the concept of workers' autonomy to account for the relational embeddedness of the good life.

3. CONCLUSION

Negri's concept of collective self-valorization entails a notion of workers' autonomy built on two qualities. On the one hand, capital operates as a selection machine that heteronomously determines which potentialities the multitude can actualize or not. Digital technologies are among its major apparatuses to effectuate this sorting of potentialities. Workers' autonomy thus *a contrario* implies workers' independence from the capitalist selection machine. Worker should seize the technical apparatus of production to expropriate capital from its position in power. On the other hand, this collective independence should lead to collective self-determination. By decoupling the multitude from capital, the multitude will itself organize the assortment of potentialities directly. Negri and Hardt see in immaterial labor and online experiments with peer-to-peer networks an opportunity to facilitate collective self-determination without the intermediation of capital. Multitudinal communism allegedly enables the multitude to select which engagements it finds valuable. Workers' autonomy, in other words, entails a collective right to be lazy: it grants the multitude free time in which it can freely cultivate its potentialities without capitalist coordination.

This concept of workers' autonomy is, however, flawed on several accounts. First, Negri's naivety about the ambivalence of the general intellect hinders him from acknowledging that capitalist imperatives are often embedded in technological design. A simple change in ownership or expropriation of private property over digital tools will not suffice to radically repurpose technological infrastructures. One must also look at the inner makeup of the technologies themselves. Second, workers' autonomy must be given a purpose beyond itself. Negri—and post-workerists in general—tend to encourage workers' autonomy for its own sake. Post-workerists understandably want to leave it to the multitude itself to decide which liberated potentialities to cultivate or not, but the perverse side-effect of this approach is that post-workerist struggles tend to be too inclusive. Almost all forms of anti-capitalist resistance are acceptable insofar as they articulate a "will to be against" capital. The mere increase in available potentialities for the multitude is equated with autonomy independently of the costs to, for instance, the stability of the social security system or whether these new opportunities are meaningful to human lives. Workers' autonomy should, in other words, be given a more specific purpose, while still respecting the multitude's democratic right to determine its own conduct. Lastly, the notion of autonomy as collective self-valorization does not consider the primary embeddedness of human beings in social relations of care. We are always already thrown into social relations not of our own making. These relations nonetheless impose obligations of care on us, out of which we cannot willfully extract ourselves. Even more important, they are largely responsible for what makes us experience our lives as meaningful. The free time acquired in struggles for autonomy is often devoted to caring for others and we need to be able to fall back on relational safety nets to securely practice our autonomy. A better notion of collective autonomy should thus be capable to reflect this chiasmic bond between autonomy and human interdependence. To that end, we turn to Ivan Illich's philosophy of technology in the next chapter.

NOTES

1. Michael Hardt, "Glossary of Concepts," in *Radical Thought in Italy: A Potential Politics*, ed. Paolo Virno and Michael Hardt (Minneapolis: University of Minnesota Press, 1996), 264.

2. Pier Vittorio Aureli, *The Project of Autonomy: Politics and Architecture within and against Capitalism* (New York: Princeton Architectural Press, 2008).

3. For the Spinozist background of this distinction in Negri, see Negri, *Subversive Spinoza*; Negri, *The Savage Anomaly*; Negri, *Spinoza for Our Time*.

4. Antonio Negri, *Marx Oltre Marx* (Rome: Manifestolibri, 1998), 223.

5. Lazzarato, *Governing by Debt*, 246. See also Maurizio Lazzarato, *Marcel Duchamp et Le Refus Du Travail: Suivi de Misère de La Sociologie* (Paris: Prairies ordinaires, 2014); Christiaens, "Neoliberalism and the Right to Be Lazy."

6. Weeks, *The Problem with Work*, 169.

7. Lafargue, *The Right to Be Lazy*.

8. Negri, *Marx Oltre Marx*, 212–13.

9. Negri, 161.

10. Negri, 203.

11. Weeks, *The Problem with Work*, 95.

12. Negri, *Marx Oltre Marx*, 222.

13. Negri, 54.

14. Negri, 217.

15. This approach has particularly gained a following in the UK. See, among others, Srnicek and Williams, *Inventing the Future* (London: Verso Books); Mason, *Postcapitalism* (New York: Farrar, Straus and Giroux); Bastani, *Fully Automated Luxury Communism*; Adam Fishwick and Nicholas J. Kiersey, eds., *Post-Capitalist Futures: Political Economy beyond Crisis and Hope* (London: Pluto Press, 2021); Kyle Lewis and Will Stronge, *Overtime: Why We Need a Shorter Working Week* (London: Verso Books, 2021).

16. Negri, *Marx Oltre Marx*, 214.

17. See Beatriz Preciado, *Testo junkie: sexe, drogue et biopolitique* (Paris: Grasset, 2008); Helen Hester, *Xenofeminism* (Cambridge: Polity Press, 2018); Bastani, *Fully Automated Luxury Communism*, 149–54.

18. Srnicek and Williams, *Inventing the Future*, 82.

19. Ravenelle, *Hustle and Gig*, 26.

20. Schor, *After the Gig*, 162.

21. Ravenelle, *Hustle and Gig*, 207.

22. Hardt and Negri, *Assembly*, 115.

23. Kate Crawford, *Atlas of AI: Power, Politics, and the Planetary Costs of Artificial Intelligence* (New Haven: Yale University Press, 2021), 223. This is also the central claim of Mueller, *Breaking Things at Work*.

24. McRobbie, "Fashion's Click and Collect: A Labour Perspective."

25. Michael Hardt, "Introduction; Laboratory Italy," in *Radical Thought in Italy: A Potential Politics*, ed. Paolo Virno and Michael Hardt (Minneapolis: University of Minnesota Press, 1996), 3.

26. See, for example, Negri, *Marx Oltre Marx*, 172.

27. Hardt and Negri, *Empire*, 215.

28. Hardt and Negri, 218.

29. Hardt and Negri obviously exempt right-wing authoritarian forms of anti-capitalism from this definition. In this case, control over human conduct would simply be passed along from capital to the state or a charismatic leader rather than to the multitude. It exchanges one form of heteronomy for another. See, for instance, Hardt and Negri, *Assembly*, 47–62.

30. Hardt and Negri, *Empire*, 301–2. Admittedly, some post-workerists, like Carlo Vercellone, have always supported the public sustenance of welfare institutions, and Negri has more recently also defended their protection from neoliberal privatisation efforts (see Negri, *From the Factory to the Metropolis*, 111.).

31. David Broder, "The Autumn and Fall of Italian Workerism," *Catalyst* 3, no. 4 (2020), https://catalyst-journal.com/2020/03/the-autumn-and-fall-of-italian-workerism.

32. Wright, *Storming Heaven*, 211.

33. Kate Soper, *Post-Growth Living: For an Alternative Hedonism* (London: Verso, 2020), 23.

34. Antonio Negri, "L'insurrezione Francese," *Euronomade* (blog), 4 December 2018, http://www.euronomade.info/?p=11351.

35. See Broder, "Autumn and Fall."

36. For more on the links between workerism and the Red Brigades, see Lumley, *States of Emergency*, 279–93; Franco Berardi Bifo, "Anatomy of Autonomy," in *Autonomia*, ed. Sylvère Lotringer and Christian Marazzi (Los Angeles: Semiotext(e), 2007), 148–71; Broder, "Autumn and Fall."

37. Harry Cleaver, "The Inversion of Class Perspective in Marxian Theory: From Valorisation to Self-Valorisation," in *Open Marxism, Volume 2; Theory and Practice*, ed. John Holloway, Werner Bonefeld, and Kosmas Psychopedis (London: Pluto Press, 1992), 126.

38. Tronti, *Workers and Capital*, xxiv.

39. Lumley, *States of Emergency*, 330–31; Gentili, *Italian Theory*, 129–43.

40. Adriana Cavarero, *Nonostante Platone: Figure Femminili Nella Filosofia Antica* (Verona: Ombre Corte, 2014), 24.

41. Judith Butler, *Notes toward a Performative Theory of Assembly*, First Harvard University Press (Cambridge, MA: Harvard University Press, 2018), 206.

42. Adriana Cavarero, *Inclinations: A Critique of Rectitude*, trans. Amanda Minervini and Adam Sitze (Stanford, CA: Stanford University Press, 2016); Luisa Muraro, *The Symbolic Order of the Mother*, trans. Timothy S. Murphy (Albany, NY: SUNY Press, 2018). For commentaries on the biopolitics of care, see Tim Christiaens, "Towards Affirmative Economic Theologies: Responses to the Problem of Evil in Contemporary Italian Thought," *Political Theology* 21, no. 7 (2 October 2020): 634–49; Tim Christiaens, "Against the Republican Foucault: How to Establish an Affirmative Biopolitics of Care," *Tijdschrift Voor Filosofie* 83, no. 4 (2021): 683–709; Tim Christiaens, "Agamben's 'Bare Life' and Grossman's Ethics of Senseless Kindness," *Journal of European Studies* 52, no. 1 (2022): 36–53.

43. Cavarero, *Inclinations*, 11.

44. Butler, *Theory of Assembly*, 108.

45. Hardt and Negri, *Empire*, 217–18.

46. Negri, *From the Factory to the Metropolis*, 145.

47. Federici, *Revolution at Point Zero*, 17.

48. Judy Wajcman, *Pressed for Time: The Acceleration of Life in Digital Capitalism* (Chicago: The University of Chicago Press, 2015), 68–69.

49. Negri and Hardt sometimes acknowledge this need in their recent, more pluralist descriptions of the multitude. Whereas in early writings, their definition of the multitude is firmly grounded in economic arguments about immaterial labour, in later writings, they stress the specificities of different social struggles that are not all necessarily or entirely grounded in economic struggles (see, for instance, Michael Hardt and Antonio Negri, *Commonwealth* (Cambridge, MA: Harvard University Press, 2011), 341; Negri and Hardt, "Empire, Twenty Years On," 85.). They argue that these different social movements should rather forge political alliances by translating their concerns into each other's vernacular. So feminists and antiracists have to translate their concerns into the economic discourse of the socialist movement, but the latter should also translate its projects into the language of feminism and antiracism.

50. For the opposite, post-workerist account that favors autonomy over relations of care, see Weeks, *The Problem with Work*, 167–68.

51. Cavarero, *Inclinations*, 7.
52. Weeks, *The Problem with Work*, 158–59.
53. Christiaens, "Affirmative Economic Theologies."

Chapter 7

Worker Autonomy as Conviviality

To improve upon Negri's notion of worker autonomy, the concept of collective autonomy, vis-à-vis technology, should emphasize the nefarious imperatives embedded in technological design, endow the acquisition of autonomy with a finality beyond itself, and respect the chiasmic intertwinement of autonomy and human interdependence. In this chapter, I propose we turn to degrowth philosophy and Ivan Illich's philosophy of technology to reconfigure our understanding of collective autonomy. Degrowth is very rarely discussed in debates about workers' autonomy and digitalization. Often, digitalization is presented as a solution to the unsustainable growth of the world economy, so environmentalist critiques of digital technology are rare, especially when the focus is on workers rather than the environment. Nonetheless, key figures in the degrowth movement, like Cornelius Castoriadis and André Gorz, come from the workers' movement, and Ivan Illich, another crucial voice in the degrowth movement, wrote explicitly about the incapacitating impact of modern technologies and how technological development would have to be rethought to serve so-called "convivial autonomy." In this chapter, I first outline how Illich's philosophy fits into the degrowth critique of modern technological and economic development. Secondly, I describe his critique of modern technology and how it applies to contemporary digital platforms. On the basis of this critique, it will become clear what Illich's notion of convivial autonomy exactly entails and how it moves beyond the limitations of Negri's approach.

1. IVAN ILLICH AS A DEGROWTH THINKER

Originally, Illich was a Catholic missionary in North and Latin America.[1] He grew disillusioned with the Church, and in 1968, when Illich strongly objected to the Vatican's refusal to condemn the use of atomic weapons, he parted from his clerical title. Illich eventually became a world-renowned cultural critic in the 1970s with incendiary studies of public medicine, the school system, and industrial technology. Today, he is mostly remembered as one the foundational thinkers of degrowth. The latter is also concerned with heteronomy, like post-workerism, but not from capital specifically. It rather locates the source of heteronomy in the imperative for economic growth, irrespectively of the mode of production that guarantees this growth.[2] Contrary to much of the Cold War rhetoric of the 1970s, Illich and subsequent degrowth thinkers insist that the difference between capitalism and communism is irrelevant for environmentalist concerns.[3] Both face the same troubles of environmental pollution, resource depletion, and social malaise due to economic hyperactivity. According to Illich, the danger of modern growth-oriented institutions is that their quantitative expansion tends to cross thresholds beyond which the gains of increased economic activity are offset by the costs. Institutions then become "counterproductive": the benefits promised no longer make up for the maintenance costs of these institutions.[4] Economic expansion comes with the promise of enhancing the people's general well-being, but it also generates social and environmental side-effects that ultimately undermine that promise. Cars, for instance, promise fast transportation, but if the supply of cars crosses a certain threshold, everyone ends up stuck in traffic; medical drugs promise health and pain relief, but some pharmaceutical products have today become so widespread that dependence on prescription drugs has itself become a public health hazard; atomic bombs promise military security, but they lead to international standoffs under the cloud of mutually assured destruction. In sum, growth-oriented institutions promise more well-being, but beyond a certain point, they devolve into their opposites.

Illich illustrates his critique of counterproductivity with the metaphor of the snail, which has later become a defining symbol for the degrowth movement:

> The snail constructs the delicate architecture of its shell by adding ever increasing spirals one after the other, but then it abruptly stops and winds back in the reverse direction. In fact, just one additional larger spiral would make the shell sixteen times bigger. Instead of being beneficial, it would overload the snail. Any increase in the snail's productivity would only be used to offset the difficulties created by the enlargement of the shell beyond its preordained limits. Once the limit to increasing spiral size has been reached, the problems of excessive growth multiply exponentially, while the snail's biological capability, in the best of cases, can only show linear growth and increase arithmetically.[5]

Just like the snail keeps the size of its shell within sustainable bounds, economic activity should be put within certain limits to avoid overburdening the environment and ourselves. The only way to avoid catastrophic counterproductivities, according to degrowth thought, is by "decolonizing the collective imagination" (i.e., by enabling ideas that promote institutions independent from infinite growth).[6] Degrowth requires new styles of communal living and new conceptions of what constitutes value and the good life.[7] Instead of imagining wealth as "having more of something," like money, one ought to find meaning in practices that carry an inherent measure of "enoughness." As long as value is measured in monetary terms, for example, governments measure their success through increases in GDP (i.e., increases in the volume of goods and services produced and consumed). They subsequently keep pushing citizens to replace noncommodified everyday activities with commodity consumption. From that perspective, grocery shopping at the supermarket is more valuable than growing your own food, mass tourism better than visiting your neighbors and hiring a nanny while you slave away at work better than raising your own children. There can consequently never be enough GDP growth. More is *ipso facto* always better. The image of the snail warns against this faith in unlimited growth. By transforming the collective understanding of value, degrowth tries to decommodify cultural life. According to André Gorz, environmental politics involves the creation of "a growing sphere of sharing within the community, of voluntary and self-organized co-operation, of increasingly extensive self-determined activities."[8] "Decommodification" sounds like a call for collective asceticism or the refusal to consume anything but absolutely necessary goods, but degrowth rather aims to (re)discover the pleasures and enjoyments that have been eroded by commodification.[9] It emphasizes the happiness in activities that cannot be bought or sold but come from noncommodified human interdependence and spontaneous sociability.

This idea of decommodified enjoyment contradicts more dominant ideas about sustainable development and techno-fixes often promoted in platform capitalism. Illich warns strongly against "the translation of values into technical tasks."[10] It masks fundamentally political debates about the good life as technocratic questions about technological development. It is tempting to avoid hard discussions about what practices are ultimately acceptable for sustainable life on Earth and focus instead on technical progress as a *deus ex machina*. Uber, for instance, calls itself a green company because ridesharing reduces urban traffic and thereby diminishes air pollution and CO_2-emissions. It has also promised to switch its services to electric cars.[11] Fewer people would supposedly need to own CO_2-emitting cars if sharing electric cars becomes cheaper. Even if we ignore the environmental costs of maintaining energy-consuming digital data centers and the mining of rare metals used in digital devices,[12] this promise is empirically false.[13] It ignores the longer-term rebound effects of techno-fixes: in a first step, Uber's services might reduce demand for polluting private cars, but afterward, the price reduction will increase demand for cheap rides, thereby nullifying the effect of limiting the total supply of cars. There will be fewer cars, but those present are used more often. Consumers might no longer own private cars, but they also stop taking public transport or their bikes if Uber rides are so cheap. Also, Uber drivers spend more time driving around aimlessly chasing new customers, annulling the effect of fewer cars on the street in absolute numbers. Ultimately, there is more rather than less inner-city traffic. Even if the Uber cars themselves do not emit greenhouse gases, the demand for electricity will go up. Instead of truly committing to zero emissions, Uber has thus merely displaced environmental pollution to less visible activities.

This rebound effect is not unique to Uber or platform capitalism. It was first described by economist William Jevons in the early twentieth century for coal consumption.[14] When coal was at risk of depletion, Jevons calculated that technological innovations promising sustainable coal consumption would not withhold further depletion. They would rather diminish the price, thereby incentivizing people to use more of it. Sustainability efforts are ultimately not environment friendly in growth-based economies because they invite to use more of the polluting resource, which cancels the energy-saving effect. As Illich argues, the problem is not lack of technical solutions but dependence on growth as a measure of prosperity. What is really required is a cultural revolution so that people would not desire energy-intensive commodities in the first place: "the only solution to the environmental crisis is the shared insight of people that they would be happier if they could work together and care for each other."[15]

In this search for radical alternatives, degrowth and post-workerism tangentially meet.[16] Both movements refer to the Lafargue's idea of liberation from work and social cooperation in the common as alternatives to capitalism.[17] For degrowth, the common represents a subsistence economy that does not need to grow to sustain human communities. The production of key resources and services, like food, energy, or transportation, should be democratically governed by local communities.[18] These can restrict output in advance to satisfy the community's determinate needs. This system not only eliminates the need for indefinite expansion but also liberates time for leisure. Once communities democratically decide how much time they would like to devote to their common subsistence, they simultaneously demarcate the supply of free time. Individuals limit their labor-time to what is required to replenish the common; the rest is open for autonomous use. Both movements hence agree on the need to liberate time from work and on the hypothesis that social cooperation for goods held in common presents an opportunity to free people from the need to subject their labor to capitalist command.

Nonetheless, the strategies for how to reach and organize the reproduction of the common are substantially different.[19] A parable from degrowth literature about the tourist and the fisherman aptly illustrates this dispute.[20] A tourist and a fisherman meet at the beach, both enjoying the sun and the breezy atmosphere. The fisherman says that if he can catch two fish today, he will not have to work for the next two days. The tourist is appalled by this seeming lack of entrepreneurship and explains that the fisherman should behave more like him. The fisherman should work harder, start a business, and eventually he will also be able to afford to enjoy a lazy afternoon at the beach. The fisherman responds, "But I'm already doing that."

Post-workerists resemble the tourist's position: one first needs to move through a capitalist stage during which society's technical capabilities are expanded, and only then is economic abundance possible. One first needs capitalist innovation to automate the labor process as much as possible to liberate free time. Degrowth argues abundance is more a subjective attitude than an objective condition of technical development.[21] Rather than reaching automation targets that make the subordination of labor to capital superfluous, degrowth emphasizes the cultural conversion to slow life independently of technical factors. Even the low-tech life of the fisherman allows for subsistence activities so long as people are happy with that level of development. Abundance lies not in expanding technical capabilities, a potentially endless process, but in desiring fewer commodities and enjoying the life into which one is gratuitously thrown. Degrowth is thus less concerned with overcoming the drudgeries of everyday subsistence work or domestic labor.[22] Post-workerism promises autonomy by emancipating workers from the realm of necessity, the kinds of labor required for everyday survival. Innovations in household appliances, for instance, must liberate people from the need to invest their time off work in domestic labor. Illich, on the other hand, cautions against the thoughtless automation of household work:

> Rising standards of living have made it more capital-intensive by providing numerous machines and gadgets . . . For a minority of women, this has meant an interesting, well-paid part-time job and free time "to write their books and go fishing." But the "new" kind of housework most present-day women perform has also become more lonely, more dull, more impersonal, more time-polluting. Valium consumption and addiction to TV soap operas have often been regarded as indicators of this new, muffled stress.[23]

Time gained through automation is, in itself, just empty time if it is not endowed with a purpose. People quickly succumb to boredom if their free time remains undefined. For Illich, housework can, however, also showcase a realm of little noncommodified pleasures and enjoyments embedded in intimate relations of care. The work one performs in the family is readily experienced as meaningful and fulfilling, even if it takes up a lot of time. The point in this version of housework is not to save time though efficient equipment but to spend it lavishly on those one cares for.

2. ILLICH'S CRITIQUE OF MODERN TECHNOLOGY

For Illich, technological development is not the unambiguous road to liberation that it is for Negri. He constructs his notion of convivial autonomy around a critique of modern so-called "manipulative tools." These are technologies that lock users in forms of heteronomy and industrial growth. But to grasp this critique, it is best to first develop a preliminary understanding of Illich's social philosophy, more specifically his notion of "vernacular culture" as the decommodified form of community disrupted by growth-oriented commodification. Illich's perspective aligns with Berardi's distinction between conjunction and connection in chapter 5. According to Berardi, human beings in bodily proximity mimetically and immanently adapt to each other's mode of existence through spontaneous interaction, just like orchids and wasps establish symbiotic collaborations through repeated encounters. An everyday human conversation, for instance, does not require external command or top-down coordination.[24] Next to the coffee machine at work or at the family dinner table, people do not need to be instructed about how to talk to each other. Individuals most often smoothly communicate in a spontaneous and balanced back-and-forth rhythm. The better they know each other, the more smoothly conversation progresses. Rarely is there a need for external intervention to regulate the conversation. This is not to say that these conversations are always power-free or harmonious agreements, but that they do not follow or implement a preestablished plan. There is room for surprise and improvisation in everyday speech.

These dialogues are not mere exchanges of explicit, propositional information either.[25] In talking, the speakers gradually learn about each other's perspective. They probe each other's reactions and tailor their own responses accordingly. In this light, human conversation is a slow calibration process in which people slowly adapt to each other's mode of existence. As Illich writes, "language [is] drawn by each one from the cultural environment, learned from the encounter with people whom the learner [can] smell and touch, love or hate."[26] In talking to someone, one does not simply learn a piece of information but integrates oneself into a common relation. One establishes a shared lifeworld.[27] For Illich, "vernacular speech spreads by practical use; it is learned from people who mean what they say and who say what they mean to the person they address in the context of everyday life."[28] Though we inhabit the same world, we have different positionalities, desires, and expectations. Through sustained communication, these differences are gradually aligned without necessarily effacing them. In dialogue, different standpoints learn to complement each other without necessarily abolishing their mutual differences. That is how life-long friends know which jokes they will like or find offensive without having to ask, how long-time colleagues silently know who will be interested in joining for lunch, how a married couple expresses its love through incessant bickering. These forms of interaction slowly give rise to a community-in-difference.

Illich calls this shared lifeworld "vernacular culture," a term that derives from the Latin *vernaculum*, meaning "homebred" in the sense of not governmentally or institutionally organized.[29] According to Illich, human meaning and purpose comes primarily from these immanent, embodied encounters. They are the constitutive building blocks for the social relationships that structure our lives.[30] These embodied bonds of care and interdependence cannot be bought or sold as commodities, yet they make the common calibration of collective life possible. It is because people are capable of directly interacting with each other and of learning to understand each other's point of view through sustained dialogue that they are capable of immanently organizing their own conduct without the need for outside intervention. Through such social bonds, human action is granted not only direction and regulation but also meaning and purpose. If humankind is ever to foster a sustainable form of life, it is, according to Illich, on the basis of the vernacular potential for immanent embodied self-organization. As David Cayley observes, "the vernacular, for Illich, is a figure of this lost spontaneity, referring, by definition, to a form of life that can be neither economised nor brought under professional control. Because such forms have only a fugitive existence in the contemporary world, he wants both to reinstate them and to ask how they were lost."[31]

However, Illich argues that modern institutions and technologies sometimes undermine vernacular culture.[32] They displace the slow back-and-forth rhythm of vernacular relations with more efficient but commodity-intensive relations, which Berardi would have called "connections." To standardize the coordination of human conduct, people are formatted into preestablished and governable relations that follow strict, preestablished rules. Instead of an embodied encounter, there is now the administrative form to coordinate collective action. The latter bypasses the slowness of collective self-organization through top-down command. Instead of, for example, steadily immersing oneself in another culture to learn the language, one hires an accredited professional instructor; instead of taking care of a horse year in year out, one buys a car and parks it in the garage; instead of democratically organizing a local farming initiative, one shops at the supermarket. These institutions all surpass the need for dialogic conjunction, but they come at the cost of counterproductivities. Illich lists through counterproductive outcomes in his writings: radical monopolization, expertocratisation, and the nocebo-effect.

Radical monopolization. Traditionally, a monopoly is a market imperfection where a single distributor dominates the supply of a particular product, for instance, when one car manufacturer dominates the industry in a given area. Radical monopolization occurs when a particular institution or technology dominates an entire domain of social practices, eclipsing noncommodified forms of intercourse and making people dependent on the commodified version of that social practice.[33] When transportation in a given territory, for example, is completely designed for cars, people cannot but buy a car to move around.[34] If roads primarily serve the needs of cars, if jobs are located far away from residential areas, if social expectations are set such that people are supposed to get anywhere within a matter of maximum a few hours, people *have* to relinquish bikes or walking and buy a car to lead socially viable lives. Such choices have a lock-in effect that makes it unrealistically hard to hold fast to noncar-based alternatives. People can refuse surrender to the radical monopoly of the car only at high personal cost. Radical monopolies thereby force commodity-dependence into the infrastructure of everyday life. As Illich writes,

> A radical monopoly goes deeper than that of any one corporation or any one government. It can take many forms. . . . Ordinary monopolies corner the market; radical monopolies disable people from doing or making things on their own. The commercial monopoly restricts the flow of commodities; the more insidious social monopoly paralyzes the output of non-marketable use-values.[35]

Radical monopolies also consolidate the logic of growth.[36] Because they erode the supply of vernacular alternatives, problems in a radical monopoly can only be solved with more of the same. Though cars promise fast transportation, traffic jams show the counterproductive results of too many cars. However, if cars' radical monopoly makes alternatives inaccessible, the only solution to traffic jams is to build more and bigger highways. However, as Jevons would have predicted, this short-term solution makes car use more attractive, which leads to even more traffic. By redirecting investments away from vernacular to car-based transportation, governments increasingly undermine the alternatives to car use until cars are the only option left.

The digital economy can also be described as a radical monopoly.[37] Platform companies' success depends on network effects, meaning their database becomes more valuable the more data it captures. Growth is, hence, written into the business model of the digital economy, and the devices to make people addicted to smartphone apps, like gamification, automatic queuing, or push notifications, are part of a strategy to keep the supply of data growing. Platform companies have an incentive to displace offline vernacular forms of social interactions and replace them with online for-profit counterparts. It would, for instance, be beneficial to Tinder or OKCupid if face-to-face flirting were to be considered inappropriate compared to online dating services. This would transfer a quintessentially embodied encounter into a commodified service provided by the platform sector. Dating platforms would get exclusive ownership over romantic social interactions and the data they generate. Privately owned platforms aim at "the gradual elimination of social spaces that can exist outside data relations."[38] They foster dependency on the provision of commodified services and disempower individuals from acquiring these goods on their own, without commercial intermediation.

Expertocratisation. Once radical monopolies are consolidated, it endows the professional experts that manage them a disproportional amount of incontestable power.[39] If entire populations are structurally dependent on access to particular commodities, professional gatekeepers decide the modalities of this access. They determine how services are provided and who gets in- or excluded. Illich's paradigmatic example is the education system: once people need official diplomas to access particular jobs and social positions, the educational class can unilaterally impose their own values and opinions as "curriculum" to which educational consumers are bound.[40] Those who accept the curriculum and obey educational standards are subsequently allowed to move up the academic ladder, while those who rebel are negatively evaluated and drop out prematurely. This practice depoliticizes social disparities insofar as technocratic elites translate contentious social cleavages into seemingly neutral differences, like educational qualifications.[41] Social inequalities are surreptitiously translated into academic inequalities.

An analogous process of expertocratisation occurs in platform capitalism. The digital infrastructure of privately owned platforms is closed off to the public through intellectual property rights and design choices meant to keep users out. Compared to traditional cell phones, Apple's iPhone has uniquely removed the screws that allow users to open the device and tinker with the phone's interior.[42] Apple even requires that the apps sold in its Appstore are exclusively made with Apple-licensed software.[43] Users are also barred from rewriting the basic protocols of Uber's app, Google's search engine, or Tinder's matching algorithms. As a result, many people nowadays use devices they are unable to understand. That right is reserved to the small elite of IT-experts and data scientists working for platform companies. According to Shoshanna Zuboff, power over the workings and designs of privately owned platforms is concentrated in a "narrow priesthood of privately employed computational specialists."[44] It is a small social circle of predominantly white men with libertarian views and engineering degrees. They live close to each other and work in a handful of companies located in the Silicon Valley area.[45] The system allows for opaque and incontestable forms of normalization and discrimination headed by a closed-off professional elite.[46] What a small non-representative group of data experts regards as the norm is surreptitiously written into platform design. That is seldomly the result of bad intentions, but rather of collective ignorance. These experts control who sees what under which conditions on the internet with minimal accountability. I have already discussed how reputational rating systems tend to disadvantage black users of Airbnb's platform, but there are many more examples of racial ignorance among platform designers leading to discriminatory outcomes. In 2021, for example, UK Uber drivers protested Uber's use of racially biased facial recognition software.[47] Uber required drivers to identify themselves through a facial recognition app, but this software malfunctioned in the recognition of black faces, leading to unjust deactivations of black drivers' profiles. This dispute was probably not the result of intentional racism on Uber's part, since the unlawful deactivation of well-performing drivers also hurts Uber's own business. It was rather the outcome of ignorant data experts relying on software only or predominantly tested on white facial recognition. Unbeknownst to themselves, data experts influence social hierarchies with their design choices. They mask systemic racial disparities as what seems like mere "bugs in the system." Once these algorithmic errors form a pattern, these are no longer one-off mistakes, but a "hidden curriculum" that expresses which bodies and faces can be considered normal and desirable or not.

Nocebo-effect. A third and final issue with manipulative technology is what Illich calls "the nocebo-effect."[48] The well-known placebo-effect occurs when medical patients get better without receiving genuine medical treatment, through the sheer power of belief. The nocebo-effect is its mirror image: people receive actual medical treatment, but in the long run it makes them worse off. For Illich, "medical procedures turn into black magic when, instead of mobilizing his self-healing powers, they transform the sick man into a limp and mystified voyeur of his own treatment."[49] The mass deployment, for instance, of antibiotics or opioid-based painkillers erodes the body's capacity to heal itself and teaches people to not take care of themselves and others in a vernacular manner. They should supposedly trust commodified health services and pills rather than their commonly developed skills embodied in folk traditions. Though medical treatment is obviously crucial to people's survival, the abstract reassurance that "science will solve all" leaves people dangerously dependent on medication and health experts. It risks imprisoning them in a sterile world entirely built according to professional medical standards. According to Illich,

> In many a village in Mexico I have seen what happens when social security arrives. For a generation people continue in their traditional beliefs; they know how to deal with death, dying, and grief. The new nurse and the doctor, thinking they know better, teach them about an evil pantheon of clinical deaths each one of which can be banned, at a price. Instead of modernising people's skills for self-care, they preach the ideal of hospital death. By their ministration they urge

the peasants to an unending search for the good death of international description, a search that will keep them consumers forever.[50]

Such overreliance is especially painful for those unable to pay for these services, as it first incapacitates people's vernacular skills and subsequently denies them access to the newly commodified service.

Ultimately, the nocebo-effect entails that people are obliged to live in a "plastic womb,"[51] an artificially created and maintained environment that protects their frail and incapacitated bodies from an outside world they can no longer master. Antibiotics, for instance, might cure some life-threatening diseases, but overuse obliges people to engage in an unwinnable arms race with drug-resistant bacteria. The deeper one travels in this plastic womb, the more exposed one becomes to threats from the outside. The dependency effect fostered by radical monopolization is, thereby, consolidated with no way back. The same has occurred, with catastrophic results, in the US opioid crisis.[52] People in economically disadvantaged regions often report pain symptoms and suffer from "deaths of despair,"[53] but rather than dealing with the underlying social problems, doctors tend to individualize and medicalize these issues. In the United States, they have prescribed addictive drugs to allow their patients to keep living in a plastic womb of painlessness while letting the underlying social and political inequalities fester. Rather than teaching patients how to independently face their problems, it was easier to make them dependent on drugs. People are still marginalized and suffering from pain, but now they are also addicted to pain medication.

Digital platforms foster their own version of the nocebo-effect, though this effect is more important in social media than in the gig economy per se. Workers rarely have a strong emotional attachment to their smartphone or their gigs that would make them crave for platform engagement. Nonetheless, they suffer from inclinations for short-term gratification leading to long-term disadvantage.[54] Especially the practice of gamifying gig work leads individuals to pursue instant dopamine hits despite the negative long-term effects on their health. Rosa accuses online media of creating a fleeting sense of "being in touch with the world" without generating any long-term effects on users' lives.[55] Smartphone apps grant workers instant access to the market where gigs are allocated, but this instant access does not translate into actual control over one's own precarious conditions. The addictive interface of apps like Uber's or Deliveroo's present the illusion of control by presenting the acquisition of work as a game, while keeping work precarious. Workers subsequently pursue the pleasure of winning a would-be video game at the cost of long-term sustainable working conditions. The repeated attempt to micro-control one's work obscures the fact that, in the long run, actually gratifying work is out of reach.

The nocebo-effect is, however, clearest in people's social media habits. Here, it is not just a matter of generating the illusion of gamified control to obscure long-term precarity, but also of inducing users to desire illusory cocoons. William Davies notes, for example, how individuals can suffer from smartphone withdrawal, showcasing the same symptoms as PTSD victims.[56] When they hear a push notification but are unable to check it, many smartphone users get unbearably anxious. They become overwhelmed with stress and the fear of missing out, fully knowing that most notifications are unimportant. It shows that people can become structurally and physically dependent on the dopamine shots they get from instant online gratification.[57] Social media bathes us in a womb of filter bubbles. The downside of this protective 'technological cocoon'[58] is that the offline world loses much of its appeal. We become unaccustomed to the slow and resistant pace of everyday life that has not passed through an Instagram filter. Offline, interactions are not specifically tailored to make us feel good about ourselves or confirm our every whim. The require the slow work of conjunction. The more one relies on online gratification techniques and the warmth of the platform womb, the less one is able to stand the coldness of analogue reality.

Even more extremely, Hartmut Rosa observes that the smartphone

> is capable of informing us, with much greater accuracy and precision than we ourselves can muster, where exactly we are at the moment, how the weather is there (temperature, humidity, barometric pressure, visibility, etc.), how the world around us is constituted, even what we did yesterday, what we will do tomorrow (appointment calendars), whether we are tired, whether we have gotten enough exercise, what we like and don't like, who our friends are, and ultimately, who we are.[59]

Our smartphone knows our lives and our environment probably much better than we ourselves do, but this comes at a cost. Technology surreptitiously takes over the thinking process itself. We can no longer think clearly without digital support systems informing us of basic information about the world and ourselves. "An inability to feel, sense, or hear ourselves has become a key symptom of this loss," according to Rosa.[60] In interviews with teenagers who use social media, Sherry Turkle confirms this diagnosis. She reports they are not only incapable of being alone without feeling a pressing anxiety to "stay connected," but they also cannot master their own thought-processes without immediately externalizing them through social media. Only by posting about their feelings, can they actually experience those sensations themselves. They need immediate feedback to think and feel. "Things move from 'I have a feeling, I want to make a call' to 'I want to have a feeling, I need to make a call,' or in her case, send a text. What is not being cultivated is the ability to be alone and reflect on one's emotions in private."[61] Thinking itself is outsourced to machines.

3. TOWARD A DEFINITION OF CONVIVIAL AUTONOMY

Despite pessimistic considerations about modern technology, Illich is not a technophobic thinker nor a one-sided critic of digital technology. On the contrary, he was even among the first, in the 1970s already, to promote the use of the internet, more specifically to connect people to form study groups outside the official education system.[62] For Illich, the internet heralded a promising route for a new common-based sharing economy, though he died too early to see this promise subverted. Illich defends so-called "convivial technologies" as an alternative to manipulative technologies. The former are technologies that augment rather than undermine human autonomy. In his opinion,

> Scientific discoveries can be used in at least two opposite ways. The first leads to specialisation of functions, institutionalisation of values and centralisation of power and turns people into accessories of bureaucracies and machines. The second enlarges the range of each person's competence, control, and initiative, limited only be other individuals' claims to an equal range of power and freedom.[63]

Though Illich criticizes the education system, cars, and TV, for instance, he favors libraries, bikes, and telephones. The question is to determine the criteria for this second form of autonomy-enhancing technology. Unfortunately, however, Illich does not demarcate a clear definition of the constituent values of convivial autonomy. He describes convivial autonomy as follows:

> To the degree that [an individual] masters his tools, he [sic] can invest the world with his meaning; to the degree that he is mastered by his tools, the shape of the tool determines his own self-image. Convivial tools are those which give each person who uses them the greatest opportunity to enrich the environment with the fruits of his or her vision.[64]

Illich's description provides three pillars: (1) the need for independence from one's tools, (2) the requirement of self-determination in mastering one's tools and environment, and (3) the potential for the world to subsequently be invested with meaning and the fruits of human vision. The work performed with convivial tools creates a lifeworld in which people are happy to dwell and call their home. These three characteristics oppose the three counter-productivities mentioned in the previous section. Where radical monopolies foster dependency, convivial technologies promote independence; where manipulative tools concentrate power among a small professional elite, convivial tools cultivate collective self-determination; where the nocebo-effect condemns individuals to a precarious and artificial plastic womb, convivial tools are embedded in vernacular practices that foster a sense of resonance and belonging in one's lifeworld. Allow me to discuss each of these criteria in greater detail.

(1) Independence. Radical monopolies make people dependent on privately owned mediating technologies to access essential social goods. Convivial technologies, on the other hand, undermine this dependency effect. One of Illich's favorite examples is the printing press in early modernity.[65] Previously, the Church had held a radical monopoly over education and information acquisition. The Church and its priestly elites determined which and how knowledge was disseminated, but the printing press enabled the mass production and circulation of books outside the confines of established institutions, giving rise to the modern scientific revolution and a surge in popular writings. Since silent reading had not yet been widespread, the reading of books in a loud voice was, furthermore, a communal vernacular practice. Popular writing was not a source of esoteric, monopolized information, but an occasion for people gathering together to listen and discuss stories. Someone would read a book aloud, while others commented on the passages read and discussed the content amongst each other. The printing press thereby encouraged the collective use of reason rather than obedient internalization of Church teachings. However, Illich adds that this practice for independent literary dissemination quickly ended with the rise of the modern nation-state.[66] The latter imposed homogenous grammatical and narrative forms on people's everyday speech to stifle the uncontrollable spread of ungoverned words. It promoted the school-taught mother tongue as an alternative to local vernacular dialects, granting a radical monopoly on proper language use to grammarians and teachers. Language acquisition and the education system in general gradually became a prerogative of the state, creating a new radical monopoly over learning in the state-licensed school system. The printing press' importance as a convivial tool was, thus, short-lived, yet Illich reminds us not to forget its roots in enabling vernacular culture to render itself independent from Church teachings.

(2) Self-determination. Autonomy not only requires independence, but also the collective capacity to pursue one's own ends rather than those of professional experts. Illich frames the aspiration for self-determination as a response to human frailty, to which technology is an answer:

> Humans, through their own fault, are weakened and must survive in an environment they themselves have damaged. Science, then, is the search for a remedy

for this painful condition. Thus, the primary emphasis is the attempt to relieve human weakness, not to control, dominate or conquer nature for the purpose of turning it into a pseudo-paradise.[67]

Human beings are fallible and finite creatures, and technology is a means to extend the range of possibilities open to individuals.[68] What is to be avoided, on the other hand, is that technology becomes a weapon for professional elites to dominate nature and the population independently from democratic input. As mentioned, vernacular culture is rooted in immanent relations of care among constitutively vulnerable beings without top-down administrative control. Convivial technologies enable communities to support each other and themselves where their sheer bodily and mental force do not suffice and where, otherwise, professional elites would dispossess people from their capacity for self-determination. Such tools grant access to potentialities beyond the limits of what a human body can do on its own in order to augment people's capacities to collectively shape their own lives. Illich contrasts libraries to the education system to illustrate this dimension.[69] The latter houses an expertocracy that imposes preestablished curricula on the population. Institutional constraints thereby dispossess the population from the ability to choose what is learned and how. Libraries, on the other hand, grant students access to learning resources without predetermining for them how to navigate themselves among the books. This grants students the liberty to set their own goals and interests, effectively expanding the reach of their curiosity.

(3) Resonance. It should be clear by now, that the capacity for collective self-determination is not a goal in itself, as for Negri, but serves to strengthen vernacular culture. Independent self-determination is not yet freedom or a good life if one does not find one's choices worthwhile. According to Illich, people should have "the freedom to make things *among which they can live.*"[70] They should be able to identify with the products of their practices on an affective level. In *Gender,* Illich devotes a section to explaining the difference between homes and apartments.[71] The latter is a spatial facility that allows for the continued survival of human beings in a plastic womb. All comforts are taken care of, but in a fundamentally sterile and anonymized setting. The apartment does not bear the imprint of its inhabitants' everyday life. "It is the address at which wires and traffic lines, postmen and police can reach and service those who are healthy, sane, and civilian, those who survive outside institutions on Valium, TV, and supermarket deliveries."[72] Making a home, on the other hand, requires a space not made *for* people, but *by* people. Its character derives from the human meanings that have sedimented in its furniture and on its walls. The pictures in the living room, the rust on the kitchen sink, and the worn-off colors of the sofa build the home's

unique character. The latter manifests long periods of vernacular community that have slowly shaped the house into a place for living and dwelling, where "to dwell means to live in the traces that past living has left."[73] Vernacular togetherness fosters tools that are not just practical but that gradually incarnate people's intimate relations. The objects in a home carry the imprint and memory of the people who lived there and the relations of care they fostered among each other.

Convivial autonomy should, in other words, serve "the poetic ability" in humankind.[74] Autonomous use of technology requires feeling invested in one's independent and self-determined work, like a poet feels invested in her writing. Illich does not have a specific name for this common reverberation between human beings and their self-instituted lifeworld, but one could use Hartmut Rosa's notion of "resonance." It is a metaphor from music theory, where "resonance" designates the responsive vibrations between two tuning forks.[75] If one starts resounding, the other responds in kind echoing the same frequency. Rosa finds this an apt description for how individuals and their surroundings ideally respond to each other's actions. Human beings find meaning in the world when they are capable of responding in kind to the vibrations of the lifeworld. This is the kind of back-and-forth adaptation that Illich identifies with vernacular culture. "The basic mode of vibrant human existence consists not in exerting control over things but in resonating with them, making them respond to us . . . and responding to them in turn."[76] People derive ontological security from the belief that they are at home in the world they have helped to create. Convivial tools should, hence, aid human beings in rendering the world more responsive to the human quest for meaning, as a craftsman learns to appreciate his material through sustained and respectful engagement with his tools.

4. CONCLUSION

In the previous chapter, I delineated Negri's notion of workers' autonomy as collective self-valorization. It emphasizes workers' independence from capital and their capacity to determine the labor process on their own accord thanks to technological innovation and automation. Problems with this account are, first, its tendency to overemphasize who owns the technical apparatus over the imperatives embedded in the technology itself; second, the reluctance to give workers' autonomy a finality beyond itself which could give determine shape to the post-capitalist future, and, lastly, the failure to couple autonomous decision making with the relations of care that give this process meaning. By the end of this chapter, one can regard Illich's notion of convivial autonomy as addressing these concerns in a fruitful manner by adding the emphasis on a vernacular culture that must be protected from manipulative tools. Firstly, Illich is less interested in who owns a particular form of technology than how the technology itself is constructed to favor either autonomy or dependency. As he writes, "the hypothesis was that machines can replace slaves," as post-workerism also promises, but "the evidence shows that, used for this purpose, machines enslave men."[77] Counterproductive tendencies, like radical monopolization, expertocratisation, and the nocebo-effect are built into the design of the general intellect. A mere change in ownership will hence not suffice for a genuine postgrowth transition for Illich. Turning to the digital gig economy in the next chapter, this means that the promotion of workers' convivial autonomy will mean dealing with platform design and not merely with legal ownership. Also, Illich's embedding of the politics for autonomy in a defense of vernacular culture gives autonomy a purpose beyond itself and a direction for its elaboration. One now knows why and to what end workers' autonomy must be encouraged. The aim is to repurpose platform technology such that it enables workers to engage in vernacular relations rather than merely formatting them in a preestablished system of connectivities. Lastly, the notion of convivial autonomy respects the chiasmic bond between autonomy and human interdependence through this focus on the vernacular. For Illich, human beings are constitutively vulnerable and finite beings who can survive and thrive in a common lifeworld by caring for each other. Autonomous convivial technology is, in this context, a means to overcome the capacities of the finite human body and mind to strengthen the capacities for care human beings develop in the vernacular interactions. What this means specifically for the digital gig economy is the focus of the next chapter.

NOTES

1. For a biography, see Todd Hartch, *The Prophet of Cuernavaca: Ivan Illich and the Crisis of the West* (Oxford: Oxford University Press, 2015); David Cayley, *Ivan Illich: An Intellectual Journey* (University Park: The Pennsylvania State University Press, 2021).

2. See Marco Derlu, "Autonomy," in *Degrowth: A Vocabulary for a New Era*, ed. Giacomo D'Alisa, Federico DeMaria, and Giorgos Kallis (London: Routledge, 2014), 55–58.

3. André Gorz, *Capitalism Socialism Ecology*, trans. Chris Turner (London: Verso Books, 1994), 4–6; Tim Jackson, *Post Growth: Life after Capitalism* (Cambridge: Polity Press, 2021), 27.

4. Ivan Illich, *Shadow Work* (London: Marion Boyars, 1981), 9. See also Silja Samerski, "Tools for Degrowth? Ivan Illich's Critique of Technology Revisited,"

Journal of Cleaner Production 197 (2018): 1637–46; Vincent Liegey and Anitra Nelson, *Exploring Degrowth: A Critical Guide* (London: Pluto Press, 2020), 34–35.

5. Ivan Illich, *Gender* (New York: Pantheon Books, 1982), 82.

6. Serge Latouche, *Petit Traité de La Décroissane Sereine* (Paris: Editions de Mille et une Nuit, 2007), 85; Liegey and Nelson, *Exploring Degrowth*, 12.

7. Latouche, *Petit Traité de La Décroissane Sereine*, 54; Soper, *Post-Growth Living*, 50.

8. Gorz, *Capitalism Socialism Ecology*, 13.

9. Soper, *Post-Growth Living*, 1.

10. Illich, *Tools for Conviviality*, 64.

11. Dara Khosrowshahi, "Driving a Green Economy," Uber Newsroom, 8 September 2020, https://www.uber.com/newsroom/driving-a-green-recovery/.

12. See Crawford, *Atlas of AI*, 23–51.

13. Schor, *After the Gig*, 114–18; Greg Bensinger, "For Uber and Lyft, the Rideshare Bubble Bursts," *New York Times*, 17 October 2021, https://www.nytimes.com/2021/10/17/opinion/uber-lyft.html.

14. Timothy Mitchell, *Carbon Democracy: Political Power in the Age of Oil* (London: Verso Books, 2013), 129.

15. Illich, *Tools for Conviviality*, 64.

16. Cleaver, "The Inversion of Class Perspective."

17. André Gorz, *Critique of Economic Reason*, trans. Gillian Handyside and Chris Turner (London: Verso Books, 1989), 58; Liegey and Nelson, *Exploring Degrowth*, 42–43.

18. Latouche, *Petit Traité de La Décroissane Sereine*, 72.

19. Soper, *Post-Growth Living*, 6.

20. Liegey and Nelson, *Exploring Degrowth*, 40–41.

21. Gorz, *Capitalism Socialism Ecology*, 58–59.

22. Soper, *Post-Growth Living*, 86.

23. Illich, *Gender*, 49–50.

24. Illich, *Shadow Work*, 38–40.

25. Ivan Illich and Barry Sanders, *ABC: The Alphabetization of the Popular Mind* (New York: Vintage Books, 1989), 53.

26. Illich, *Shadow Work*, 66.

27. On the notion of lifeworld in degrowth, see Gorz, *Critique of Economic Reason*, 173–80.

28. Illich, *Shadow Work*, 71.

29. Illich, 24.

30. For the Christian theological background of Illich's theory of vernacular culture, see Ivan Illich and David Cayley, *The Rivers North of the Future: The Testament of Ivan Illich* (Toronto: House of Anansi, 2005); Ivan Illich, *Powerless Church and Other Selected Writings, 1955–1985* (University Park: The Pennsylvania State University press, 2018).

31. Cayley, *Ivan Illich*, 289.

32. Illich, *Shadow Work*, 24.

33. Illich, *Tools for Conviviality*, 65.

34. Ivan Illich, "Energy and Equity," in *Toward a History of Needs* (New York, NY: Pantheon Books, 1978), 130.
35. Ivan Illich, *Medical Nemesis: The Expropriation of Health* (New York: Pantheon Books, 1982), 42.
36. Illich, *Tools for Conviviality*, 22.
37. See Christiaens, "Convivial Autonomy and Platform Capitalism."
38. Couldry and Mejias, *The Costs of Connection*, 107.
39. Ivan Illich, *Disabling Professions* (London: Marion Boyars, 1987), 15.
40. Ivan Illich, *Deschooling Society* (London: Marion Boyars, 2002), 41.
41. Illich, *Disabling Professions*, 12.
42. Mueller, *Breaking Things at Work*, 132.
43. Tarleton Gillespie, *Custodians of the Internet* (New Haven: Yale University Press, 2018), 80.
44. Zuboff, *The Age of Surveillance Capitalism*, 189.
45. Gillespie, *Custodians*, 119.
46. Couldry and Mejias, *The Costs of Connection*, 144. For more on discriminatory algorithms, see Eubanks, *Automating Inequality*; Safiya Umoja Noble, *Algorithms of Oppression: How Search Engines Reinforce Racism* (New York: New York University Press, 2018); Crawford, *Atlas of AI*, 123–49.
47. Robert Booth, "Ex-Uber Driver Takes Legal Action over 'Racist' Face-Recognition Software," The Guardian, 5 October 2021, https://www.theguardian.com/technology/2021/oct/05/ex-uber-driver-takes-legal-action-over-racist-face-recognition-software.
48. Illich, *Medical Nemesis*, 114.
49. Illich, 114.
50. Illich, 204–5.
51. Illich, 257.
52. William Davies, *Nervous States: Democracy and the Decline of Reason*, First American edition (New York: W.W. Norton & Company, 2018), 106–7.
53. See Anne Case and Angus Deaton, *Deaths of Despair and the Future of Capitalism* (Princeton, NJ: Princeton University Press, 2021).
54. Jones, *Work without the Worker*, 59.
55. Hartmut Rosa, *Resonance: A Sociology of the Relationship to the World*, trans. James Wagner (Medford, MA: Polity Press, 2019), 92.
56. Davies, *Nervous States*, 112.
57. Sherry Turkle, *Alone Together: Why We Expect More from Technology and Less from Each Other* (New York: Basic Books, 2011), 227.
58. Turkle, 228.
59. Rosa, *Resonance*, 430–31.
60. Rosa, 431.
61. Turkle, *Alone Together*, 176.
62. See Illich, *Deschooling Society*, 72–104.
63. Illich, *Tools for Conviviality*, 12.
64. Illich, 34.
65. Illich, 79; Illich, *Shadow Work*, 70.

66. Illich, *Shadow Work*, 33–34.
67. Illich, 84.
68. Samerski, "Tools for Degrowth," 1640.
69. Illich, *Shadow Work*, 16–17.
70. Illich, *Tools for Conviviality*, 24. My emphasis.
71. Illich, *Gender*, 118–26.
72. Illich, 120.
73. Illich, 119.
74. Illich, *Tools for Conviviality*, 75.
75. Rosa, *Resonance*, 164.
76. Hartmut Rosa, *The Uncontrollability of the World*, trans. James Wagner (Cambridge: Polity Press, 2020), 31.
77. Illich, *Tools for Conviviality*, 23.

Chapter 8

Toward Convivial Platform Labor

Our present problem is taking the conditions of production substantially as we find them, to reintroduce into industry the communal spirit by re-fashioning industrialism in such a way as to set the communal motives free to operate.

—*G.D.H. Cole*

8.1 REKINDLING THE PROMISE OF THE SHARING ECONOMY

Early internet enthusiasts presented the advent of the web as an emancipatory promise. Technical advancement would maximize opportunities for collective autonomy. People would be able to communicate with each other for free across the globe without having to submit to any centralized authority. With the invention of digital platforms, people would even acquire the quasi-divine power to create and curate their own worlds *ex nihilo*. In the 2010s, this promise got a new inflexion with the emergence of the so-called "sharing economy." Digital connection could purportedly be harnessed to share idle resources. Instead of booking expensive hotel rooms, tourists could couch surf via Airbnb; instead of everyone owning a car, people could share rides with Uber; instead of renting and decorating expensive office space, start-up companies could share predecorated free space with WeWork. The sharing economy also promised more autonomy for workers. The latter would supposedly be able to get rid of their boss, download an app, and start working for themselves on their own terms. However, the promise remained unfulfilled. The sharing economy quickly devolved into mere rhetoric to justify the emergence of a precarious digital gig economy. Privately owned platforms like Uber, Deliveroo, or TaskRabbit have turned the sharing economy into an algocracy where algorithms take absolute control rather than introducing a realm of freedom for workers. In the gig economy, workers are at the mercy of unaccountable artificial intelligence that monitors their work more meticulously than a human supervisor ever could have. Workers' autonomy is structurally impeded by exploitation, alienation, and the exhaustion of the workforce.

Post-workerists often argue for "platform expropriation" (i.e., workers seizing digital platforms through revolutionary struggle and making them serve workers themselves).[1] But not only does it remain unclear how workers' struggles in the streets of London or Mumbai could expropriate gaseous global corporations with HQs in Silicon Valley, but they also fail to explain how workers' autonomy would be organized beyond the horizon of the revolution, as discussed in chapter 6. More attention is required to the institutional framework of labor platforms. I have argued that Illich's notion of convivial autonomy presents an occasion to rethink this institutional dimension and rekindle the promise of the sharing economy, but this also lacks an institutional dimension. The concept of convivial autonomy values technologies respectful of personal independence, collective self-determination, and the longing for resonant relationships, but which forms of governance does that require? What should the digital gig economy look like to guarantee workers' convivial autonomy?

I will focus on one institutional proposal in particular: the platform cooperative. The central idea of platform cooperativism is that the nature of digital information as common goods is ideal for the establishment of user cooperatives.[2] Ownership and control over digital platforms should be allocated to digital users themselves. This keeps free markets in place but annuls the capital/labor-hierarchy within the firm in favor of workers' direct democratic self-governance. As already mentioned, social cooperation in the digital realm is a common. The online multitude does not require central direction to organize itself. Monetary value often derives from legal technicalities, like copyright laws, that render digital information *artificially* scarce and opaque, but in itself digital information can be free and transparent to all. Platform cooperativists apply this idea to the governance of all digital platforms, though I am mainly interested in its application to labor platforms. The knowledge and resources for how to make digital labor platforms is held in common and can be used to support cooperatives rather than privately owned corporations.[3] Platform cooperativism combines the emphasis on solidarity and bottom-up democratization from the cooperativist movement with the digital freedoms from hacker culture.[4] According to Zygmuntowski, "the core premise of platform cooperativism, then, is to clone the 'technological heart' of the new, digital platforms . . . while redesigning algorithms and the ownership structure so that they become transparent, democratic, and revenue-distributive in nature."⁵ Digital information wants to be free and cooperatives are the best institution to govern this free flow of information.

A few examples to illustrate the practice of platform cooperativism. Stocksy United is a highly successful global cooperative that accepts and distributes royalty-free stock photography. Photographers can get a profile on Stocksy to exhibit their work and, in exchange, Stocksy takes a cut from photographers' revenue—a cut much lower than that of its competitors. The multitude of artists hire a limited staff to run the company, but all major decisions are democratically enacted. Another famous platform cooperative is Fairbnb, a cooperative alternative to Airbnb. It is a home-sharing platform, started in 2016 in Amsterdam, Venice, and Bologna, aiming to amend some of Airbnb's flaws. To combat the gentrifying and alienating effects of Airbnb on city centers, some municipal governments chose to partner up with Fairbnb to provide tourists with an ethical alternative.⁶ Hosts govern the platform directly and Fairbnb commits itself to environmentally sustainable urban travel. CoopCycle, thirdly, is a cooperative started in France that puts delivery couriers in control of their own platforms. It was founded after the Nuits Debout protests of 2015 as a way of institutionalizing some of the democratic aspirations of the movement. It is less interested in organizing food delivery itself, but rather distributes the software and knowhow to local initiatives with which the latter can establish their own food delivery apps. It thereby supports local workers to set up their own cooperative alternatives to Deliveroo or UberEats across the world.

In what follows, I will first respond to some preliminary criticisms to platform cooperativism. Especially Marxists often accuse cooperativists of being politically and economically naïve because capitalist firms can easily parasitize on the value produced by non-capitalist cooperatives and the discipline of capitalist competition ultimately forces cooperatives to become just as exploitative as their corporate counterparts. Afterward, I highlight how cooperatives can engender a workplace culture conducive to convivial autonomy by reviving the legacy of guild socialism as evinced by British socialist G. D. H. Cole. By encouraging adherence to a common artisanal identity, cooperatives can create among workers the preliminary conditions of possibility for the formation of convivial communities. Lastly, I will explain how each of Illich's criteria of convivial autonomy—independence, collective self-determination, and resonance—are reflected in the institutional design of such guild-like platform cooperatives.

8.2 PRELIMINARY CRITICISMS

Platform cooperativism is contested, especially among Marxists.[7] The first problem concerns the potential for capitalist parasitism. Since platform cooperativism promotes the governance of digital space as a common, it is easy for private corporations to extract data and knowledge from their cooperative competitors and privatize these resources. If cooperatives come up with innovative designs or amass valuable data without calling upon intellectual property law to privatize these goods, corporate rivals can simply copy this information for their own purposes. Privately owned platforms could outcompete platform cooperatives by combining the latter's open-access data with their own. To this particular challenge, there is, however, an easy solution: not all commons should be open access. Proponents of platform cooperativism argue that cooperatives should only share digital common goods with other cooperatives, while demanding a fee from capitalist firms that wish to access the same information. The latter, subsequently, have to pay rent to the cooperatives.[8] By establishing so-called "peer production licenses,"[9] platform cooperatives can internally organize as commoners, while externally fending off competitors. Not all common goods have to be open access.

The second, more troublesome worry is that cooperatives are embedded in capitalist market structures and thus eventually "forced to become their own capitalists," as Marx wrote about nineteenth-century cooperatives.[10] Capitalism imposes competitive pressures on all firms alike, meaning that companies that refuse to exploit, alienate, or fatigue workers tend to be outcompeted by others that do. Economic survival allegedly depends on *systemic* ruthlessness, independently of whether managers *want* to oppress their workers. Cooperatives are purportedly doomed to either remain loyal to their principles but be outcompeted or abandon their ideals and become just as oppressive as any other capitalist firm. According to Rosa Luxemburg, workers "are obliged to play the role of capitalist entrepreneur toward themselves—a contradiction that accounts for the usual failure of cooperatives in production, which either become pure capitalist enterprises or, if the workers' interests continue to predominate, end by dissolving."[11] In the case of digital platforms, cooperativism allegedly hesitates between presenting itself as a more efficient alternative to privately owned platforms (e.g. Resonance, a cooperative alternative to Spotify) or as a radical postcapitalist alternative (e.g. Fairbnb).[12] Cooperative platforms purportedly have to choose between their founding ideals and the reality of capitalist competition.

The applicability of this argument to the platform economy is, however, doubtful. In contrast to nineteenth-century industrial capitalism, today's digital markets do not function under ordinary competitive conditions. Privately owned platforms are often backed by billions of venture capital and count on legal loopholes in labor law to stay financially afloat. Their business model is thus more fragile than that of nineteenth-century capitalist manufacturers. Companies like Uber or Deliveroo cannot operate under conditions of pure competition either. They need not only external investments but also government regulations that exempt them from laws that apply to competitors. *Ergo*, the more labor protections workers acquire through judicial decisions and legal reform and the fewer venture capitalists invest in the digital gig economy, the worse privately owned platforms' financial prospects become. In multiple countries, workers have won legal cases against platform companies. It is certainly not clear whether platform companies will keep profiting from the legal loopholes their business model depends on. Moreover, both Uber's and Deliveroo's stocks flopped when they were first sold on the open financial markets.[13] Commentators have sometimes explained this disappointing financial performance as a consequence of investors' moral concerns about labor practices in the digital gig economy. Given that Amazon's or Zalando's stock prices do not suffer from the same problem, however, it is much more likely that financial investors do not believe in the long-term viability of labor platforms.[14]

From this perspective, platform cooperatives appear not as genuine competitors of privately owned platforms but as substitutes that can step in whenever the latter crash. Cooperatives do not have to outcompete their corporate rivals. Whenever the venture capital investments dry out, there should just be a cooperative ready to take over. The latter can be financed either through public-common partnerships or through collaborations with factions of capital more sympathetic to ethical consumption.[15] Local governments and ethical companies can form a temporary counterweight to venture capital until privately owned platforms run out of investments. Especially due to digital markets' monopolistic tendencies, it matters to be first on the scene when cracks appear in the system. Whichever company gets into the game first, will probably amass most users and possess the most valuable database. In 2016, for example, the city of Austin in Texas experienced such a shift from private to cooperative platforms in the ride-hailing sector.[16] Uber and Lyft had left the city overnight due to a legal dispute with the municipal government.[17] Both knew their operations would not be profitable if they had to abide by new municipal regulations, so it was for them financially impossible to stay. The city used this economic vacuum as an opportunity to invest in more sustainable alternative platforms: a nonprofit called "RideAustin" and a worker cooperative called "ATX." These initiatives thrived in the environment created, yet abandoned by their corporate predecessors. They show that platform cooperativism is a sustainable organizational form, granted that they constitute successors to rather than competitors of privately-owned platforms.

8.3 FOSTERING A COMMUNITY OF PLATFORM ARTISANS

There is a third problem that requires separate attention. Cooperatives promise to abolish the capital/labor hierarchy in workplace governance, but the empirical record shows that new hierarchies often emerge. Cooperatives sometimes reproduce social inequalities of class, race, and gender in their own internal governance.[18] If ownership of capital no longer guarantees status, people often invent new ways to distinguish themselves from the crowd, which undoes cooperativists' good intentions. Juliet Schor, for instance, mentions the unfortunate demise of an urban food-sharing cooperative due to implicit classism.[19] The members reveled in food snobbism to showcase their individual cultural capital, but this practice pushed out anyone who did not conform to the latest trends in hipster cuisine. Outsiders were surreptitiously kept out through the ruthless application of an implicit and opaque rulebook about food trends. Ultimately, the project was unsuccessful, and the members gave up. Internal elitism also haunts digital cooperative initiatives.[20] Wikipedia, for instance, is officially a peer-to-peer network run by its own members, but, in reality, rigid hierarchies dominated by middle-class white men curate the platform.[21] Such hierarchies tend to homogenize and hierarchize rather than diversify and equalize Wikipedia's user base. Democratic intentions do not automatically translate into democratic platforms. This risk is particularly worrisome for the digital gig economy, where the workforce is exceptionally diverse and disadvantaged. If cooperatives require membership homogeneity and reproduce internal hierarchies, platform workers might not be the ideal subjects for the cooperativist project.

I honestly do not believe this obstacle can be entirely eliminated. It would be naïve to assume that any institutional form would ever be able to overcome all forms of social conflict in favor of an absolute reconciliation between individual freedom and collective equality.[22] Fostering human autonomy while simultaneously imposing strictly equal power relations is probably unrealistic. But inequality can be managed if social homogeneity and internal hierarchy are established on acceptable grounds, namely through the promotion of a shared artisanal identity. Insofar as hierarchy is established on merit and skills on which there exists consensus among the cooperative's members, the unequal distribution of authority can be considered legitimate. I take inspiration from British twentieth-century socialist thinker G. D. H. Cole's proposal of guild socialism.[23] Cole comes from a long British tradition of cooperativism and craftsmanship linked to thinkers like Robert Owen and William Morris. According to Cole, the mere takeover of the means of production by conquering the state apparatus—as the Russian revolutionaries had done under Lenin—was insufficient to emancipate the working class. This strategy rather replaced capitalist with bureaucratic domination. Cole envisioned a socialist system where the state apparatus would be accompanied by a system of worker-controlled guilds in charge of particular economic sectors. These guilds would be organized in a federative structure with decision-making powers allocated to local worker councils as much as possible. The guilds would ensure workers' democratic control of the sphere of production, while the state would represent other collective interests, like those of consumers. I focus on Cole's reinterpretation of the guild system. In essence, Cole's aim was to embed wage and trade relations in a moral economy of craftmanship.[24] Monetary value should be considered secondary for the coordination of the sphere of production. More important are workers' own professional values about what is to be considered "good work." The guild-system provided an institutional framework for this embedding of labor markets.

The starting position of urban workers in the Middle Ages was not too dissimilar from the predicament of gig workers today. Most workers were migrants from the countryside with minimal skills and personal connections. A major challenge was the lack of support networks and steady incomes, which led workers in the hands of exploitative employers and precarious work arrangements.[25] Workers could not count on a social safety net to secure their sustenance, which pushed them into temporary gig work. There were hardly any official labor contracts or governments willing to enforce minimal labor standards. In response, workers established guilds to protect their interests. The latter provided security by promoting solidarity among peers and mutual aid networks: guilds would provide loans to impoverished members and pay out compensations to the widows of deceased members. To justify these practices of collective solidarity guilds relied on shared responsibilities and aspirations.[26] They organized disparate migratory workers by forming their own common ethos and professional hierarchies. Members were willing to perform their civic duties toward the group because it meant belonging in a professional community. The guilds' internal organization was very hierarchical, but this inequality was based on skill, seniority, and craftmanship, rather than ownership of capital.[27] Artisan-masters were responsible for their own workshops and students.[28] Workers' coordination derived from high-trust relationships built on mutual respect for each other's professional skills. Members invested in their professional reputation to earn peers' respect. A worker could, for instance, only ascend the social ladder by completing a masterpiece and gaining acceptance by his superiors. The guilds might not have been the utopias of radical democratic equality, but they were remarkably effective in the collective organization of work. As Sennett observes,

> The medieval workshop was a home held together more by honour than by love. The master in this house based his authority, concretely, on the transference of skills. This was the surrogate parent's role in child development. He did not "give" love; he was paid to do his particular kind of fathering. . . . In goldsmithing, the child was inducted into an adult code of honour that widened his horizons beyond that of the individual house.[29]

The guild provided a communal space where young workers were gradually educated into a shared artisanal culture. The latter made top-down regulation less necessary in everyday situations. Members shared the same standards of what constituted good work, so guild masters could often trust their students to commit to professional expectations spontaneously. The workforce became increasingly homogenous, not thanks to classist or ethnic forms of exclusion but thanks to these shared communal commitments. All workers shared the same professional values and were bound together through bonds of mutual aid and solidarity.

A similar potential for a guild-like culture of artisans exists in the digital gig economy. The fact that Uber drivers or Deliveroo couriers can spontaneously self-identify as platform workers—rather than primarily according to national or linguistic identity, for instance—shows the potential for a common artisanal ethos. Today already, they often take pride in performing qualitatively good work. Taxi driving or food delivery can be a *métier*, which renders platform work potentially a professional vocation, as was the case in the medieval guild system. The community of photographers connected to Stocksy United are a poignant example. They collaborate across continents because they share an artistic identity with common values and quality standards. This identity also determines internal hierarchies, since successful members have a better professional reputation and gain more income from the platform than others.[30] These inequalities are, however, generally accepted since they are based on professional standing rather than private wealth. Members agree on how good work ought to be evaluated and remunerated without much need for explicit coordination.

Just like the medieval guilds, the platform cooperatives that require such forms of shared collective identity tend to be exclusive when it comes to membership. Aspiring members need to prove their commitment to the professional community. Once a member, workers often have to cultivate civic duties, like spending time in the daily governance of the community and investing in its everyday expenses.[31] One should first prove one's willingness to adapt to the community culture before one is accepted. In the Middle Ages, practices like the masterpiece performed this role of initiation. Today's cooperatives usually accept a subjective expression of allegiance and the investment of money and time. Bauwens, Kostakis, and Pazaitis illustrate this with a discourse analysis of the founding documents of the New Zealand cooperative, Enspiral.[32] The latter is a network of cooperative platforms that emerged from the New Zealand Occupy Wall Street (OWS) faction. It started with Joshua Vial, a freelance computer specialist, but quickly he drew the attention of like-minded colleagues, and today Enspiral is an ecosystem of digital cooperatives that contains a freelance accounting platform (Enspiral Accounting), open-access, decision-making software development (Loomio), a web-development school (Dev Academy), and so on. All members and partner organizations have to share the ethos and commitments of the original OWS inspiration. The marketing material and official documents repeatedly stress the need for "high-trust relationships," "shared values," and "the collective personal sense of commitment." People usually only sacrifice time and energy to endeavors in which they are emotionally involved, so it is crucial for cooperatives with diverse crowds to encourage these forms of emotional involvement. Enspiral is able to keep a diverse community of platforms together by first demanding their commitment to cooperativist principles. This might seem exclusivist at first, but it ensures members will later be willing to perform the civic duties required of them to keep the cooperative alive.

In sum, platform cooperatives can be considered a viable alternative to privately-owned platforms. They can shield themselves from parasitic corporations by establishing peer-licensed production certificates. The latter allow the common use of digital resources for cooperativist organizations, while capitalist outsiders must pay a fee to get access to the same information. The risk of platform cooperatives turning into ruthless exploiters of labor, like their corporate counterparts, is less troubling given that the digital economy does not operate on classically capitalist principles of free market competition. Privately owned platforms rely on venture capital and legal loopholes to stay financially afloat. Struggles for workers' rights directly undermine the financial viability of these companies and paves the way for cooperative alternatives—potentially financed by, for instance, public-common partnerships—to step in when privately owned platforms go bankrupt. Lastly, cooperative businesses tend to require social homogeneity and internal hierarchies to operate successfully. Rather than trying to deny this inclination, I have argued to recall the tradition of guild socialism and plead for a shared ethos of craftmanship with an internal hierarchy based on skill and professional merit. By transposing the culture of craftmanship to platform labor, platform cooperatives could foster a common artisanal identity to workers as a basis for workplace coordination. In the remainder of the chapter, I will explain how this system conforms to Illich's criteria of convivial autonomy, namely workers' independence, collective self-determination, and resonance.

8.4 WORKERS' INDEPENDENCE AND LABOR RIGHTS

Privately owned platforms promote radical monopolism and users' dependency on commodified services. They infiltrate a social field and transform it into a database. They also employ psychological techniques to make workers work more and harder. Because platform workers are often independent contractors without access to the algorithms that govern their work, they can only rarely contest this dependency. Convivial autonomy, on the other hand, "rules out certain levels of power, compulsion, and programming."[33] In a cooperativist system built on professional identity and common ownership and control of digital platforms, workers would presumably grant themselves official employee status by default. The legal self-recognition of workers as employees in a cooperative can create the basis for workers' independence from algorithmic control.[34] Privately owned platforms' profitability often relies on denying workers employee status, but cooperatives need not be bound by the same limitations. Once workers are their own boss, they themselves decide what rights they enjoy, what responsibilities can be expected of them as professional workers, and how disputes between workers and the platform must be adjudicated.[35] They can democratically decide what data the platform extracts and analyses, how much of the work is gamified, and how addictive interfaces can be.

Platform cooperatives could grant workers more independence from the platform by recognizing their "right to log off."[36] Workers would be able to log off the platform at no cost or penalty. This is part of a larger trend in labor relations toward establishing workers' right to disconnect.[37] The latter has already been established in France and Portugal by law, and in Germany some companies have introduced it voluntarily. To a large extent, workers' malaise comes from the incessant obligation to read e-mails, check smartphone notifications, and scan multiple platforms in search for gigs. Privately owned platforms also often penalize workers for logging off or for withdrawing their labor-power at the moments when the latter would profit the platform company. Cooperative platforms limit this incentive for overwork because those affected by the policy are also its makers. By owning the platform themselves, workers can fairly balance the need for having a continuous workforce available with the danger of overwork. This system secures the social reproduction of the workforce since workers themselves decide on the separation between labor time and leisure.

How such a structure would limit the chances of workers' fatigue is obvious, but it would also restrain the excesses of exploitation and alienation previously addressed. With regard to exploitation, if workers retain the capacity to limit their interactions with the platform and the data they share, it is harder for digital platforms to establish radical monopolies over social fields. Platforms cannot cannibalize entire social fields if users can, at any moment, choose to log off without consequences. It creates more space for nonplatform alternatives. The Austin ride-hailing cooperative, ATX, offers a good illustration. It was created in collaboration with the local municipality and was part of a coordinated effort to manage the urban transportation sector. It was not designed to displace public transport or the bicycle. ATX created a ride-hailing platform that only undermined corporate alternatives, but not the more desirable forms of urban transportation. The same power to withhold platform engagement also restrains the potential for alienation. In privately owned platforms, workers contribute to their own subordination by producing the data that subsequently informs the algorithms that steer their conduct. With the right to log off, however, workers can choose not to be mined for data harmful to their autonomy.

8.5 COLLECTIVE SELF-DETERMINATION AND THE LIBRARY OF BASIC PROTOCOLS

The algorithms coordinating the labor process are often the sole dominion of a select group of computer scientists in Silicon Valley. They decide what data is analyzed and how it is used to discipline the workforce, without democratic accountability from the workers subjected to their regulations. By allowing workers themselves to govern the labor process, cooperatives obviously overcome this lack of collective self-determination. A good example of this effort is provided by the French cooperative platform CoopCycle.[38] It is a global federation of cooperative food delivery platforms started in France after the Nuits Debout protests of 2015. The latter was a radical-democratic movement that called for, among others, the democratization of the workplace. CoopCycle has tried to implement these values and now has member organizations in cities across the world. It provides local food delivery cooperatives software support to set up their own food delivery app. The most difficult part of launching a food delivery cooperative is not finding workers or restaurants, but to develop a well-performing platform that efficiently allocates tasks to individual couriers. CoopCycle, however, works hard to avoid the formation of a narrow elite of IT experts in control of local initiatives. By predominantly providing the basic protocols for a platform, CoopCycle distributes the building blocks for food delivery apps without predetermining how its algorithms are supposed to coordinate the workforce. The eventual platform itself is created in collaboration with the local groups themselves. CoopCycle allows local groups to adapt the algorithms to their own context but offers help from in-house IT experts on the technicalities.[39] As Scholz states, the backend of platform cooperatives must be "accessible to the workers so that they can understand the parameters and patterns that govern their working environment."[40]

Scholz's proposal of rendering platform software publicly available recalls Illich's example of libraries as convivial technologies. Instead of unilaterally imposing a biased and preestablished curriculum on all students alike, like the school system, libraries grant access to a wealth of resources in which individuals can find their own way to education. With all resources accessible, individuals can continuously select and adapt their learning process without having to conform to a predetermined curriculum. Similarly, CoopCycle offers workers a library of basic protocols that workers can further develop to fit their specific needs. The algorithms are not set in stone but can be revised according to how workers wish to collectively govern their labor. They combine the aspiration for self-determination from the cooperative movement with the free-software ideals from hacker culture, where the free appropriation and modification of software is a long-standing habit.[41] They turn software into Simondonian "open objects."[42] Digital technologies, and algorithms in particular, are too often designed as "closed objects" (i.e., technologies whose makeup is closed to users' modification attempts). With most Big Tech corporations, the corporate programmers write the basic infrastructure of digital platforms while users have to obey those unilaterally imposed settings as part of the terms and conditions. We cannot reconfigure an Apple iPhone, Uber's pricing algorithm, or Deliveroo's allocation software. These are all fenced-off intellectual property. However, the algorithms underlying the operations of platform companies could and should become vehicles for workers' collective self-organization. As Scholz argues, "free software developers could publish core protocols and then allow various independent open-source projects to build their own different back-end and front-end components."[43] Open objects are tools that invite users' attempt at creative modifications. Instead of delivering finished products, platform providers like CoopCycle produce starter's packages that allow local cooperatives to code their own work schedule. These procedures allow workers to eliminate discriminatory or unfair imperatives from their platforms. As in the medieval guild system, it allows workers to autonomously set the standards for their own labor.

8.6 RESONANCE AND GRASSROOTS SOLIDARITIES

Manipulative technologies in the digital gig economy mobilize addictive interfaces to gamify the working experience. They provide short-term virtual gratification with long-term disadvantages and disappointment, a process which Illich links to the nocebo-effect in medicine. Early enthusiasts of the sharing economy, however, promoted the promise of gig work as an opportunity to establish new meaningful relationships between strangers.[44] One would allegedly find new friends and authentic relationships by having the algorithm of Airbnb or TaskRabbit match complete strangers. Workers quickly discovered that this was false: gig work is predominantly anonymous and too exhausting and alienating to spark genuine human contact. Convivial, resonant technologies, on the other hand, should follow up on the promise of fostering community through digital means, for the promise is not entirely dishonest. Especially in the digital economy, where social cooperation is the main resource of collective wealth, stimulating a sense of genuine community is crucial for the economy's long-term survival.[45]

The guild-like system of platform cooperativism is especially promising on the level of resonant relationships. The medieval guild system provided workers not only a personal support network built on shared values and professional commitments but also an opportunity for developing resonant relationships with the products of their labor.[46] Workers found meaning in the work they performed for the sake of the work itself and that they could regard as an expression of personal self-realization. Individual flourishing and collective coordination largely overlapped. According to Jacques Le Goff, "each man's new consciousness of himself came to him only through the *estate* to which he belonged, the professional group of which he was a part, or the trade in which he engaged. . . . It offered itself in the form of a *vocation*."[47] Insofar as platform labor can be reconceived as a craft, a similar sense of vocation can develop in the digital gig economy. Even today, it is not uncommon for platform workers like Deliveroo couriers to mention they find genuine joy and pride in their labor. Many Deliveroo workers like their job insofar as it allows them to work outside on their bikes. For them, food delivery services literally help them turning their hobby into a profession.

However, not only resonant relationships with one's labor is important; also resonance with one's peers is important to develop a thriving artisanal community. Despite recent bad press, even the staunchest critics admit that online media can generate genuine belonging across time and space.[48] The original promise of the internet and peer-to-peer networks was that they primarily offered "a mode of relationship that allows human beings to be connected and organised in networks to collaborate, produce and share."[49] Even in the digital gig economy today there are already enclaves of resonant communities, but they often exist outside the confines of the tightly controlled worker apps themselves. As Phil Jones argues, "work can offer nourishing forms of community," and the artisanal ethos of the guild previously discussed is one way of institutionalizing this imagined community.[50]

Many gig workers turn to online support for a to find the workplace resonance they lack during their work.⁵¹ In times of trouble—or just for human interaction—workers often establish WhatsApp groups or Facebook communities. As Maffie writes,

While many gig workers may work alone and enjoy the entrepreneurialism of this industry, when a conflict with a customer occurs, they are often unaware of their responsibilities or how to handle the situation. Without co-workers or a union to ask for support, workers turn to their most immediate community: an online network like Facebook. Once part of this group, however, many find that they share grievances with other drivers and enjoy the comradery and support of their digital colleagues.⁵²

Also, Amazon workers meet through online confessionals where they collectively bond over workplace injustices.⁵³ AMT workers have even launched their own platform, TurkerNation, to support each other and organize.⁵⁴ Sometimes, these initiatives also find their way offline. Food delivery apps like Deliveroo's, for example, encourage workers to gather on public squares or in streets close to restaurants to wait for new orders.⁵⁵ These informal meeting spaces generate opportunities for face-to-face contact. The few times that gig workers have succeeded to politically organize, it has often come from these forms of "invisible organization."⁵⁶

Platform cooperatives internalize these grassroots solidarities from the digital platforms already available. Several co-ops are the direct products of collective resistance movements that promoted the implementation of meaningful social relations at work: CoopCycle arose from the Nuits Debout protests in France and Enspiral from Occupy Wall Street in New Zealand. Platform cooperative Loomio even directly produces open-source software to facilitate horizontal decision making in cooperative structures.⁵⁷ Once they are established, they also encourage the cultivation of a common ethos that fosters the creation of resonant relations. Once workers share a collective sense of commitment to the work they perform and their coworkers, they can use the platform as a tool to enhance their common bond. Fernandez-Trujillo Moares, for instance, reports that, in Spain, workers at a Spanish food delivery co-op, refer to each other as "friends" rather than colleagues or competitive rivals.⁵⁸ Rather than the platform's algorithms formatting individuals into preestablished connective networks, genuine resonant relationships developed through everyday democratic involvement determine the platform's algorithmic processes. This might sound utopian, but it is, in reality, the product of hard democratic work. These friendships do not emerge out of nowhere. The day-to-day collaboration required to make a cooperative functional fosters sustained human relationships. Gig workers subsequently become more than mere disconnected pieces of labor-time that algorithms can rearrange at will. They become an organized community that, through collective decision-making, submits the platform's algorithms to its own will. This might come at the cost of exclusivity, where only those who share the ethos and values of the cooperative can join, but it creates the opportunity for collaborative empowerment among workers absent in the current digital gig economy.

8.7 CODA

The rhetoric of the sharing economy promises workers an escape from submission to a boss in favor of a more autonomous working life. By advertising the benefits of entrepreneurial conduct, platform companies have lured many workers at the bottom of the labor market into an experimental venture of labor market deregulation and renewed forms of exploitation. Many gig workers quickly discovered that their digitalized working lives were much less autonomous and entrepreneurial than they had expected. They have primarily substituted their human boss for algorithmic control that is even less receptive to workers' attempts at resistance. Platform cooperatives provide a template for how to improve working conditions in the digital economy today. This is not to say that all platforms must be transformed into cooperatives, but that cooperatives reveal what kind of practices and institutional arrangements encourage workers' autonomy. Platform cooperatives put workers themselves at the helm of the digital infrastructure that coordinates their labor. Whereas platform technology today is predominantly manipulative, because they have to guarantee profits to digital corporations at the cost of workers' well-being, platform cooperatives trigger our political imagination to think about how digital technologies can be used to enhance workers' self-mastery. In so doing, they foster what Illich has called "convivial autonomy": they sustain human independence from digital technology, enhance opportunities for collective self-determination, and support the creation of networks of resonant relationships. For those looking to improve our digital working lives, engaging with the tradition of platform cooperativism seems like a good start.

NOTES

1. Cant, *Riding for Deliveroo*, 150; Jamie Woodcock, *The Fight against Platform Capitalism: An Inquiry into the Global Struggles of the Gig Economy* (London: University of Westminster Press, 2021), 92.

2. See, among others, Trebor Scholz, "Platform Cooperativism vs. the Sharing Economy," Medium, 5 December 2014, https://medium.com/@trebors/platform-cooperativism-vs-the-sharing-economy-2ea737f1b5ad; Trebor Scholz, "Platform

Cooperativism: Challenging the Corporate Sharing Economy' (Rosa Luxemburg Stiftung, 2016); Scholz, *Uberworked and Underpaid*, 148–75; Kessler, *Gigged*, 208–13; Nathan Schneider, "An Internet of Ownership: Democratic Design for the Online Economy," *The Sociological Review* 66, no. 2 (2018): 320–40; Francisco Fernandez-Trujillo Moares, "Delivery Cooperatives, an Alternative to the Great Platforms of the Digital Economy," in *Sharing Society. The Impact of Collaborative Collective Actions in the Transformation of Contemporary Societies*, ed. Benjamin Tejerina (Bilbao: Universidad del País Vasco/Euskal Herriko Unibertsitatea, 2019), 162–71; Nicoli and Paltrinieri, "Platform Cooperativism'; Morshed Mannan and Simon Pek, "Solidarity in the Sharing Economy: The Role of Platform Cooperatives at the Base of the Pyramid," in *Sharing Economy at the Base of the Pyramid*, ed. Israr Qureshi, Babita Bhatt, and Mani Shukla Direndra (New York: Springer, 2021), 249–79.

3. Scholz, "Platform Cooperativism," 14.

4. See McKenzie Wark, *A Hacker Manifesto* (Cambridge, MA: Harvard University Press, 2009); Michel Bauwens, Vasilis Kostakis, and Alex Pazaitis, *Peer to Peer: The Commons Manifesto* (London: University of Westminster Press, 2019).

5. Jan Zygmuntowski, "Commoning in the Digital Era: Platform Cooperativism as a Counter to Cognitive Capitalism," *Praktyka Teoretyczna* 1, no. 27 (2018): 181.

6. Schor, *After the Gig*, 171–74; James Muldoon, *Platform Socialism* (London: Polity Press, 2022), 104.

7. Srnicek, *Platform Capitalism*, 127; Woodcock and Graham, *The Gig Economy*, 139; Papadimitropoulos, "Platform Capitalism, Platform Cooperativism, and the Commons," 255.

8. Michel Bauwens and Vasilis Kostakis, "From the Communism of Capital to Capital for the Commons: Towards an Open Co-Operativism," *TripleC: Communication, Capitalism & Critique* 12, no. 1 (2014): 356–61.

9. Michel Bauwens, "Thesis on Digital Labor in an Emerging P2P Economy," in *Digital Labor: The Internet as Playground and Factory*, ed. Trebor Scholz (London: Routledge, 2012), 389.

10. Karl Marx, *Capital: Vol. 3*, trans. David Fernbach (London: Penguin, 1992), 571.

11. Rosa Luxemburg, "Reform or Revolution," Marxist Internet Archive, 1999, https://www.marxists.org/archive/luxemburg/1900/reform-revolution/index.htm.

12. Marisol Sandoval, "Entrepreneurial Activism? Platform Cooperativism between Subversion and Co-Optation," *Critical Sociology* 46, no. 6 (2019): 801–17; Cant, *Riding for Deliveroo*, 149.

13. Schor, *After the Gig*, 151.

14. Herman Loos, *Homo Deliveroo: Dwangarbeider van de Weg* (Antwerpen: EPO Uitgeverij, 2021), 126.

15. Scholz, "Platform Cooperativism," 21–23; Bauwens, Kostakis, and Pazaitis, *Commons Manifesto*, 12–19; Muldoon, *Platform Socialism*, 104–5.

16. Yifat Solel, "If Uber Were a Cooperative: A Democratically Biased Analysis of Platform Economy," *Law & Ethics of Human Rights* 13, no. 2 (2019): 239–62.

17. Ultimately, Uber and Lyft returned to Austin after successfully lobbying with the Texas State Government to overrule the municipality's regulations of the ride-hailing sector.

18. Sandoval, "Entrepreneurial Activism," 811; Arvidsson, *Changemakers*, 67; Muldoon, *Platform Socialism*, 106.

19. Schor, *After the Gig*, 173–74.

20. Mueller, *Breaking Things at Work*, 112.

21. Schneider, "An Internet of Ownership," 327.

22. For an application to cooperative governance, see Denise Kasparian, *Co-Operative Struggles: Work Conflicts in Argentina's New Worker Co-Operatives*, trans. Ian Barnett (Leiden: Brill, 2022); Tim Christiaens, "Worker Co-Operatives for the 21st Century," *Critical Sociology*, 2022.

23. George D. H Cole, *Guild Socialism Restated* (London: Routledge, 2017); George D. H Cole, *Self-Government in Industry* (London: Routledge, 2017). See also Muldoon, *Platform Socialism*, 80–100.

24. For the concept of moral economy, see Edward P. Thompson, "The Moral Economy of the English Crowd in the Eighteenth Century," *Past and Present*, 50 (1971): 76–136.

25. Gervase Rosser, *The Art of Solidarity in the Middle Ages: Guilds in England 1250–1550* (Oxford: Oxford University Press, 2015), 6; Arvidsson, *Changemakers*, 115.

26. Rosser, *The Art of Solidarity*, 192.

27. Rosser, 161. See also Richard Sennett, *The Craftsman* (London: Penguin, 2009), 55–65.

28. Cole, *Guild Socialism*, 43.

29. Sennett, *The Craftsman*, 64.

30. Schor, *After the Gig*, 166–67.

31. Bauwens, Kostakis, and Pazaitis, *Commons Manifesto*, 39.

32. Alex Pazaitis, Vasilis Kostakis, and Michel Bauwens, "Digital Economy and the Rise of Open Cooperativism: The Case of Enspiral," *Transfer*, 2017, 1–17.

33. Illich, *Tools for Conviviality*, 30.

34. This claim is also made by people outside the cooperativist movement. See, among others, Aloisi and De Stefano, *Il Tuo Capo è Un Algoritmo*, 185–90; Woodcock and Graham, *The Gig Economy*, 124–30.

35. Scholz, "Platform Cooperativism," 13.

36. Scholz, 20; Scholz, *Uberworked and Underpaid*, 183.

37. Rob Kitchin and Alistair Fraser, *Slow Computing: Why We Need Balanced Digital Lives* (Bristol: Bristol University Press, 2020), 109–13; Joana Ramiro, "Everyone Should Have a Right to Disconnect from Work," Jacobin, 22 November 2021, https://jacobinmag.com/2021/11/portugal-right-to-disconnect-law-work-time/.

38. For a history of CoopCycle, see Ana Sofia Acosta Alvarado, Laura Aufrère, and Cynthia Srnec, "CoopCycle, Un Projet de Plateforme Socialisée et de Régulation de La Livraison à Vélo," HAL Archives Ouvertes, 4 October 2021, https://hal.archives-ouvertes.fr/hal-03364001/document.

39. As Scholz and Schneider mention, the best way to make this truly democratic is by encouraging workers themselves to acquire basic IT-skills so they would be able to directly curate the platform according to their own design, without the mediation of experts holding a monopoly on specific necessary skills. Enspiral does this through one of its member organisations, Dev Academy, a cooperative that provides software development education. See Scholz, "Platform Cooperativism," 26; Scholz, *Uberworked and Underpaid*, 191; Schneider, "An Internet of Ownership," 331; Pazaitis, Kostakis, and Bauwens, "Digital Economy," 7.

40. Scholz, "Platform Cooperativism," 23.

41. Mueller, *Breaking Things at Work*, 108.

42. Gilbert Simondon, "La Mentalité Technique," in *Sur La Technique* (Paris: Presses Universitaires de Paris, 2014), 312–13; Christiaens, "Digital Biopolitics and the Problem of Fatigue in Platform Capitalism," 89–90.

43. Scholz, "Platform Cooperativism," 23.

44. Schor, *After the Gig*, 111.

45. Arvidsson, *Changemakers*, 66.

46. See also Rosa, *Resonance*, 233–38.

47. Jacques Le Goff, *Time, Work, & Culture in the Middle Ages* (Chicago: Chicago University Press, 1995), 114.

48. See, for example, Turkle, *Alone Together*, 238.

49. Bauwens, Kostakis, and Pazaitis, *Commons Manifesto*, 2.

50. Jones, *Work without the Worker*, 107.

51. Scholz, *Uberworked and Underpaid*, 166; Heiland and Schaupp, "Breaking Digital Atomisation," 141.

52. Michael David Maffie, "The Role of Digital Communities in Organizing Gig Workers," *Industrial Relations* 59, no. 1 (2020): 132.

53. Delfanti, *Warehouse*, 151.

54. Scholz, *Uberworked and Underpaid*, 169; Kessler, *Gigged*, 35.

55. Cant, *Riding for Deliveroo*, 132; Jones, *Work without the Worker*, 85.

56. Cant, *Riding for Deliveroo*, 130. In some cities, like Athens, political activists have played a key role in fostering these bedrocks of political organisation and mutual aid networks. See, for instance, Woodcock, *The Fight against Platform Capitalism*, 76–77. For more literature on the politics of gig workers and how they organise, see Woodcock and Graham, *The Gig Economy*, 67–94; Gianluca Iazzolino, "'Going Karura': Colliding Subjectivities and Labour Struggle in Nairobi's Gig Economy," *Economy and Space* Online First (n.d.).

57. Scholz, "Platform Cooperativism," 24.

58. Fernandez-Trujillo Moares, "Delivery Cooperatives," 167.

Index

absenteeism, 7
absolute surplus value, 22
Adorno, Theodor W., 7, 22
AI. *See* artificial intelligence
Airbnb, 1–3, 102; algorithmic coordination by, 5; rating systems and, 60, 65–66, 68–71; response rate and commitment rate of, 74n27; superhost system of, 33
airspace aesthetic, 69
algorithmic control, 5, 30–31
alienation, 59–61, 144; ambivalence of general intellect and, 61–66; conclusion to, 71–72; general intellect and, 66–71
Alquati, Romano, 6
Amazon, 1–3, 11, 24–25, 31, 41, 53, 148; COVID-19 pandemic and, 76; growth-before-profit model of, 4–5; tracking algorithms by, 33
Amazon Mechanical Turk (AMT), 32, 70, 89, 148
antibiotics, 125
anti-capitalism, 110, 111n29
Apple, 25, 27, 123
Arbeitskraft. *See* labor-power
artificial intelligence (AI), 49–51, 64
artisans, platform, 140–43
Arvidsson, Adam, 41, 42–43

asignifying semiotics, 30
Assembly (Negri and Hardt), 12, 25
ATX, 139, 145
Aureli, Pier Vittorio, 96
Aurora, 57n52
Austin, Texas, 139, 145
authenticity, 98
autodeterminazione. *See* self-determination
automation, 62–63, 98, 100, 119
autonomist Marxism, 16n45, 95
autonomous working conditions, 11
autonomy, 95–96; collective, 104, 109, 115; convivial, 11–13, 115, 127–30, 136, 144, 149; multitudinal, 101; objections to, 102–9; as self-legislation, 6; as self-valorization, 96–101; struggle for, 6–10; of workers, 109
autoriduzione, 7, 23

Back to the Future (film), 49
Badger, Adam, 50
barriers to entry, 5
Bauwens, Michel, 12, 142
becoming-rent of profit, 45–47
behavioural modification, 33
Bentham, Jeremy, 33

Berardi, Franco "Bifo," 12, 31, 76, 120, 121
biases, 68
Birch, Kean, 40, 47, 49
Black Mirror (TV series), 59
brand management, 34
Braverman, Harry, 22
Broder, David, 104
"bullshit" jobs, 6
Butler, Judith, 106–7

Caffentzis, George, 75
Cant, Callum, 11
capital: accumulation, 28, 46; assembly-line production and, 20; labor-power and, 8–9; multitude and, 45, 98, 102, 104; venture, 4, 50–53, 139
capitalism, 63, 76, 87, 96, 107, 138; anti-capitalism, 110, 111n29; capitalist development, 8; capitalist modernity, 64; growth and, 80; industrial, 97, 138; platform, 41; post-Fordist, 69, 98; social subjection in, 29; wages and, 42
Capital: Volume I (Marx), 9, 21, 62, 77, 78
car driving, 30
Care.com, 39, 44
care labor, 107
Castoriadis, Cornelius, 12, 115
Catholic Church, 29, 115–16, 128
Cavarero, Adriana, 106, 108
Cayley, David, 121
Chayka, Kyle, 69
Chen, Julie, 88
Christophers, Brett, 43
Classe Operaia (journal), 6
Cleaver, Harry, 105
click work, 41
closed objects, 146
coal consumption, 118
Cochrane, D. T., 40, 47, 49
co-creation projects, 26
Cold War, 116
Cole, G. D. H., 13, 135, 137, 140–41

collective autonomy, 104, 109, 115
collective bargaining, 69
collective planning, 99
collective self-determination, 102, 145–46
Colleoni, Elanor, 41, 42–43
commitment rate, of Airbnb, 74n27
the common, 39
Commonwealth (Negri and Hardt), 11
communism: cyborg, 62, 64–65; libertarian, 99; tenets of, 97
conducting materials, 79
connections, 90, 121
convivial autonomy, 11–13, 115, 127–30, 136, 144, 149
convivial technologies, 127, 129
CoopCycle, 137, 145–46
cooperation: abstract, 31; affective, 98; cognitive, 98. *See also* social cooperation
core competences, 28, 34
COVID-19 pandemic, 76
Crawford, Kate, 102
cyborg communism, 62, 64–65
cynicism, 69

Dalla Costa, Mariarosa, 24, 86, 87
data, 56n27; online transactions extracting, 3–4
dating platforms, 47–48
Davies, William, 126
decommodification, 117
degrowth, 115–16
Deleuze, Gilles, 9, 25
Deliveroo, 1, 2, 5, 24, 39, 53, 70
democratization, 136
deskilling, 21, 32
digital capture: enclave rent and, 47–50; financial rent and, 50–53; of social cooperation, 39–41
digital gig economy, 1–2; convivial autonomy in, 11–13; defined, 2–6. *See also specific topics*
digital media, 26, 41
digital rating systems, 59–60, 65–71

digital reputation metric, 67
digital surveillance, of work, 2
digital Taylorism, 25
digital technology, 6, 19, 102; digitalization, 32; post-Fordism and, 28–34
divine creation, 51

Economic and Philosophical Manuscripts of 1844 (Marx), 66, 78
economic value, 41
Empire (Negri and Hardt), 9–12, 25, 104
employment: nonstandard contracts, 27; as personal identity source, 62; traditional, 2; unemployment compared to, 63
enclave rent, 40; digital capture and, 47–50
Enspiral, 143
entry barriers, 5
European Commission, 14n3
exhaustion, 75
expertocratisation, 123
exploitation, 39–40, 144; becoming-rent of profit and, 45–47; conclusion to, 54; digital capture and enclave rent, 47–50; digital capture and financial rent, 50–53; free labor and, 41–45

Facebook, 4, 41, 53, 148; free labor and, 42–43; Like-button of, 45–46
facial recognition, by Uber, 124
factory jobs, 9
factory-society, 19
Fairbnb, 137
Fathers and Sons (Turgenev), 103
fatigue: physical and mental, 80–85; problem of, 77–80
fear, 69
Federici, Silvia, 24, 86, 108
feminism and feminist movement, 23, 86, 106
financial rent, 50–53
Fiverr, 29
Five Star Movement, 105

Ford, Henry, 20
Fordism, 19; assembly-line production, 20; industrial factory under, 20–24; "wages for housework" and, 86–87. *See also* post-Fordism
Foucault, Michel, 9
Foxconn, 27
"The Fragment on Machines" (Marx), 61, 73n7
France, 105, 137, 144
Frankfurt School, 7, 8, 22
free labor, 40, 41–45
Fuchs, Christian, 11, 55n15
function creep, 48, 49–50

Gender (Illich), 129
gendered signifying semiotics, 29
gender relations, 87
gene editing, 100, 104
general intellect, 25, 60, 73n15; alienation and, 66–71; ambivalence of, 61–66
General Motors, 21
gentrification, 72n4; response rate and commitment rate of Airbnb, 74n27
The German Ideology (Marx), 78
Germany, 144
Global Financial Crisis (2007), 1, 2, 75
globalization, 32
global North, 2, 5, 9
global South, 2, 5
Google, 11, 41, 53
Gorz, André, 12, 115, 117
grassroots solidarities, 146–49
growth, 75–77; conclusion, 89–90; degrowth, 115–16; problem of fatigue and, 77–80; radical monopolies and, 122; social reproduction and, 85–89
growth-before-profit model, 4–5
Grundrisse, 36n20, 61
Guattari, Félix, 9
guild socialism, 137, 140, 143

Hardt, Michael, 76, 97, 102–4, 107; *Assembly* by, 12, 25; *Commonwealth* by, 11; *Empire* by, 9–12, 25, 104; on exploitation, 45; general intellect and, 73n15; *Multitude* by, 11; right-wing authoritarian anti-capitalism and, 111n29. *See also* multitude
Hegelianism, 77
Helmholtz, Hermann von, 77
Hobbes, Thomas, 10
Horkheimer, Max, 7
hormone therapies, 100, 104
housework, 107, 119; domestic labor, 24, 86–87
housing market, 65, 72n4
human awareness, bypassing, 31, 33

Illich, Ivan, 13, 115–20, 129; modern technology and, 120–27; philosophy of technology of, 6, 11, 115–20
immaterial labor, 9, 24, 26, 44, 98, 102
independence, 128
independent contractors, 2, 14n3
industrial capitalism, 97, 138
industrial factory, under Fordism, 20–24
industrial labor, 63
intellectual property rights, 99
internet, 12, 41
invisible organization, 148
iPhone, 11, 27, 123
isolation, social, 88
Italy, 6, 7, 86, 105

James, Selma, 24
Jevons, William, 118, 122
Jones, Phil, 147
just-in-time production, 27

Kalanick, Travis, 53
Keynes, John Maynard, 20
Kostakis, Vasilis, 142

labor: care, 107; conditions of, 27; domestic, 24, 86–87; free, 40, 41–45; immaterial, 9, 24, 26, 44, 98, 102; industrial, 63; subsumption of, 21; surplus, 67
labor market, 70
labor-power (*Arbeitskraft*), 42, 76, 78, 85; capital and, 8–9; reproduction of, 77, 87–88; of women, 23–24
labor productivity, intensifying, 21, 22
labor rights, 144–49
labor theory of value, 41, 43–45
Lafargue, Paul, 97, 100, 118
Lane, Don, 75
language, 128; asignifying semiotics and, 30; signifying semiotics and, 28–29; vernacular culture and, 120–21, 129
laziness, 97
Lazzarato, Maurizio, 19, 25–26, 28, 30, 51, 97
lean manufacturing, 27
Le Goff, Jacques, 147
Leibniz, Gottfried Wilhelm, 51–53
libertarian communism, 99
libraries, 13, 129
Like-button, of Facebook, 45–46
living labor, 8
Loach, Ken, 75
Lonzi, Carla, 86
Loomio, 148
Lorde, Audre, 102
Luxemburg, Rosa, 138

machines: as means of labour, 61; social, 19, 20, 27; subjugation, 28, 30
Maffie, Michael David, 148
male-breadwinner model, 23
manipulative tools, 120
manufacturing, lean, 27
Marazzi, Christian, 40
marketing, 34
Marx, Karl, 6, 9, 19–21, 28–29, 62; alienation and, 66, 71–72; fatigue and, 77–80; general intellect and, 60; *Grundrisse* and, 36n20; labor theory of value, 41

Marx beyond Marx (Negri), 95, 96–97, 101
Marxism, 6–7, 43; autonomist, 16n45, 95
mass consumerism, 22
mass production, 20
McJobs, 5
means of labour, machines as, 61
media: digital, 26, 41; social, 26, 42, 45, 126
men, as breadwinners, 23
mental exhaustion, 75, 80–85
Middle Ages, 141, 142
Minca, Claudio, 74n27
Moares, Fernandez-Trujillo, 148
modernity, capitalist, 64
modern technology, 120–27
monetary value, 136, 141
monopolization, radical, 122–25, 128
monopoly, of Uber, 4
Moreno Zacarés, Javier, 46
Morris, William, 140
Moulier Boutang, Yann, 40, 45, 51–52
multitude, 10–12, 76, 99, 109–10, 112n49; capital and, 45, 98, 102, 104; as collective subject, 106; self-valorization and, 107; sociability of, 46; social cooperation of, 25, 40, 47, 56n33, 81, 100
Multitude (Negri and Hardt), 11
multitudinal autonomy, 101; collective autonomy, 104, 109, 115
multitudinal wealth, 98
Muraro, Luisa, 106
Musk, Elon, 53

Negri, Antonio, 6, 39, 76, 95–104, 107, 109; *Assembly* by, 12, 25; *Commonwealth* by, 11; *Empire* by, 9–10, 11–12, 25, 104; on exploitation, 45; general intellect and, 73n15; *Marx beyond Marx* by, 95, 96–97, 101; *Multitude* by, 11; right-wing authoritarian anti-capitalism and, 111n29. *See also* multitude
Netflix, 31
network effects, 4
Neumann, Adam, 14n12, 53
New Zealand, 143, 148
nocebo-effect, 124–26, 146
nonstandard employment contracts, 27
"Nosedive" (*Black Mirror* episode), 59
Nuits Debout protests (2015), 137, 145, 148

Occupy Wall Street (OWS), 143, 148
OKCupid, 123
omnipotentiality, 70
online peer-to-peer networks, 99
online ratings, 68
online transactions, data extracted from, 3–4
open-access research networks, 99
open objects, 146
opioid crisis, US, 124
opportunism, 69
overproduction, 20
Owen, Robert, 140
OWS. *See* Occupy Wall Street

pandemic, COVID-19, 76
panopticon, 33
Panzieri, Raniero, 6, 73n7
Paypal, 53
Pazaitis, Alex, 142
peer-licensed production certificates, 138, 143
Pepsi, 49
personal identity, employment as source of, 62
philosophy of technology, 6, 11
physical exhaustion, 75, 80–85
platform artisans, 140–43
platform capitalism, 41
platform cooperativism, 137–39
platform expropriation, 136
platform lock-in, 47
political economy, 6

Portugal, 144
post-Fordism, 24–28, 56n33, 69; digital technology and, 28–34; exploitation and, 39–40, 44; social cooperation under, 99
post-Fordist capitalism, 69, 98
postwar working class, 7
post-workerism, 6–10, 16n45, 25, 95, 105, 118–19, 136
potentiality, 97
power: potentiality and, 97; power-signs, 30; relations, 28. *See also* labor-power
price: discrimination, 48–49; value *versus*, 55n15
privatization, 47
production: assembly-line, 20; just-in-time, 27; mass, 20; overproduction, 20; peer-licensed certificates, 143; peer production licenses, 138; value, 41–42
profit: becoming-rent of, 45–47; growth-before-profit model, 4–5
profitability, 4
"The Project of Autonomy" (Aureli), 96
promotional partnerships, 48, 49
Proposition 22 (California referendum), 14n3, 52
psycho-physical adaptation, of workers, 30–32

Quaderni Rossi (journal), 6, 73n7

radicalism, 104
radical monopolization, 122–25, 128
ratings: digital systems, 59–60, 65–71; online, 68
real socialism, 99
Red Brigades, 105
resonance, 129, 130, 146–49
response rate, of Airbnb, 74n27
revolutionary faddism, 104
RideAustin, 139
rifiuto del lavoro (work refusal), 7, 97

rights: intellectual property, 99; labor, 2–3, 64, 97–98, 144–45; right to log off, 64, 144; of workers, 143
right-wing authoritarian anti-capitalism, 111n29
Roelofson, Maartje, 74n27
Romanticism, 77
Rosa, Hartmut, 125, 126, 130
Rousseau, Jean-Jacques, 107

salario al lavoro domestico ("wages for housework"), 24, 86
Schneider, Nathan, 151n39
Scholz, Trebor, 11, 64, 145–46, 151n39
Schor, Juliet, 140
second law of thermodynamics, 77
self-determination, 100, 104, 106–8, 128–29; collective, 102, 145–46
self-government, 100
self-legislation, autonomy as, 6
self-organization, 10, 12
self-valorization: autonomy as, 96–101; collective, 130
Sennett, Richard, 141–42
service work, 63–64
sharing economy, 1, 135–37
Sharma, Sara, 88
signifying semiotics, 28–29
Simondon, Gilbert, 146
slacking, 22
slavery, 86
sleep deprivation, 88
Smalls, Chris, 76
smartphone technology, 64, 126
social cooperation, 1, 60, 98–99, 101, 136; digital capture of, 39–41; immaterial labor and, 26; internet and, 12; of multitude, 25, 40, 47, 56n33, 81, 100; technology and, 25
social isolation, 88
social machines, 19, 20, 27
social media, 26, 42, 45, 126
social reproduction, 77, 85–89
social security, 79
social subjection, 28, 29

social value, 62
Softbank, 14n12
Solmi, Renato, 73n7
Sorry We Missed You (film), 75
South Park (TV series), 59
Spinoza, Baruch, 10
spontaneous voluntary networks, 89
Srnicek, Nick, 43, 100
Starbucks, 32
start-up companies, 53; digital start-ups, 4
Stocksy United, 137, 142
Sun, Ping, 88
superhost system, Airbnb, 33
supplemental earners, 60
surplus labor, 67
surplus value, 45; absolute, 22

TaskRabbit, 1, 135, 147
Taylor, Frederick, 21
Taylorism, 21, 25
technological developments, 19
technological exceptionalism, 4
technology: convivial, 127, 129; digital, 6, 19, 28–34, 102; modern, 120–27; philosophy of, 6, 11; platform, 33; smartphone, 64, 126; social cooperation and, 25
Terranova, Tiziana, 41
Tesla, 53
thermodynamics, 77, 78
Tinder, 123
total monopolization, 48
tourism, 72n4
tracking algorithms, 33
traditional employment, 2
Tronti, Mario, 6–9, 11, 22, 105
Turgenev, Ivan, 95, 103
TurkerNation, 89, 148
Turkle, Sherry, 126

Uber, 1–3, 11, 25, 41, 70, 88, 117–18; abstract cooperation by, 31; algorithmic coordination by, 5; Aurora and, 57n52; behavioural modification and, 33; enclave rent and, 40, 48–50; exploitation by, 39–40, 43–44; facial recognition by, 124; independent contractors and, 28; monopoly of, 4; Proposition 22 (California referendum), 14n3, 52; rating systems and, 60; safe-driving reports of, 33–34; venture capital and, 50–53
"Uber-for-X"-companies, 3
uberization, of work, 2
unemployment, 63
United States, opioid crisis in, 124
urban workers, 141

value: absolute surplus, 22; economic, 41; labor theory of, 41, 43–45; monetary, 136, 141; price *versus*, 55n15; production, 41–42; realizing, 44; social, 62; surplus, 45
Van Doorn, Niels, 50
Vatican, 116
venture capital, 4, 50–53, 139
Vercellone, Carlo, 40, 46, 56n33
vernacular culture, 120–21, 129
Vial, Joshua, 143
Virno, Paolo, 27, 60–62, 68–69, 96

wages, 42
"wages for housework" (*salario al lavoro domestico*), 24, 86
Walmart, 25, 27, 31
wealth, multitudinal, 98
Wendling, Amy, 80
Western societies, as work-centered, 62
WeWork, 14n12, 53
WhatsApp, 51
Wikipedia, 99, 100, 140
Williams, Alex, 100
women: domestic labor by, 24, 86–87; labor-power of, 23–24; work by, 64, 107–8
Woodcock, Jamie, 11
work: click work, 41; digital surveillance of, 2; household, 119;

service, 63–64; uberization of, 2; by women, 64, 107–8
work-centered, Western societies as, 62
workday, prolonging, 21–22, 66–67
workerism, 6–7
workers: autonomy of, 109; independence of, 144–49; psycho-physical adaptation of, 30–32; rights of, 143; urban, 141
Workers and Capital (Tronti), 6–7, 11, 105

working class, 79, 86; factory-society and, 19; resistance by, 7–8
World War II, 7

Yellow Vest movement, 105
"You're Not Yelping" (*South Park* episode), 59
YouTube, 41

Zuboff, Shoshanna, 123
Zygmuntowski, Jan, 136

www.ingramcontent.com/pod-product-compliance
Lightning Source LLC
Chambersburg PA
CBHW021851300426
44115CB00005B/108